"Groundbreaking! Unique in the literature, *Trans-Kin* is a profound tool that encourages understanding and acceptance of the transgender community and their loved ones. The poignant, liberating histories bear witness to complicated issues and are healing to all involved. This book sheds new light on topics often publicly ignored or misunderstood. It is a long-awaited resource, highly recommended."
—Carol Grever, Author, *My Husband Is Gay* and *When Your Spouse Comes Out*

"These bright voices of families and partners of transsexual and transgender people round out the picture and provide dynamic perspectives on what it means to be human and to live in a society that is just beginning to come to grips with the range of human variation that has always been here, but has often been made invisible or erased for the convenience of others. The status quo no longer reigns; long live the unexpected, the creative and the loving reality of *Trans-Kin*!"
—Jamison Green, Author of *Becoming a Visible Man*

"If you are someone who loves a person who is gender variant but needs to understand more, then *Trans-Kin* is the book for you! Such diversity of race, ethnicity and geography provides a sense of how common transgender is in every culture and in all kinds of families. The personal stories are poignantly and even humorously shared with intimate details that might not happen in a classroom or lecture hall. The appendix provides a comprehensive glossary and resource lists as well as a pronoun guide. A fascinating and compelling read about an often misunderstood topic!"
—Jean Hodges, National Vice-President of PFLAG

"Get a different picture of ourselves by looking at our community and all those in it. Trans people, no longer isolated case studies or unusual clinical rarities, are taking our place as a force for change — usually positive — within webs of relationships and the larger world. This compendium by Whitley and Hubbard gives everyone something to think about!"
—Rev. Malcolm Himschoot, featured in video, *Call Me Malcolm*

"Often overlooked, underserved and misunderstood, the significant others, family members, friends and allies of transgender and transsexual people have their own unique experiences that sometimes fade into the background when discussion turns to trans issues. *Trans-Kin: A Guide for Family and Friends of Transgender People* offers a diverse collection of voices that all too frequently go unheard. Featuring the personal stories of SOFFAs, from nationally known activists to everyday people, *Trans-Kin* provides a window into the world of our loved ones, friends and supporters and lets them know that they are not alone."

—Matt Kailey, trans activist and author of *Just Add Hormones: An Insider's Guide to the Transsexual Experience* and *Teeny Weenies and Other Short Subjects*

"Speaking from a wide spectrum of relationships to trans people and informed by an even wider array of experiences, *Trans-Kin* is a comprehensive, nuanced and informative anthology. Honest and deeply thoughtful, these testimonies open readers to new possibilities of transformation, gender and sexuality. They also remind us all of the many ways that family, friendship and romantic love, inspire and challenge people to imagine, create and re-create community and connection, while still continuously forging their own identities as uniquely individual people."

—Max Wolf Valerio, author of *The Testosterone Files*

TRANS-KIN

A Guide for Family & Friends
of Transgender People

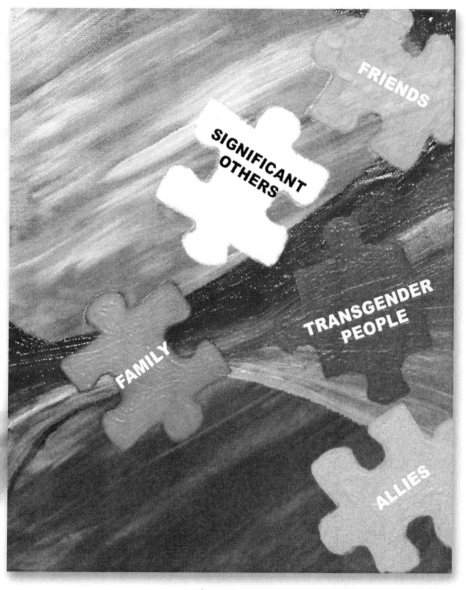

FRIENDS

SIGNIFICANT OTHERS

TRANSGENDER PEOPLE

FAMILY

ALLIES

Edited by
Eleanor A. Hubbard and Cameron T. Whitley

Design by
Concepts Unlimited
www.ConceptsUnlimitedInc.com

Cover art by
Cameron T. Whitley

 Published by
Bolder Press
PO Box 3719
Boulder, CO 80307
www.Trans-Kin.com

ISBN-13: 978-0-615-63067-0   (pbk)

ISBN-10: 0-615-63067-7

12   13   14   15   16   0 9 8 7 6 5 4 3 2 1

Printed in the USA

Dedication

American author and poet, Oliver Wendell Holmes (1809-1894) once noted that, "Language is the blood of the soul into which thoughts run and out of which they grow." It is with great courage that our contributors have shared their words and have trusted us with their stories, metaphorical pieces of their souls, so that others may grow. It is for this reason, that we dedicate this book to the many authors and artists who have made *Trans-Kin* possible. We feel honored to have worked with so many wonderful people and humbled by this experience. This book is a trans-kin community work of art.

Table of Contents

Acknowledgments

We would be derelict if we did not mention those who were invaluable in helping us complete this anthology. Natasha Hubbard worked tirelessly to make this anthology accessible to those who don't know the language of transgender issues, but want to understand their transgender loved one. Pam McKinnie created the "look" of the book, working to translate our ideas into a visual reality. Carol Grever was a constant support, champion and dear friend. Our spouses (Melanie and Dennis) could not have been more supportive. We know they will be as happy to see this project come to fruition as we are.

Trans-Kin: A Guide for Family and Friends of Transgender People has been a joy and a privilege to work on and a dream fulfilled. Not only have we been invited to share in the stories and journeys of hundreds around the world, but this transgender man (Cameron) and strong ally (Eleanor) have also found a sense of peace and joy in our own journeys. We sense this has been true for the other authors in this anthology. They tell their stories as a testimony to their own journeys and to assist others in finding a path less traveled.

Preface

This anthology is a unique sampling of Trans-Kin voices, as they tell about their lives and their experiences. Yet we are fully aware of the many voices that are missing from these pages. Our sample is designed to start a conversation within and between our communities about the need for SOFFA visibility. In this vein, we hope that this will only be one of many texts, which explores the experience of Trans-Kin and hopefully one of many editions of this text. We think the very presence of this book will encourage others to share their stories, adding to the wealth of knowledge collected from shared experiences.

Our anthology has five sections: Significant Others, Family members, Friends, Allies and Transgender persons. In the first four sections, we detail the layered emotions and personal processes of Trans-Kin to the transgender community. The relationships showcased are varied, including mother, twin sister, friend, significant other, father, teacher, counselor and minister. Repeatedly the theme of invisibility is present as these individuals describe the collective processes of coming to terms with the transgender identification of a loved one. Some of the stories are filled with joy while others convey deep personal loss, and many stories combine these feelings creatively. The final section of this anthology is by design shorter. Our intent was always to focus on SOFFAs not the transgender person, yet a few trans people's stories of their relationships with their SOFFAs convinced us of the need for this section as well.

As you read through articles in this book, you might encounter terms you are unfamiliar with: there is a glossary in the appendix providing definitions of words used in the transgender community. Hopefully you will want to experience more than just reading about other SOFFAs' stories, so also in the appendix, we have included lists of other resources: books, videos and organizations, that will help you on your journey. You will probably have many questions about the trans experience, which you may not be able to ask your transgender loved one, so throughout the book, you will find answers to questions you may be wondering about; for instance, What pronouns should I use with a transgender person? and What will my transgender loved ones look like after their transition? You will also discover the artwork of poets and visual artists that enliven this book on page after page. We hope that it stimulates your visual and sensory awareness just as much as the stories stimulate your thoughts. We are deeply honored that our artists allowed their art in this forum, and we thank them for their gifts to this anthology as well.

Eleanor and Cameron

Introduction

Cameron Thomas Whitley and Eleanor A. Hubbard

Cameron T. Whitley and Eleanor A. Hubbard, the co-editors of *Trans-Kin: A Guide to Family and Friends*, have extensive personal and professional experience with the transgender community. They are also longtime friends, having met at the University of Colorado and worked together on several projects. Cameron, a transgender man, is currently working on his Ph.D. in Sociology; Eleanor, an ally of the transgender community, is a Senior Instructor in the Department of Sociology at the University of Colorado at Boulder. Together, they created this resource for SOFFAs (Significant Others, Family members, Friends and Allies) recognizing the need for a guide to help SOFFAs tread new ground in coming to terms with the transgender status of a loved one. The purpose of this guide is to provide a safe space for SOFFAs to share their own journeys, in some ways similar and in other ways quite different, from their transgender loved one.

Cameron, while working on his Ph.D., runs a transgender support group in his community. As an undergraduate at the University of Colorado, he founded TransForm, a student support and social group for transgender students. TransForm, as well as offering support services and a safe space to explore gender non-conformity, was a successful advocate for establishing gender-neutral bathrooms around campus. Cameron has also served as a board member for several non-profit volunteer organizations, presented at national conferences and engaged in consulting work, all related to transgender equality and inclusion.

Eleanor, semi-retired from teaching at the University of Colorado, was well known for her courses in sex, gender, sexuality, race and pop culture. She has also twice taught on Semester at Sea, traveling around the world and introducing students to how these concepts are different in different parts of the world. In addition, she is the Founder and CEO of DiversityWorks, a diversity training and consulting firm. She also has served on many non-profit volunteer boards working for equality and inclusion of marginalized groups.

Cameron and Eleanor connected in the early years of Cameron's undergraduate career over a scholarly interest in sex, gender and sexuality. As Cameron and Eleanor worked together on a variety of projects, they had frequent conversations about transgender issues: sex and gender, body image and the representation of transgender people in the media, to name a few. A recurring theme in this dialogue concerned the difficulties trans people face in explaining their journey to the people they care most about and how the significant others, family members, friends and allies of transgender persons process their own journey when coming to terms with the transgender status of a loved one. It was out of these discussions that the idea emerged for an anthology to guide family and friends of trans folks through their own transition process. It all came together when Cameron and Eleanor discovered the term SOFFA: they would gather and document personal narratives, thought-provoking stories and the individual journeys of those with transgender loved ones. We have called these people Trans-Kin, the kinship of the transgender person.

Trans-Kin tread much of the same ground as transgender persons do: they experience an assortment of feelings as they come to terms with the transgender status of a loved one. This process is exemplified by their own coming-out experience where they divulge the transition of a loved one to others around them. As their loved one transitions physically, as well as emotionally, psychologically and spiritually, Trans-Kin often experience a need for a safe space to explore their own emotions and potential identity challenges. Our society has provided few such places. As resources grow and expand for transgender members, so too must the resources for their Trans-Kin. This is our intention for the Trans-Kin anthology.

$$\star \quad \star \quad \star \quad \star \quad \star$$

During the final weeks of preparing this book for publication, we became even more convinced of its necessity, as we heard of cases from around the globe that spoke to the need of such a resource. In 2012, Tennessee State Representative Richard Floyd proposed a law that would ban transgender people from using dressing rooms and restrooms that do not match the gender on their birth certificates. He said, "This bill ... is not personal, but it is intended to protect. I have a wife, three daughters, two grand-daughters, and there is no way, if some man thought he was a women ..., I would stand there and allow that." Rep. Floyd came up with his proposed bill after reading about a woman in Texas who claimed she was fired from Macy's, after attempting to stop a transgender teen from using the women's dressing room. He said,

> It could happen here. If I was standing at a (women's) dressing room and a man tried to go in there — I don't care if he thinks he's a woman and tries on clothes with them in there

— I'd just try to stomp a mud-hole in him and then stomp him dry. Don't ask me to adjust to their perverted way of thinking and put my family at risk. We cannot continue to let these people dominate how society acts. There is a potential for pedophiles and molesters to come into the restroom and claim the same thing.

The many ways in which Rep. Floyd is mistaken about transgender people will be addressed throughout this book, but for now suffice it to say there is no evidence that transgender people are pedophiles and molesters or that those who are, have used cross-dressing as a way to have access to dressing rooms. Fortunately the bill was withdrawn almost immediately.

The fallacies that Rep. Floyd articulated as a public figure are not uncommon in our society. These misconceptions specifically affect not only trans persons but also their SOFFAs. In fact, the generalized transgender person Rep. Floyd intends to assault is someone's daughter, sister, friend or possibly spouse. This blatant stigmatizing, hurtful as it is for the trans community and their kin, also legitimizes transphobia by a person in power. This is a scary thought, one that reaches into the hearts of many SOFFAs, including the ones we were so fortunate to interact with in the preparation of this book. We have tried to give voice to the mother, sister or friend, worried every time their transgender loved one walks out the door, that their transgender loved one might be assaulted, even killed, by individuals who share a similar misconceived point-of-view as Rep. Floyd.

Another example: Govan High School in the UK allegedly kicked Jamie Love, a 17-year-old transgender student, out of class. Jamie, who was born male came to school dressed in girl's clothing and accessories: tights, shorts, make-up and hair extensions. Jamie spoke to school officials about plans to wear female clothing, mentioning feeling "trapped in a boy's body." Upon Jamie's arrival, school officials indicated that Jamie was troublesome in class and proceeded to ask Jamie to leave. Jamie's mother said, "Jamie has done nothing wrong here. He has every right to express himself the way he wants and I will stand by him. Imagine the fear and confusion other trans teens experienced at Govan High School, and throughout the UK, as well as their SOFFAs, as a result of Jamie's expulsion.

One final example: one of our original authors chose not to include her submission because she said, "The atmosphere is just too toxic," in the state in which she lives. She was afraid that her son would be too easy to identify and placed in danger. Of course we agreed not to include her piece, but were saddened by her revelation. These three examples, out of the many we could include, emboldened us and renewed our commitment to Trans-Kin: Significant Others, Family, Friends and Allies of the transgender community.

At the same time, we are pleased that real progress has been made in our society toward a more equitable treatment of transgender people. In 2012, Jenna Talackova, Miss Universe Canada, was removed from the Miss Universe finals because she had gender reassignment surgery when she was 19 and was not "born female." However, the organization re-considered, and Ms. Talackova will be allowed to compete, as long as she passes unspecified "gender recognition requirements." Also On August 29, 2011, *Dancing with the Stars* announced that Chaz Bono, a F2M (female to male) transgender person and son of Cher Bono, was to be a contestant on the show. Although there was an attempt to protest his casting, he successfully found a large fan base, well beyond week six, when he was voted off. Transgender stories have also been featured in the last few years in *Newsweek*, and on *20/20*, *Oprah* and *America's Next Top Model*. Other resources include a new book by psychologist Dr. Ehrensaft, titled *Gender Born, Gender Made*, which encourages parents of transgender children to allow them to be more gender-creative. We have included many such resources: books, videos, organizations and a glossary of terms at the end of this book, but the most important resource for trans-kin, we anticipate, will be listening and responding to people who are in similar situations.

Our intention for this anthology is to encourage Trans-Kin to experience their own transitional process and be strong in telling their own stories, which may be similar but are often different than their transgender loved one. Many such loving Trans-Kin express themselves in this anthology, but they also ask profound questions about gender, identity and social support networks, as well as the transitional process they are thrown into when their trans loved one comes out. We hope Trans-Kin and transgender people as well, will find herein a place of safety, a place to share common stories, and move through their own process. We dedicate *Trans-Kin: A Guide to Family and Friends of Transgender People* to our strong, dedicated, vulnerable and delightful authors.

Cameron's Story:
Please God, Make Me a Boy

"You're not a boy," he screamed at me. I was five or six, and yet I can still feel the power of those words rising from Paul's stomach and exiting out his lips. Paul and I were best friends. We were the same age and played together nearly every day during the summer. I told him to call me Alex and stop using my female name, because I knew that both boys and girls could be named Alex. On this particular day, though, something had changed. Gender made its mark on Paul, and we could no longer be the same: he established his position as a boy and pushed me forcefully into being a girl. Following his words, I erupted into tears and decided that I would never play with Paul again. I cried in private and never told my parents what had happened.

We all have "aha" moments, instances where time stops and something changes, something is realized or something must be let go. This was, perhaps, my first dawning moment. For some reason, up until that point, I did not realize that I would grow up to be a woman. Inside I had always felt like a boy and would eventually become a man.

After all, each morning I woke up to meet my father in the bathroom, as he smeared shaving cream on our faces. Then he took the dull side of his razor and ran it over my face clearing the shaving cream away. "Dad, someday I'm going to have my own razor and shave all the time," I asserted with pride. He looked at me and smiled with a little chuckle never challenging my gender identity.

It was the mid 80s. I was the typical tomboy. I loved sports and my GI Joes, hated dresses and enjoyed spending time with my dad in the garage. However, I also enjoyed playing with Barbies and working on creative projects with my mom. At that point, I didn't even realize what it meant to be a boy or a girl (I'm not so sure that I fully understand these categories now). But what I did know was that if I was a boy, I wouldn't have to wear dresses and I could have short hair. Beyond these things, at such a young age, I didn't see much difference. My parents believed, and I was taught from a young age that a girl could do or be anything she wanted. My parents placed few restrictions on my interests and let me wear boys' clothes to school. As I grew older and classmates taunted me, my home was a place of refuge, and my mother was my inspiration and closest friend.

Still, neither my parents nor any of my friends knew my deepest secret. One of my earliest memories is praying to God that he would change me into a boy. While we didn't attend church that often, I had been taught, "God answers prayers." If that were the case, if God really did listen and answer our prayers, he would hear my plea and change me into a boy. I knew that as a boy, I could have a girlfriend, and I liked girls. I had yet to understand the difference between sexual orientation and gender identity, but still each night, I would start with my standard prayer of "Now I lay me down to sleep ... " followed by an extensive prayer to end my suffering and transform me into a boy.

"God, I know that lots of people are suffering, but I really want to be a boy, and I know you can make me into one. I promise to be really good. Please change me into a boy tonight...." Because I knew that my prayer was not normal and that other kids my age were not wishing for the same thing, I never mentioned these prayers to my family although I confided in a few friends while playing childhood games, so that when we played house, they would let me be the dad or brother.

Yet, each morning, I awoke to my same body, the same confusion and unable to find a place for kids like me. I kept asking myself, "Where does someone like me fit in?" When no answer came, I attempted suicide during my senior year in high school. I couldn't manage the depression, confusion and anxiety that I lived with on a daily basis.

I could not resolve my gender and sexual orientation confusion. It was even too much to think about being gay. I knew that I was attracted to women, but I continued to date men and some women. I prayed that my attraction to women was only a phase that would eventually resolve itself when I found the "right" man. Truthfully, I didn't feel gay; I just felt that I was meant to be a boy and that somehow God had mixed up the packaging. While I had lots of gay friends in high school, our perceptions of our bodies and attractions didn't seem to match. My gay friends didn't share the same mind and body disconnect that I had felt from such a young age.

My life wasn't easy growing up in a small western town with a population of less than thirty thousand. My local library did not own any transgender texts, and my family, like most families then, did not have Internet access. So I watched daytime television and saw transsexuals sensationalized, carnival characters parading around on a public stage for the amusement of the audience. Then I met my first transgender friend, Helen. This encounter was a breath of fresh air for me. Helen was not like the transsexuals I had seen on TV, but a successful, brilliant, talented and beautiful woman. We became instant friends, as she freely shared information about her transgender journey. I was intrigued. Never had I heard someone express the same feelings and internal struggles that were my unique burden. It was as if the missing piece of my identity puzzle was found. I came out to myself as a transgender guy as an eighteen-year-old fledgling in college. While I had always had "boy feelings," I now had a word for how my mind and emotions were disconnected from my body.

In college, I was able to network socially with other gender non-conforming friends, and I was able to find my story on numerous websites and recognize the normality of my experience as expressed by others. Now, more than 10 years later, it is clear that the environment for transgender individuals has changed significantly; there are many more resources available for transgender people and their transitional journey.

Two years passed from the time I came out to myself as a transgender man and the moment when I revealed this fact to my family. My father passed away when I was 11, and my relationship with my mother was extremely important. I wanted to be open and honest with her, while providing her resources to face the jagged road that my identity would place her on. Coming out to my mother was not an easy process. We struggled together. So, I searched for parallel stories about her future journey, a map, as one of the authors in this anthology suggests. Alas, I found nothing. I could not find a source that would allay her fears, or a group that would help her process her emotions. I felt like a failure. I could not provide a resource for my mother, the woman who had spent her entire life providing for my needs and cultivating my creative curiosity. At the time, she had become comfortable with my identity as queer, but the shock of my transgender status was a second numbing blow. Although, the journey has not been easy for her, she continues to delight in her son's newfound freedom, passion for life and renewed determination.

"*It* was as if the missing piece of my identity puzzle was found."

In college, I was fortunate to not only come to terms with my transgender identity, but to also find a mentor and friend in Eleanor. Initially as my professor, Eleanor created a classroom where my identity and perspective was valid. She encouraged my self-exploration and supported me in my undergraduate honors thesis where the idea for this book was able to unfold. Over the years, we have remained close, sharing moments of great joy and times of struggle. Eleanor has always been one of my biggest supporters, cheerleaders and allies. For that and so much more, I am truly grateful. As I developed my voice as a transgender man, I enjoyed community education and transgender advocacy. I spent time cultivating relationships, serving on various non-profit boards, conducting transgender 101 workshops and writing pieces for a number of books. In the depth of my heart, I did this for my mother and for the thousands of mothers like mine who fear for the safety and future of their transgender children.

While I continue to run support groups, respond to speaking requests and support organizations in providing safe and affirming environments for transgender individuals and their SOFFAs, my life is awkwardly typical. I always dreamed of this moment, when my presence as a man would not be questioned, and now here it is. It has been well over 10 years since I publically came out as a transgender man and started this profoundly amazing journey. My physical transition ended years ago. Rarely do I consider my transgender status or the fact that I was not born with a male body. It does not come up in daily conversations, nor do most people around me even know. However, my mother still encounters times when she must contemplate 'coming out' as the mother of a transgender son. My transgender status is not something that I try to keep secret, but it is no longer the center of my life. Today, my life is filled with a bounty of wonderful friends, a loving and supportive family, a rescue Yorkie (Pal), and a beautiful wife who shares my passion for living and desire to create change.

"Fleur" by Melanie Whitley © 2012

When my husband and I were first dating he began to call me sunflower; as time went on this name transitioned to mon fleur and then simply to fleur. This term of endearment has given me much joy, and I painted this picture for him as a thank you for these simple words of love.

Eleanor's Story:
An Ally From the Classroom

I am a 70 + year old grandmother, as well as a retired teacher. I have not worn a dress, skirt or high heels in at least four decades, because I prefer comfortable clothes and shoes. I also prefer a short haircut that requires little or no work to maintain. In the last few years, I am on occasion addressed as sir, particularly if a person approaches me from behind. Even though the person is usually embarrassed and apologizes, I enjoy confusing others about gender. One reason is that I am confident I am a woman, even though I usually present myself as androgynous and often break feminine societal norms. Nobody seems to care how I present myself; this is not true for my good friend and colleague, Cameron.

I taught gender studies in the Sociology Department at the University of Colorado at Boulder for 20 years until I retired in 2006. During those years, I learned a great deal (I thought) about transgender issues. I often invited Terri, a M2F (male-to-female) post-operative transgender person to speak to my class. She would tell my students that from a very early age, she felt like a woman, trapped in the body of a man. Terri openly discussed her counseling, cross-dressing, hormone replacement therapy and costly operations she undertook to align her body with her perceived gender.

Terri was a beautiful woman, who emphasized her curves in her attire. She wore stilettos, and in almost every way, presented herself as more feminine than I ever have. Still in order to achieve her feminine persona, Terri experienced severe suffering not only in the hormone treatments and surgical interventions, but also in her family, work, and personal relationships. She lived in constant fear that danger could be around any corner because transgender people are at more risk for assault and even murder, just because they live as the person they perceive themselves to be not as the gender they were assigned at birth. Life was difficult in many ways for Terri, but she felt fulfilled and contented that she was now the person she was meant to be.

Cameron was the next transgender person I met. He called me the summer after his freshman year at the University of Colorado, informing me that he was a F2M (female-to-male) transgender person and asked me to supervise an independent study of transgender issues. When Cameron walked into my office, he was definitely not my image of a man; he was short, skinny and smooth-faced. He could have passed easily as a young boy or a young girl; he was as androgynous as I. Now hormone therapy has helped Cameron achieve a more muscular body, a lower voice and more body hair, including the need to shave. He too feels fulfilled and content with his achieved gender.

Through the years Cameron and I have developed a relationship not only as teacher-student, but also as colleague and friend. Watching him grow and develop into the man he believed he was born to be has been exciting. Cameron has helped me understand more concretely about the gendered world we live in: the strict gender boundaries that transgender people transgress to become their true selves. He also shared with me the times he was assaulted for presenting himself as a man and reminded me that safe places for people like me, who mostly follow the gender norms, are often unsafe for transgender people. I go to the public bathroom marked women, for instance, and nobody has ever questioned my right to be there, and often if the line is too long, I go to the men's bathroom, again without being questioned. When he started transitioning, Cameron did not share this same basic right. He was often harassed in bathrooms regardless of which one he selected. In those early years, he found friends and allies to stand guard outside restrooms, constantly in fear of how people would react to his presence.

Of course, Cameron and Terri provide only a limited lens into the world of gender diversity, and the transgender world is filled with a plethora of individuals and often quite different paths. Trans-Kin are also individuals who experience diverse journeys. I certainly honor and respect everyone who is struggling with loving transgender individuals. For me though, it was a   no-brainer. Becoming an ally of transgender people, while learning about Cameron's life and struggles and standing beside him, seemed very natural.

Still being an ally of any marginalized group is both rewarding and challenging. My curiosity is triggered by the stories of those who live on the margins, whether it is because of their race, class, sexual orientation, age or gender. As a sociologist, I recognize that persons living on the margins often understand our society better than those of us who "fit" societal norms. Because I have engaged in self-education and been taught about the processes and structures of our society by those who are marginalized, I am (hopefully) a better teacher and, as Dr. Ehrensaft says, a more gender creative person.

The first step to becoming an ally is about self-education, but more is required. Those of us, like myself, who may 'play' with gender presentation, but don't identify as transgender, live relatively easily within societal gender norms and as a result reap benefits denied to transgender persons. Our families probably don't disown us, and we probably won't be fired for not dressing "appropriately." Too often these things do happen to transgender people. My privilege allows me to transgress gender norms relatively easily, but it also gives me the opportunity to stand beside those who transgress with greater consequences. That's what being an ally means to me: challenging gender norms by using my privilege to make changes.

Some of the ways I ally myself with transgender people: I share my understandings of gender and transgender issues with others who live inside gender borders; I confront social structures that marginalize Cameron and work toward more equitable treatment for all transgender people; and I speak out against media injustices directed toward people who live across the gender spectrum. My life is richer because I know Cameron, and because I am an ally of all transgender people.

"*My* privilege allows me to transgress gender norms relatively easily, but it also gives me the opportunity to stand beside those who transgress with greater consequences."

When Cameron and I decided to co-edit this anthology, I thought I knew a great deal about gender diversity and the transgender community. What I am learning through the stories of SOFFAs is that Trans-Kin are also marginalized, only because they love the transgender people in their lives. The SOFFA journey, like the transgender journey, is often dangerous, confusing and confrontational as well. It is not an instant destination, but a forever journey: a process of reflection, coming to terms with, empowerment and coming-out. Cameron and I hope that in a small way this anthology will help to create a better-traveled path for significant others, family members, friends and allies and their transgender loved ones.

"Behind Closed Eyes" by Jackie Frances © 2012

FAQ

Q. What does it mean when someone says they are transgender?

A. Transgender is a term for people who perceive themselves born into the wrong body. It may also be used as an umbrella term to include anyone who does not fit well into the gender they were assigned at birth, what gender they identify with and how they present themselves.

Q. My loved one just told me she is transgender and handed me this book. I am devastated, what should I do?

A. Read the section of the book that is relevant to you. Pick it up and lay it down as you need too. Scan all the resources that are available in the appendix and try them out. We know that this is a difficult experience as we have been through it. But we also know, as you sample articles from this book, you will be comforted to know you are not alone. Hang in there, and as they say, it will get better.

Q. What is all this F2M stuff? Is cisgender a word? Genderqueer sounds like a slam, is it?

A. Like everyone, trans people use a kind of shorthand to describe themselves and their experiences. F2M (female-to-male) means an individual was born female, but identifies as male and M2F (male-to-female) means an individual was born male, but identifies as female. Cisgender is a term sometimes used to refer to people who are not transgender. Genderqueer is a term used proudly by those in the transgender community who do not fit or choose not to fit into society's gender norms. Check out our glossary at the back of the book; don't let the terms hang you up.

Q. Isn't being transgender morally wrong?

A. We don't think so, nor do many faith communities (see Burke, Hassler, Monroe and Nicewander articles in the Ally section), but different people have different opinions about this one. Many trans people are religious and active in a faith community where they are accepted. But if you are in a faith community that believes that your trans loved one is "going to hell," you will probably have a hard time reconciling your faith with your love for someone. Remember questioning religious assumptions is not wrong, and you and your trans loved one can agree to disagree (see article by Mark Miller in the section on Families).

Q. Is a trans person psychologically damaged? Can gender identity be changed?

A. NO! and NO! Trans people are as psychologically healthy as the rest of us, meaning like all people, some have "baggage." Being treated badly because of one's gender identity may cause psychological problems, but they can be worked through with a good therapist. By all good scientific evidence, being trans is not psychologically damaging nor can gender identity be changed (see the American Psychological Association website; www.apa.org/topics/sexuality/transgender.aspx).

Q. Does conversion therapy work?

A. Some groups of conservative Christians believe that gender identity is not fixed, can be changed and have developed therapies to change GLBT people. We do not think this is possible, and all good scientific research agrees. We also believe conversion or restorative therapy does not work, and it almost always does more harm than good, because of the negative stereotypes used (see the American Psychological Association website: www.apa.org/topics/sexuality/orientation.aspx).

Q. My friend George, who lives in Cincinnati, is transgender. Do you know him?

A. Coincidentally, some transgender people do know each other, but it is not as common as you might think. If you want to have a conversation with a transgender person, it might be best to look for common interests rather than assuming all transgender people know each other.

12.31.11 — from the daily shots of the
"random morning series" by dylan scholinski,
© 2012, www.dylanscholinski.com

"*It's* not always easy, and it's certainly not simple, but our relationship has lasted, and so have many relationships of people we know."

—Cat Moran,
significant other of a trans man

SIGNIFICANT OTHERS

Significant Others

All relationships take work. As William Shakespeare wrote, "The course of true love never did run smooth." The most intimate relationship is one's life-partner, significant other or spouse, and the one with the most potential for conflict. When a partner comes out as transgender, additional challenges may present themselves. Couples may be faced with the process of a partner physically transitioning, the mental and emotional components of coming to terms with this transition and if (and how) the relationship can continue. Communicating the decisions the partners make about their relationship to others is also a challenge. You will find all of these issues and more discussed in this section.

Like non-transgender relationships, some remain strong (Hall, Whitley), while others decide to separate (Star). Some have heart-breaking stories of domestic violence (Gates) and "broken" relationships (Harris), while another finds joy in a transgender partner giving birth and raising children (Beatie). One's sexual orientation as a lesbian is challenged when she discovers her love for a transgender man (Cowan), while another actively explores relationships with transgender men (voltz). Additionally, all couples experience reactions from family, friends and community members regarding their relationships, a topic that is different, but not unique for couples with one or more transgender partners (Moran). These stories together tell of joy, self-discovery and loss, the same components that are present in all relationships regardless of transgender status. What is unique about this section is that significant others share their unique insights into being a significant other to a transgender person(s).

Stones

In darkness
he'd held them always.
Hiding in his closet
he filled his secret sack,
bravado wrapping reality.
I stood outside,
shielded by ignorance
while he added
stone after stone
to that bag.
Each one a lie,
told and retold
till he believed himself.

Intimations of truth
pulled me in
to share his shadow.
Night and day melded
as we huddled there
a long, long time.
Slowly, he emptied his sack
now too heavy to bear.
One by one,
he gave stones to me.
Stone after stone shifted
from his bag to mine.

I could barely lift the load
when at last
he cracked the closet door.
Sudden sunshine flooded
light on his empty sack,
mine, full of stones.

It took years to dole them out,
one for each friend,
each loved one, betrayed.
No life escapes pain.
I still carry
a pocketful of pebbles.
Memories don't die,
but my bag for secrets
is folded and flat,
finally empty.

Carol Grever

Carol has been a successful businesswoman and English professor and now writes professionally. She's authored two books *(My Husband Is Gay* and *When Your Spouse Comes Out)* and produced a documentary on straight spouse recovery *(One Gay, One Straight: Complicated Marriages)*. A recognized spokesperson on straight spouse issues, she's appeared on major network TV shows, including *The Oprah Winfrey Show, Anderson Cooper 360, The Early Show* and *Good Morning America*. Read more about her work online at www.carolgrever.com and www.straightspouseconnection.com

FAQ

Q. My significant other just told me he is trans. Does that mean he is gay?

A. Gender and sexual identity are not the same. Trans persons may be gay, straight or bi-sexual; it is best to let him tell you his sexual identity rather than assume it.

Q. How did my significant other choose his new name?

A. Every trans person is different. Why don't you just ask? However, he may choose not to share this information.

Q. Why did my significant other wait so long to tell me, when she says now that she has always known she was different? Why didn't she tell me before we got married?

A. Trans people often spend a long time trying to overcome their transgender feelings. It is not easy to come out in a world that is not supportive of transgender people. Some trans people try to live their lives by avoiding their transgender status, perhaps they get married and have children, but the feelings never go away. If you are married to a person who has come out, this does not mean that the person was deceiving you. More than likely, the individual has only now fully come to terms with her transgender status. However, it is not surprising that you feel betrayed. Picking up this book is a good start. You may want to find someone you can confide in, perhaps a good therapist to work through your feelings.

Q. Could my significant other just cross-dress in the privacy of our home? Why does he need to "come out?"

A. Cross-dressing is not the same as being transgender. Some people enjoy cross-dressing in private, others in public; they may or may not be transgender. Transgender people must live as the gender they perceive themselves to be to become psychologically healthy people. Cross-dressing is not the answer.

Q. **I feel like I am in a closet now that my trans significant other has come out? Should I tell my family and friends that she is trans, and if so how?**

A. Now you know, and it may become a heavy burden (see Carol Grever's poem, *Stones*, pg 18-19). What to do about what you know is a very personal decision; only you know the time and place to share this personal information. There are many factors to consider though: where you live, your family dynamics and the concerns of your trans significant other, to name just a few. But the feeling of being in a closet (unable to share who you really are with the significant people in your life) is very uncomfortable. It was for your trans loved one, and it will be for you too. What trans people often do is think carefully about who will be most accepting of their decision. This is the person they usually tell first, in order to practice coming out. You may need some assistance to decide when and how to come out of your closet. National organizations like PFLAG (Parents, Friends of Lesbians and Gays) and TYFA (TransYouthFamilyAllies) and others found in the resources section, as well as a good therapist can help with this process.

Q. **Is my significant other in danger?**

A. Perhaps, but maybe not. Transgender people may be victims of hate crimes because of their gender presentation. Statistics show that trans people are targeted more in the early stages of transitioning when they may appear more ambiguous. Unfortunately, not all states and cities recognize gender identity as a protected class of individuals or consider the harassment of a transgender person a hate crime. Your significant other has probably weighed these issues and is aware of the possibility for harassment and violence. If you are concerned about safety, perhaps you could share this with your significant other and together you could brainstorm some ways to 'be safe.' Ideas might include; not walking at night, meeting people in public places, not disclosing personal information to strangers, particularly online, etc. If you or your partner is verbally harassed, fired from a job or physically attacked, there are organizations that can help (see Lambda Legal in the resources section).

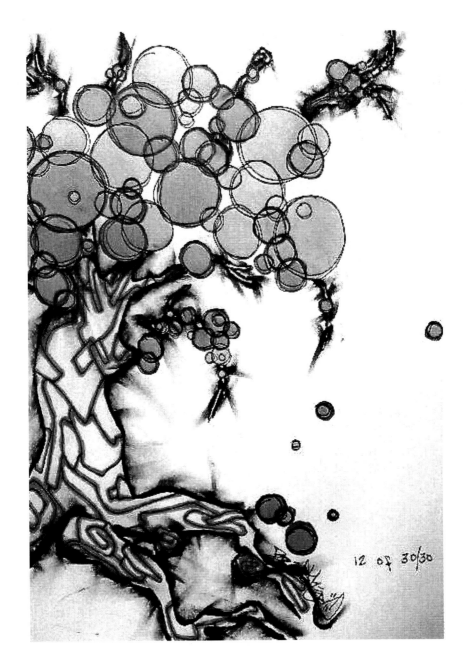

"No. 12 — November Challenge"
by Troy Jones © 2012

A personal challenge to draw 30 drawings in 30 days: 8.5×6 in. colored paper, the smudges were made with my fingers as I applied ink with a fountain pen.

My Life With Thomas, the Pregnant Man

Nancy Beatie

Interviewed by Eleanor A. Hubbard

Nancy is the mother of five, three of whom were birthed by her husband Thomas. She and Thomas run a successful business. Thomas told his story in the book, *Labor of Love*. For a picture of Nancy, Thomas and their three children, check out Thomas' website. http://www.definenormal.com/PregnantMan/Home.html

* * * * *

What first attracted you to Thomas and was it different than other kinds of attractions you have felt?

I have known him for so long, around January 1991, it is hard to remember. We both worked in the same gym and we said hi, bye and walked past each other. But this one day, I was working behind the desk, and he walked by and I was like, oh my gosh. He had his hair super short, and he looked just like he was supposed to look, in my mind. My heart started beating fast. We have known each other for 21 years, and we have been together for 14. We have been married for nine. At that point, Thomas was Tracy and working as a female model. I was too old; I am 12 years older than him.

He had a crush on me when he was 16 years old. He was too young for me, and I was already in a relationship, and so was he. We had to go through those relationships and learn from our mistakes. I had been married for several years to a terrible guy and have two children from him, my older daughters. But I have been attracted to lots of different people. Everybody is so different, and I am glad Thomas was attracted to me. It was different though, because of who he is. I am not attracted to a gender, but to the person.

I have gone back and forth between the genders. Gender doesn't matter to me, it is who the person is, who they are inside and up in their head.

What concerns, if any, did you have contemplating a relationship with Thomas?

I was able to go through the change, the whole process with Thomas. I met him as a female model, but when I saw him in the gym that day he was already changing. I got to go to all the surgeries and the hormone treatments, that's when I learned about gender. Wow, a person sure can change. He used to be more emotional, not so much anymore. Hormones can really change you, the hair on his body, physically, mentally. He always looked like a guy, and he walked like a guy when he was a model. It was kind of funny. He was really pretty too. Check out the photos of him in his book. But this kind of confused me keeping sex and gender straight. Thomas keeps teaching me, as well as other transgender people.

Another transgender couple reached out to us, and we just had them over for dinner last week. They played with our children. They are very cool, and we liked them a lot. We have met a few other couples online, and one couple is going to visit us in March. We really had a lot of friends when we lived in Hawaii, but when Thomas went through his change, a lot of them dropped off. Then we moved to a small town in Oregon and made friends with our neighbors, and we were just Thomas and Nancy, the old lady and the young guy.

When Thomas and I got together, my older daughters were still living at home with me. I had left my husband and had a relationship with a girl for three years. Then I decided to take a year off from all relationships and just be by myself. Then I met Thomas and he moved in; my daughters were very religious, and they weren't very happy. One of my daughters is gay, and she has been in a relationship for four years with her girlfriend. But back then they thought we were going to hell, and they would cry for me and pray. But then they got to know him, warmed up more to him and it got better.

What concerns did your family and friends express, as you contemplated a relationship with Thomas?

I have a really large family, but just a few years ago I found out who my real father was. My mother was ok with Thomas because he is a man. My mom has gone back and forth between women and men as well, so it wasn't huge. My mother was married to this icky guy, and he would say mean things and call Thomas a circus freak. But it didn't stop me, what my family thought wouldn't stop me.

My mother died in a car accident, although our relationship had stopped years before that. We were going to go see her, because I wanted to see her before she died, but then she died in this car accident.

I don't have a relationship with my dad, because he stopped talking to me. He is stuck in his ways. My second daughter is in a relationship with a woman, and my dad thinks this is just a phase she is going through. My dad never really got to know Thomas well, although he does know that Thomas was Tracy. Even though Thomas was female and we were in a relationship, it is weird that he still thinks my daughter is just going through a phase and will eventually be with a man. I tried to tell my dad, "No, she loves her," but he seems to just tolerate her relationship.

With Thomas' family, it was awkward. His dad is a mean person. He's always treated Thomas badly, like Thomas describes in his book. He was not supportive of our business, not supportive of Thomas or Thomas' change, or any of his relationships. Thomas has a little brother and an older brother and none of them support him either.

We don't have a lot of friends, just a few that we don't see every day, or every week or even every month. Our neighbors reached out to us, and we made some friends. The woman who works at our daycare has babysat for us a couple of times, and we really like her.

Since you and Thomas decided to have children, has your relationship changed with each other and with your family and friends?

Susan is 3 ½, Austin is 2 ½ and Jensen is 1 ½, and they are the prettiest children in the world! Although Thomas delivered them, I got to breastfeed them and bonded with them, which was wonderful. I went on hormones and other herbs to do that. They are very happy babies and they love us. Susan has known for a long time that she came from inside daddy. As she got bigger and bigger, she had to come out, and then she says, here I am. Then she says, she was in daddy's tummy and Austin and Jensen were in daddy's tummy too. Then I show her pictures of when I was pregnant with my children, her sisters, and she says they were in your tummy. She is getting it. She knows that she has a vagina and her brothers have peepees, and when she can understand abstract concepts, it is just going to flow right through. We are always going to tell the truth. We want our children to know where they came from and everything. Hopefully, one day when they are 18, the donor, if he wants to, will form a relationship with them as well. All of our children came from the same donor's sperm, and I feel it is very important to know where your genes came from.

None of our family thought we should get pregnant. Some thought we wouldn't be good parents; others thought we should adopt. My older daughters were jealous at first, of having more brothers and sisters, but then they came around and were here when Susan was born. We lost friends, but the neighborhood was great. They gave Thomas a baby shower. He wore slacks and a button up shirt and his tummy was just bulging. I think there were over 55 people there. We had games and it was fun. I am still amazed that all those people went to such a fuss for one man: my husband.

We had to adopt all of our children, and it cost a lot of money. The hospital was so confused they didn't know what to do. They were going to put us down as domestic partners, with Thomas as the mother and me as the father. That was not right because we are married and could have caused potential legal issues for us with having official paperwork listing our marriage and genders as something other than what our original paperwork says. The hospital wanted us to use a birth certificate form specifying a same-sex parental relationship and would have listed Thomas as a female. This would have caused conflicting legal documents and could well cause a problem if Thomas were to die, then my parental rights could have easily been challenged by my father-in-law. We did hire an attorney to ensure that the birth certificates properly listed me as the mother and Thomas as the father.

When I was born, they put this man's name as my father and 42 years later, Thomas and I figured out he wasn't my dad. So how hard is it to say Thomas is the father. The hospital said, but fathers can't give birth, but we said, he just did. All of Thomas' documents, his passport, birth certificate, driver's license, all say male. So at the hospital he can't say he is female, that is just ridiculous, and it cost us thousands of dollars per child to adopt our children.

Between Thomas and I, having three children close in ages, is really rewarding but extremely tough. First off, we didn't sleep together during all the pregnancies, because he was afraid there would be a miscarriage. Now we sleep in separate rooms and switch off. I will have the babies and he will sleep, and then switch every other night. It's tough on a relationship because we have to find time for us. We have a date night.

I think our family is just like every other family, a little different, but only because of us. If you know who we actually are, we are just the same, nothing different. Hopefully, we are just as grounded as most people are. We are a mommy and a daddy and isn't that what family is all about.

What do you intend to teach your children about transgender issues?

Our children haven't been bullied at school yet, but when that comes, we will talk to them about how everyone gets bullied. I was bullied, because I wore tomboy clothes. They will be able to deal with it. We have talked to the director of the pre-school they go to and let her know who we are. They were not weirded out, and everyone treats us really nice.

Children learn to hate somebody from their parents. If the parents teach their children it is ok that men get pregnant, that there are transgender people, then it is ok. There are gay people too; two mommies and two daddies, there are all kinds of different families. I think in my older children's generation, it is going to be way more cool.

Because you were publicized heavily when Thomas was pregnant, what has changed if anything?

A lot of people call and ask us what to do, and we say that the most important thing is to go see a doctor, and see if they are capable of having a baby. Then we are all for it, because we think people should not have to be sterilized to become who they are. We just got an email this morning from a man in Israel who said thank you. You are such a great inspiration, I don't know if I would have gotten enough courage to get pregnant without you, and now the baby is 16 days old. He is the first F2M in Israel to have a baby, a little baby boy. People call us and they are shy, indicating they didn't think we would answer the phone and don't know what to say.

If we can help other families, and if they ask, particularly the younger ones, we tell them it is ok, they can have families. Some organizations think you have to give up your reproductive rights to be transgender. It is just not true. Thomas never faltered on his maleness when he was pregnant. He never felt he was female because he was pregnant. Who says it is a female thing to have a baby. It is a human thing. I had a hysterectomy, does that make me a man now. Thomas blends in, obviously not when he was pregnant, but he is certainly blending in now. He just did a karate tournament and kicked butt.

Anyone who contacted us in person or sent us letters was positive. It is the emails where people don't have to show their faces that just rant and rave and swear. There have been death threats and kidnapping threats against our children. It has been scary. Many transgender people, with some incredible exceptions, badmouthed us, because they told us we were an embarrassment to the community.

As to being on television, it was positive that we got to tell our own story and could educate people, about people like us and our family. We could give hope to people who are transgender who think there is no hope to have family.

Heather and her spouse

A Lesbian Who Hates Men Dating a Man Who Hates Lesbians

Heather Cowan

Heather is a linguist from New Mexico and is now married to the man referenced in this article. She is a feminist and is committed to anti-racism and anti-oppression. She produces many lesbian, women and queer-oriented events through her involvement in Women in Movement in New Mexico. She involves herself in local and national politics, as she believes "Dissent is Patriotic!"

$$\star \quad \star \quad \star \quad \star \quad \star$$

"I have a boyfriend for the first time in nine years," I say to people. Depending on how well they know me or how they perceive me, this statement means something different.

Group A: People who don't know me at all. To these people, that statement means: Oh my god! How awful! She's been single for NINE years. What's wrong with her? Is she hideously ugly? Was she going to become a nun? Poor thing. Well, good for her. At least she's found someone now (to a subset of people with empathy). Yeah, let's see if it lasts…(to a subset of these people who are also cynics).

Group B: People who don't actually know me, but have a general perception of me and my affiliation with the queer community: Oh, so she's not a lesbian anymore. Well, whatever. We don't need people like her in our community anyway. Stupid breeders.

Group C: People who actually know me: Ha Ha Ha. They laugh and joke about how odd it is that I have a boyfriend. Who'da ever thunk it?

So, have you guessed it? Yes, that's right. My boyfriend is trans. And he doesn't really hate lesbians; he used to think he was one! And I don't hate men; I'm a feminist, so it's usually assumed I hate men. Occasionally I get calls from ex-girlfriends. They go something like this:

Me: Hello?

Ex: Hey. It's (insert name here).

Me: Oh, hey. How's it going?

Ex: Great. Things are good.

Me: Excellent. How's (insert ex's new girlfriend's name here)?

Ex: Oh she's great. We're great. We're really great. (*in my head: great…*)

Me: What's up?

Ex: Oh, I was just calling to see how you are.

Me: I'm good. Thanks. (This dissolves into a very boring conversation about work, school, family, whatever.)

Me: Well, um, it was good talking to you?

Ex: Uh, yeah. You too.

(Why is she being so weird? What the hell is going on?)

Ex: Well, have a good life.

(What? What is she talking about?)

Me: What? What are you talking about?

Ex: What do you mean?

Me: What do I mean? Have a good life? What?!

Ex: Well, (insert ex's friend's girlfriend's co-worker's girlfriend's name here) told me you're with a boy.

Me: Oh. Oh lord. Yes, I'm dating a boy.

Ex: Yeah, so what? You weren't going to tell me?

Me: Well, we hadn't talked in a while. It hadn't really occurred to me to call you every time I started dating someone new.

Ex: Well, I thought we were friends.

Me: Okay. It sounds like you're maybe a little hurt that I didn't update you on my life. I'm sorry. If it makes you feel better, I've been pretty busy, not really been in touch with a lot of people.

Ex: Well, it's just that that's pretty big. I mean, you're dating a boy (said like I'm dating a leper). And well, when we were together, it was so important for you to be friends with your exes. *(Well, of course I had to be friendly with them! There are only 10 lesbians here, and I've slept with all of them. If I weren't friendly, I'd get cut every time I went to the lesbian bar!)* And, well, it's just, I thought we were still friends. I still care about you.

Me: *(uh-huh)* I still care about you too. You know that.

(Conversation then dissolves into the drawn out lesbian processing that we're so fond of.)

My current situation (humorous as I find it to be) is actually indicative of a broader issue within queer communities. Trans people have to deal with where they fit in after they transition within lesbian, gay or queer communities. As feminists within these communities, we give lip service to how gender and sexuality are on a continuum, but enter in trans folk (who may or may not identify as queer anymore) and all of a sudden, it's the gender police. I don't want to play this game, not for anyone else, and I certainly don't want the gender police coming down on me because the person I am dating excludes me from the lesbian community. These are not new issues. Trans people have been dealing with these issues forever! And now, our queer communities are starting to catch up. Safe, exclusive spaces for gays and lesbians (while still needed) are no longer serving our communities to the fullest. I (as a lesbian) miss out on the perspectives of trans people (and gay men) whenever I immerse myself in 'women's only' space. This is reminiscent of white people continuing to miss out on the perspectives and knowledge that people of color bring to the table whenever we buy into the current white dominated field of politics, academia, religion, etc. Our herstory is lacking because what everyone is taught in school is still from the perspective of the dominant culture leaving out the contributions of countless others! Our own perceptions of society become clouded in the lack of information presented to us. For the last six years, I've been a board member on an all-volunteer, non-profit lesbian production company. One of our main events was a women's music festival that until 2003 was advertised as a "women's only" event. And we got a lot of flack from some members of the lesbian community when there were…(have a seat now)…BOYS on the dance floor!!

We, as a board, within our own group and as part of larger discussions with the community, processed for at least a year (if not longer) about what our events are gaining and missing from being "women's only" spaces. In victory, we determined that the separatism (that is still valued, and in some communities incredibly needed) in our community has become disrespectful and oppressive.

Questions surfaced over these discussions. Were we causing pain by gender policing our events and denying entrance based on gender presentation or identity? Was it fair to deny entrance to a person on the basis of gender when their friends were attending the same party? Obviously, it was disrespectful to force select persons to disclose their own personal history (that may be painful) in order for us to see them as "acceptable" within our community spaces; for a guy to have to say to perfect strangers, "Hey, I was born a girl" in order to be allowed access to a queer event (and vice versa, although gay men's events don't often have the same reputation as being separatist as compared to lesbian events). These are some of the questions that led us to allow everyone access to our events without fear of "gender policing." At a minimum, this reduced discomfort for some members within the community. There are still some "women's only" spaces in my community. Dances I used to love! The people who organize these events are not transphobic, everyone is very accepting of trans guys at these events. However, the key difference for the trans guys at these events is that they transitioned in the community! Everyone knows them from the lesbian community and accepted their identities, using the right pronouns, new names and such as they transitioned to be men.

My boyfriend moved here from out of state. He did not transition in this community and was not offered the same acceptance as those who transitioned and remained here during this process. I'm sure they'd accept him — if they knew his history. But, how is that fair to him? He doesn't identify as a lesbian, and it certainly is not my place to disclose information about him to people he doesn't know. Although, believe me, I didn't quite understand this concept at first and disclosed this aspect of his life to several people. He was kind, patient and understanding and explained to me that if it's only okay for me to date a guy if I've told them he's trans then, for these people, they don't see him as a guy. They see him as a "guy," or a trans guy. Or worst case scenario, just a butch lesbian.

"Am I still allowed to participate in the lesbian community now that I'm dating a guy?"

So, why isn't it okay for lesbians to date guys? Ha ha. I know this seems obvious, right? Because the definition of lesbian states that, lesbians date women. And it's seen as a betrayal if a lesbian 'moves out' of the community, as she is then seen as embracing heterosexual privilege or has seemingly had a choice in the scenario. Even if, it was solely out of love. As I have done. Does my identity change if the person I'm dating changes their gender? If I choose to date someone whose perceived gender changed before I met them? Is my identity dependent upon my partner's identity? His identity doesn't change because he is dating me, he doesn't become a lesbian. Is it anti-feminist to assume that my identity is dependent on my partner's? Although, I believe ostracizing a member of a community because they no longer appear to 'fit' is anti-feminist, I also understand the semantics involved in this. Lesbians are women who date women. I no longer date women, so who am I now? I don't feel like 'lesbian' fits me anymore. I've always liked 'queer' because I'm definitely oh so queer. But, where does that place me in my 'lesbian' community? Especially now, that I am often perceived as heterosexual. Have I betrayed my community by 'moving out' and embracing a man I love? Where am I on this continuum of sexuality? Where does this place me in terms of my community involvement and activism? Am I still allowed to participate in the lesbian community now that I'm dating a guy? Is it hypocrisy that I would still produce queer events, ride in the pride parade, march in the dyke march? And where is my boyfriend allowed? Queer events, why not? Pride parade, sure.

But, picture the dyke march. My best friends marched by my side, despite the fact they don't identify as dykes. Their presence was not questioned, solely because they were female. But, would it be okay if I wanted my partner to march with me? Probably not. Unless we disclosed his history to an entire group of people we do not know. Or would it just be that we would have to disclose and disclose and disclose every time we passed a new dyke that we hadn't already disclosed to? What about the potential for violence, harassment or angry looks? Lesbians are just people too, some of whom are violent (or racist, sexist, classist, whatever). People can be very defensive when something very precious to them (like a hard sought and won safe lesbian space) feels threatened. I don't want to make my boyfriend or myself uncomfortable any more than I want to make members of my community uncomfortable. But, wait, what is my community anyway?

"Untitled" by Liam Madden © 2011

Things That Matter

Flora Gates

Flora is a Chicana activist and writer. Raised in Southern California, Flora now calls Colorado home (even though she misses the beach dearly). Flora enjoys learning and adventure and has a passion for anything that involves intersections of identity. A sociologist at heart, she has done research on race/sexuality/identity. Flora hopes to continue writing and to one day soon publish a novel. That, and change the world.

For over two years, I was in a relationship with an individual who I'll refer to as James. James was a transgender man. Many years have passed since this relationship, and to this day I look at myself in the mirror and I wonder why I stayed in it so long. I'm sure there are a number of people who can relate to this story, people who may or may not be in a relationship with a transgender person. James was abusive. As twisted as it sounds to admit to myself and to anyone else, something about his danger and something about "his edge" attracted me to him. I thought that I could be the one he could take care of, the one he could love, perhaps the one to break his destructive patterns. I have to say, this man did have a reputation.

It was not his transition from female to male or the use of testosterone that made him abusive. However, the worst part about his attempts at rationalizing his abusive behavior is that he would blame the testosterone. James was abusive from the early stages when we were dating, when he was not transitioning, to the final days of our relationship when he had fully transitioned. Perhaps, I thought it was the need to transition that made him so angry. I wanted to be supportive, so I stayed. I rationalized that he consumed alcohol because of this need and that when he had transitioned our lives would be different. He would no longer get angry. He was really great when he wasn't angry. I wanted to be supportive. I loved him when he was sober, when the anger didn't take over. When I look back now, I know that James, regardless of his desire to transition, was an abusive man.

I remember what went through my mind when I saw him; I wondered "who is that individual?" I wasn't sure which pronoun to use or if I even needed to use just one. I was intrigued. I don't know if it was the way he carried himself or what attracted me to this person.

What I do know is that I have always been attracted to people who transcended gender. I don't have a whole lot of early childhood memories. However, I can recall telling my mom when I was a small child that men would one day wear dresses. She looked at me perplexed. I remember her look almost as if it were yesterday, even though 25 years have since passed. It was not only a look of disagreement, but also a look of warning, a look that signaled that my sense of gender was not appropriate for my Mexican-American family. I remember many instances like this, where I attempted to skirt along the edge of the divide by playing with trucks when my sisters played with dolls...until I got my trucks taken away from me. This was not an appropriate toy for a girl.

I grew up in East Los Angeles in the projects in the borderlands between gang life and Hollywood, where Catholicism is like syrup. I watched from behind my screen door as a man died on my front lawn, shot to death for his jacket, and I had family members who were addicts. I found my safety at school, in my writing and in my dreams. My hero was and always will be my uncle, a gay man. In 1994, my life would abruptly change. The Northridge Earthquake hit, and we lost everything. In a matter of minutes my home became a tent in the park, and I had lost my safe spaces. Over the course of the next few weeks, we found ourselves in Colorado staying with my great-grandmother. I didn't know what culture shock was like until the moment when one short plane ride took me from inner city madness to open fields and cows.

In high school I dated men who often identified as bisexual and engaged in cross-dressing. One wore a dress out in public, and I recall the daily harassment that he endured. I kept his secret from my family. I enjoyed his transgression. Myself, I often adorned jeans, t-shirts and glitter. I wore boxers underneath my baggy jeans, and on most mornings, I took time to carefully apply vibrant eye shadow and glitter on my eyes. The divide between masculine/feminine and male/female has always been blurry for me. I can't say that I have ever felt "female enough," but I also can't say that I have ever felt "like a man." I wore a dress when my sister got married, and I haven't worn one since. It has been four years. Not that I will never wear a dress again, but it is just not how I feel most comfortable. I enjoyed being in my sister's wedding, and she had a wonderful and beautiful ceremony, but the best way to describe how I felt that day is like I was in drag. On most days, looking at me, what you see is a female and feminine, but perhaps not a "traditional" Chicana. When I look in the mirror, I see me.

Being Chicana, I have gained most of my inspiration to be myself and be okay with my construction of gender fluidity from writers like Emma Perez, Cherrie Moraga, Carla Trujillo, Ana Castillo and Gloria Anzaldua. These women have paved the way for Chicanas/Latinas to interrogate the edges and to transgress the binaries.

As James and I got to know each other better, we talked about our worldviews and our transgressive identities. James embraced and even celebrated my gender fluidness, and I embraced and celebrated his. I listened to his stories from childhood, and he shared his gender journey with me. What I found in James was a best friend, but what haunted James was an addiction to alcohol/prescription drugs and a propensity for abuse. Our relationship had all of the signs of an abusive situation, but he justified his actions through his transition. Before transitioning, he would assert that it was his need to transition that drove him to violence. He was angry about his situation. He swore that once he was able to start the transition process that things would improve. I trusted him.

Like most abusive relationships, things were often great. These moments were scuffed with tar from his anger and violence on seemingly rare occasions. When things were bad, they were really bad. I wanted to support James, and I loved him. I loved the man I knew without the abuse, as I held on to the hope that things would really be different. I wanted to support him so I stayed. My family and friends were concerned from the beginning. They warned me from the very beginning that it was not a good situation. They saw him as a loose cannon and a controlling man. They saw past his charm that blinded my brown eyes. On a few occasions, I remember telling him that I was going to leave, and then he would take my phone and my purse and sit in front of the door of our small apartment.

When he started testosterone he was happier. He talked about how the testosterone would give him the body he had always desired, but nothing changed. He continued to drink, heavily. He continued to be abusive. It was not worse, but it was not better. Repeatedly he would apologize for his behavior. The tears would come, and I don't even know how many times the words "I'm sorry" passed through his lips and into my naïve ears. He would say that he was still adjusting to the testosterone, that he was starting to feel more and more like himself. Again and again I would forgive him.

After years of this cycle, I finally developed the courage to leave. It was not an easy process. The first time I attempted to leave he attacked me and downed a bottle of drugs so that I would be forced to stay, to get him medical help, to call 911. He claimed that he could not live without me. I called 911, paramedics came and took him to the hospital. As they were ripping off his clothing to give him the medical attention he needed and pumping his stomach, two officers approached me on the front sidewalk and asked me a few questions. They took a statement from me about what happened and asked me some questions about his medical and mental health history. They asked about his emergency contacts, his one and only emergency contact was me. Then the officers asked me if he was abusive in any way. I thought about it for what was probably only 10 seconds (but felt like eternity), and I told them "no."

To this day, I regret not telling the truth. But yet again, I wanted so badly to protect him. A short time later, I went to the hospital to see him. He was in pretty bad shape for three long days, and then he got better. We went home and, yet again, he told me how sorry he was, and he told me that I had to promise not to leave him. As he pleaded for my forgiveness, I knew with all of my heart and my entire mind that it was time to leave. Four days later, I packed my car with whatever I could fit (including my dog and cat), drove away and never looked back. Through a local shelter and legal help, I was finally free of him. Free of the abuse and free of the manipulation. What mattered most was that now I was safe and I was free. What took longer to free myself of was the shame.

To this day, certain things will remind me of that time in my life and remind me of the situation, whether it is a song or a place or the smell of his cologne. I had an experience two years ago where I was walking through the mall and walked passed Abercrombie and Fitch, a store. As I passed by the entrance, I got a big whiff of Fierce (their men's cologne) and had what was almost a full-on flashback. But through prayer and through a supportive network of friends, I have learned to enjoy the present, and I have learned to move passed the horrific memories that were once my reality.

I somehow rationalized all of it and kept telling myself that it would get better. I had wanted to be fully supportive. In doing so, I had allowed this man to use and abuse me for far too long. One of the first times I opened up about the whole James situation, I was talking with a friend from church. She was a woman who was older than me, and she was extremely wise. She was in an abusive marriage for much of her life. She told me that although I endured abuse for way too long, that I should be glad I got out before years turned into decades. This woman spoke from a place of truth, and through our lessons learned from our past relationships, we had a really deep connection. I learned so very much from the relationship and the years that have followed since leaving James.

I had placed myself second to all of his needs during his transitional time. It took me years to deal with the issues that this relationship caused, years for me to trust someone again. I learned that regardless of gender identity or transitional status, abuse exists in every community. I learned that if and when I am in a relationship, my needs and my safety are as important as my partner's. I learned that leaving an abusive relationship (even if the person is transgender) does not mean that I am not supportive of the transitional process of my partner. It means that I care enough about myself to leave an abusive situation.

> "*I* learned that leaving an abusive relationship (even if the person is transgender) does not mean that I am not supportive of the transitional process of my partner. It means that I care enough about myself to leave an abusive situation."

Today, I am in a healthy and a loving relationship. My current partner is a gender transgressor as well. Performing in drag shows, my partner uses gender to deconstruct gender norms and raise money for various charities. Even in the aftermath of this situation from many years ago, my alliance to those in the transgender community has not changed with the recognition that it was not James' transition that made him an abuser. James, like most abusers, had a difficult childhood. He needed help to deal with his anger. It is my hope, my prayer, that James has found the help that he needed.

$\star$ $\star$ $\star$ $\star$ $\star$

As some of us may know, transgender and gender variant individuals have been victims of horrendous and senseless acts of violence. There's an entire day set aside to mourn deaths that have resulted in such violence, to celebrate lives and to think about what we can do to change the sad reality that people are often targeted for their gender identity/expression. Each November, when the National Transgender Day of Remembrance rolls around, the most important thing we can do is act, and then, to take those actions and weave them into our daily lives, actions and conversations.

What is an ally? Allies matter. An ally stands up, speaks up, holds up and owns up. An ally stands up for those that need someone to stand up for them...period. They speak up for those who don't have a voice, they stand up for those whose voices are so tired...tired of continuously and tirelessly trying to explain and justify who they are. They hold up their friends, their family, their partners, their communities and strangers. They own up, owning up to their actions and their words, reflexive of how their actions may help or harm others, whether or not it was ever intentional.

We all need allies. I needed allies when I was in a relationship with James. My allies included individuals from the transgender community, people who I owe so much gratitude to. Beyond being an ally for a specific group, it is about being an ally to those around you. Being an ally, to me, is about recognizing inequality and being ready to address it, regardless of how hard it may be. I will continue to be an ally to my transgender friends and community members. I will also continue to speak out about domestic violence and how it affects all individuals regardless of one's chosen or birth identity. It is not always easy, but the difficulties outweigh the consequences of not speaking up. I am sitting here, wrapping up this piece on Martin Luther King, Jr. Day and cannot help but be reminded that this day marks the 18-year anniversary of the Northridge Earthquake. However, more importantly, I also cannot help but be reminded of one of my favorite quotes that encompasses the very essence of what an ally should be:

Our lives begin to end the day we become silent about things that matter.
—Dr. Martin Luther King Jr.

"The Archer's Violin" by Autumn Yamamoto © 2012

Dylan and Miriam

Change One Thing and You Change Everything

Miriam Hall

Miriam is the wife of a transgender person. She teaches writing and writes in Madison, Wisconsin and also teaches Miksang Contemplative Photography. She has two poetry chapbooks: *At Home Here* and *Dreams of Movement*, through Finishing Line Press. She is working on two memoirs entitled *Bermuda Triangles* and *I Call Him Madeline*, from which this essay is a selection. Find her at www.herspiral.com

⋆   ⋆   ⋆   ⋆   ⋆

I used to play a game as a budding bi-girl. I wasn't the only one — for all I know, queer kids still play it. It was a guessing game called "Dyke or twelve-year-old boy?" Basically, to look at someone from a distance and determine if they were a she or he, baby butch dyke or small boy. The aim of this guessing game was, ostensibly, to turn around our expectations and perceptions of gender and sexuality and to poke a tiny bit of fun at our own community.

Then I got my first girlfriend who had a boy's ass — flat, thin-hipped — and well-developed breasts on top. She was woman above, but total boy below. From the back you'd think "twelve-year-old boy," from the front, not even "dyke," but "Hot Mama." She hated the guessing game, not just that I did it but that others did it, too; found it disparaging, and pointed out to me, after all, that looks are only as accurate as a book cover and even then, often not even as good as a cover. She was right; she still is. On my own, a few years later, I began to, and still do, dissect the concept of "gaydar" for the same reasons — not to become humorless, but to be aware of the new positions, restrictions and roles such ideas enforce within the queer community. I always fail to fit someone's gaydar anyway, still do, being bisexual, trisexual or whatever I am — a bit of both, a bit of neither, some of all, none at all.

Recently, I only have eyes for trans women. With my spouse in the very early stages of becoming one, I see a trans woman in more women than who actually are. I do see trans women, but I also often think that a slim-hipped and large-breasted, long-fingered or very tall woman with barely-there-hair is trans, when in fact, she is not. I have actually begun to personally feel the "pain of the game," this guessing game, that is naming even if only in hope for community, even in a positive light. How risky my assumptions are and how tight they show my mind to truly be — grasping for some order, sanity, in changing identities.

A few nights ago I asked my spouse how he feels about being diagnosed with gender dysphoria. "It seems society is what is disordered about gender!" I charge ahead, before he can answer indignant and angry me. I spit out a friend's story of an acquaintance of hers rattling in my head — how he self-medicated with illegal hormones and even castrated himself and yet still lives as a man, a ½ man, in fact, scared to lose his daughter if he fully transitions, yet now fully abandoned by friends, family and himself. He isn't crazy, or if he is, he was only driven that way in response to society's expectations. Then again, what is insanity, if not non-conformity, of the mind, body and/or spirit? I keep piling out my opinions and rant as he listens.

My spouse waits patiently through me answering my own question and recounting this tale, then responds. "Me? Personally, I don't mind. I *feel* fucked up. I am going to get help because of it. Sure, I'm angry that this is in the DSM, sad that I am seen as insane, in some sense, to have been born in a wrongly gendered body. But anger and sadness aren't going to be my life or to eat me alive." We both sit in silence as I drive, the image of the friend's acquaintance half-eaten in his indecision and loneliness in our mind's eyes. The ambiguity of being forced to wait in the middle, to not move one way or the other, angers me more than even the binary [gender binary assumes that there are two and only two genders] itself.

I recall our first date, the long conversation over bottles of wine about — at the time — political ideology and our personal leanings, how we're both now "less left" than we used to be but also more spacious, more aware of nuance, of differences. My spouse wants a gender to be sure — a female gender — to be a she, her, hers — not to be ze or zer, as has become the possibility for the newer generations of genderqueer folk. Of course he thinks, as do I, that we should all be able to have the choice to match and represent as our true gender — whether binary or not. It just so happens that my spouse wants his body to match his very female, very lesbian mind and soul — and that, of course, can be another troublesome area in terms of society's versions of sanity.

"But homosexuality used to be in the DSM," I refute, knowing his moderate opinion of wanting to fit in isn't weak at all, is in fact, a strength of his; knowing what he wants, working from a confident and centered place, from where he can fight the oncoming gender storm. I want to play devil's radical queer advocate anyway.

"And one day transgender and transsexual won't be in it," is his answer, and I relax. Being married to someone who, weeks ago, was determined disordered, dysphoric, but not delusional (according to a four hour therapy session and two hour MMPI test), put me firmly, finally, in the place where I can accept that I am, in fact, no longer even "just bisexual," but all out queer — trisexual —even while vanilla monogamous. The new therapist who gave my spouse his diagnosis was clear — while gender dysphoria is in the DSM, they tested my spouse to make sure he's not delusional (implication: that would be "crazy," — and even the therapist grimaced an ironic, sad face at this) in order to authorize him to move forward with hormones and eventually, if he desires, surgery.

"But anger and sadness aren't going to be my life or to eat me alive."

It's a funny position to be in (funny as in odd, and, occasionally, as in ha ha), and my spouse tells me horror stories he's read or heard of people who are deemed not "stable" enough (either because of their transness, because of other trauma, or from being in the closet so long) to transition, or of those who refuse to fit the Harry Benjamin Standards of Care. There are those who study for the same "exams" he just took, in order to "pass," and of course those who refuse the whole structure all together — who don't want to enter the legal and sanity-judging Olympics of changing gender. They choose their own way, staying male legally but always presenting as female, or going to Thailand, (which, having just adopted a version of the MMPI and Harry Benjamin Standards, will no longer be an option in a few months) and/or use hormones illegally, independently found. Some try harder than he has to, to fit in, some see how ridiculous the whole circus of being authorized just disordered enough to transition without being so delusional as to not be allowed to do it is, and they do it their own way.

"I am aware," he says, "due to not a lot of effort on my behalf — that I was lucky enough to pass the test, to be determined disordered but not insane. Many people can't pass that test and are left in the dysphoric gender ditch." He is clearly relieved and also aware of his privilege.

I become aware, too, of how others have looked at me, this demi-dyke that I am, for many years now. I begin to observe and digest my own privilege — as most of my lesbian friends see it — that I can "pass" or "choose to pass" as some would put it. Be with a man and fit in. Be with a woman and make a statement, as if it were that simple. I feel a tinge of regret for my young queer games — wish that I didn't still play them sometimes, pointing out someone I am sure is queer to a friend from the window in the car next to me. Am I labeling because I want community or to single others out?

But mostly my spouse's situation reminds me to feel gratitude, even if it is a mixed feeling. Salve for anger and permission for action. For a moment, I feel it too — after all, if he's been deemed not delusional that also releases me from a fear I hadn't known I had, that in supporting his maybe-delusions for the last three years of being together, I, too, would have been delusional. Though my spouse has always been really good about separating fantasy from fetish and fetish from reality; part of me, truly, was always a bit worried and wanting an outsider expert to tell us we are ok. This temporary relief, this modicum of ironic acceptance — we are taking it where we can get it, while so many others won't have it offered to them at all.

"This is insane," a close friend said in first response to my telling him that my spouse will be changing gender, "but I support you two all the way."

Pre-publication note from the writer: At this time, checking the final edit, I hesitate to change the gender of my spouse, who now identifies most of the time as female. I now fully think of her as female, and it grates on me to leave all the "he" and "his" in this piece. And yet, it was true to the time, so I leave her gender as it was then. This in itself is a lot of the experience of having a transgender person in my life.

"No. 24 — November Challenge" by Troy Jones © 2012

Kieran

The Broken Man
Kieran Harris

Kieran was born and raised in British Columbia, Canada and became a supporter and ally to the transgender community at an early age. She currently lives and works out of Vancouver, running her own photography business and caring for her dog, two cats and two snakes.

Anyone could see that he was broken. I think in a way that was my attraction to him. I've always been attracted to broken people, I want to mend them, help them find peace and truth in the pit of despair that they are consumed by. I don't mean the emo [overly emotional] kids who are so common today, following a trend of depression and self-injury for the sake of being cool, but truly broken people, people who have been through so much.

Something in me found him. Something looked at him and saw that he needed to be mended. The first time I ever saw him was at a queer event, the first weekend that I was ever exposed to the thought that not only were there other people out there — that I had already known — but they congregated, met up and spent time together, that I could be safe somewhere without hiding who I was. I saw him and had no idea if he was a gay boy or an incredibly butch girl. The concept that he could be something else was foreign to me at that point, but I was attracted nonetheless. I had always claimed bisexual so one-way or the other, I was "safe." It would be exactly a year before I got to speak to and spend time with him again and over a year before we started our relationship, but I thought of him on and off the whole time, curious about this handsome creature.

It was September third when we made it official, and we were inseparable. If he wasn't at my house for the night, I was at his. It didn't take long to fall into a routine that we were both comfortable with and yet…

Every day was a struggle; every day he showed me that he was a survivor. I watched as he crawled from my bed to dress, readying himself to make his way to work in the darkened hours of the early morning. He left every morning with food, coffee and a kiss, and my words of love in his ears. It wasn't enough, it would never be enough, but I like to think that it helped him get through the daily grind. Later the hours changed, and so my schedule changed, and we woke closer to noon. Still he left with food, coffee and a kiss, and still my words of love followed him down the hall. He came home to dinner; no matter what hour his work brought him back into my arms. Some days he came home looking defeated, some days he came home bursting with pride and joy, some days in physical pain from the long hours of labor. But he always came home. For the short months that he was mine, we had love.

"*B*ut he lives as the man he truly is. As the man I see, the man I loved. In the end, that will be all that matters. He is a good man, better than any that were born as such. And I am lucky to know him."

He lived in constant fear of being found out. The labor industry, be it construction or warehouse work, is unforgiving, and he knew that if he was outed it would make life even more difficult than his ruined knees and tired back already had. I watched him switch jobs over and over to avoid the shame of people discovering him. I sometimes wonder if it would have been as bad as he feared, bad as we both feared.

The nights were hard sometimes. He had nightmares of a time before me, terrible nightmares of tortures nobody should have to endure. He once told me that he endured them so that nobody else would have to. That he was picked for these terrible things because the fates knew he could survive them. Sometimes I think he was right, but to this day, I would give anything to go back and endure them in his place, chase that haunted look from his eyes. No matter what expression he wears, his eyes are haunted. The nightmares were frightening; he fought and swung, took out a night table and nearly took me out as well one night, when I tried to calm him down. Why the gods chose him to endure, to suffer, I will never know. Perhaps it's better that way, let them have their mysteries.

I remember going out one night with him to a local bar. He picked me up at work, surprised me when I wasn't expecting him and took me to a bar commonly frequented by the lesbian crowd. It should have been a safe haven for someone like him, for a couple like us. But instead I had a drink dumped on me after disagreeing with one girl's opinion on "what" I was dating. Not who. What. It was the first time since we'd started dating, that I realized that not everybody saw him as a man, not the way I did. I'd never thought of him as anything else even though he hadn't begun his physical transition. He had been living as a man since before I ever even met him and that was enough for me. For the first time, that night, I was confused, lost. It didn't last long and it was easy to return to viewing him exactly as he was, a man, no matter what anyone said. But for a few days afterwards, something in me tried to doubt, tried to ask questions.

Not all the times were dark. We had our good times, (I learned the hard way that compression vests [worn under clothing to compress the breasts of F2M trans so that they present as men] and dryers do NOT get along well) our laughs over strange day-to-day situations. To say that living and loving with my broken man was always hard, was always saddening, would be a lie. He had his first birthday cake in years with me, and we had wonderful times watching movies together, being together. I taught him how to play Guild Wars, ensuring that he would be just as geeky and addicted as I was, then had to learn how to entice him from the computer to the bedroom.

Nothing in me has or ever will see him as anything but male. I can't. He is so much more and yet, he is simply a man. What he looks like when he undresses, what ID tries to tell me, they are of no consequence. To me. To him…

My broken man looks in mirrors and hates what he sees. He looks in mirrors and sees the fatal mistake that was made in his creation. He looks in the mirror and sees the woman's body that has plagued him from his youth. But he lives as the man he truly is. As the man I see, the man I loved. In the end, that will be all that matters. He is a good man, better than any that were born as such. And I am lucky to know him.

Charlie and Cat

The Relationship That Is Surviving Transition

Cat Moran

SIGNIFICANT OTHERS

Cat graduated with honors from the Advertising Design program at the Fashion Institute of Technology. Cat promptly decided that phe (Cat prefers gender-neutral pronouns) was actually a writer rather than an art director. Phe spends per free time hugging treehuggers and baking cookies from scratch. Cat can be contacted through per website, www.mcatmoran.com

$\ast$ $\ast$ $\ast$ $\ast$ $\ast$

My partner, Charlie, and I met almost five years ago at NYC's Dyke March. We converged on Washington Square Park with scores of queers, and we danced and drummed and made eyes at each other.

Charlie is a trans man, and at the time, I was a bisexual-identified cis-woman [gender identity matches assigned gender]. Shortly after meeting him and beginning to hang out with more trans and gender variant folks, I realized that "bisexual" limited things to the gender binary, and I certainly didn't. Rather, I was a queer woman.

Early in Charlie's medical transition, before his top surgery and in the early days of his testosterone therapy, we would sometimes be treated as a lesbian couple. One chain restaurant that we frequented had a particularly problematic waiter who we affectionately referred to as "DudeBro." The first time that DudeBro served us, he was attentive, and it was clear that he read us as a couple. We figured that we were "passing" — Charlie passing as male, and me passing as straight.

On our next visit, however, we were seated with another waitperson. DudeBro walked by our table and gave us a friendly, yet stomach dropping, "Hey girls, how's it going?" It was hard to shake him and his mis-gendering from that day forward. He always seemed so friendly and bubbly about it that we wondered what he was thinking, if he was conjuring up thoughts of the fetishization of lesbians, or if he was so pleased with himself because he "treated some gays just like everyone else today!" When we were feeling like giving him the benefit of the doubt, we wondered if someone he's close to might be gay.

While we flubbed the first few times we saw him, after that, we managed to speed up our response times. One of us would let out an incredulous, "Did he just call us ladies?" and we would chortle, since DudeBro, and any other person who might have addressed us that way, was clearly mistaken.

Sometimes, during this process of transition, it has been obvious that someone has known that Charlie is trans, and their kindness has not wavered at all. When Charlie had top surgery, I waited for 4½ hours in a waiting room by myself, and finally, I was allowed back into recovery to see him. After a while, a nurse told us that Charlie could have some juice, and after naming apple, grape, cranberry, she finished with, "And ice pops."

"You didn't tell me they had ice pops!" Charlie said.

The nurse smiled and brought him an ice pop, and I held it for him since it hurt to move his arms. He decided he was finished about halfway through, and I absentmindedly licked at the second half of it.

A young, scruffy nurse walking by stopped outside our curtain and said, "You know, I can get you your own ice pop so you don't have to share."

We laughed. "That's ok, he decided he was done with it, so I thought I'd finish it," I said.

"She's lying!" Charlie burst out. "She stole my popsicle! I'm bedridden and I can't move and so she stole it!"

We all laughed, and Charlie admitted he was kidding and I wasn't, in fact, a popsicle thief, but the nurse seemed to take a liking to us. A while later, he saw that we were leaving, and he offered to take a photo of the two of us.

> "*I*t's not always easy, and it's certainly not simple, but our relationship has lasted, and so have many relationships of people we know."

"You're probably busy doing important things," I told him.

"This is an important day," he said. It was ridiculously touching, and I am honestly glad we have that photo of a groggy post-op Charlie and I.

There have been other moments like these, where I have smiled so hard that my face hurt because of the kindness that others have shown us. And there have been many, many times when I have been uncomfortable, for myself, and even more for Charlie, like with the waiter in the restaurant. There have even been times that were scary for us, though I'm relieved to say that most of them are events that we're now able to laugh about later.

The more time I spent in the trans community, among friends who accepted me, the more I realized that I, too, did not identify as cisgender. Looking back, I realize that I have always been a bit of a gender anarchist, though I didn't have the words to describe my identity until I found community. Now, I identify as genderqueer, and I present more androgynously. Between my presentation and Charlie being further in his medical transition, we now get read completely differently than we once did!

One of the first times that we got mistaken for two cisgender guys was in a situation that made me very nervous. We were only a mile or two from home, and we got pulled over for having a headlight out.

"How're you boys doing tonight?" the cop asked.

I thought I must have misheard him. Charlie answered for us. "We're good."

"You live around here?" he asked.

"Yup," Charlie said. "Right over there." He motioned towards the traffic light up ahead.

"How about you?" the cop asked me.

I realized that the cop was not viewing us as a couple, and that I hadn't misheard him. He thought we were two young guys, perhaps out to cause some trouble.

"Where are you off to tonight?" he asked. It was the weekend, a Saturday night, perhaps eleven o'clock.

"Just home," we answered.

"You sure?" he asked. "Not headed out to party tonight?"

He wasn't asking in a way that was condescending. Instead, he asked in a way that was almost accompanied with a "wink, wink, nudge, nudge," or that the follow-up question would be, "Aren't ya going to go try to nail some chicks tonight?"

"No sir," Charlie answered. When I realized that the cop thought I was a cis-male, I zipped my lips. My voice is low for a female-assigned-at-birth person, but I worried that if I spoke too much, the cop would realize his "mistake." If this happened, I was scared that he would get angry and cause trouble for us.

"Well, you have a tail light out," the cop said, putting his arm on the top of the car. "Make sure you get that fixed this weekend, you hear?"

"Yes sir," Charlie said. We drove off and I finally exhaled. As soon as the flashing lights were out of the rearview mirror, we were able to laugh about it, but in the moment, it had been nerve-wracking.

Over time, these kinds of negative incidents have lessened, and when they do happen, we deal with them with more grace. Also over time, there has been more of an understanding from society about transgender and gender variant people, and less people say the "wrong" things, and more people act in solidarity with us.

What has not changed during all of this is our relationship. Some people told me in the beginning that a relationship could not survive transition. I know that this isn't true. It's not always easy, and it's certainly not simple, but our relationship has lasted, and so have many relationships of people we know. Listen to your partner. Learn from your mistakes. Find community (the internet counts!). Love, above all.

"Sleepy Joe" by Autumn Yamamoto © 2012

Mina

Change
Is Good
Araminta Star

Araminta wears many hats. She leads a boisterous life with her life partner, Abner, her whippet Devo, and her portly cat, Pandora. She teaches College English courses at various colleges, as well as writing at the adult education level. She advises a campus club devoted to celebrating GLBTQ diversity. In addition, she helped to found UU Theatre where she served for a time as Artistic Director, producing many plays that dealt with transgender issues, like *Hidden: A Gender* by Kate Bornstein, and *Looking For Normal* by Jane Anderson. In her "spare time," Mina is a board member for the Literacy Volunteers of Androscoggin County, and she freelances as a writer and editor for various publications. Her debut novel, *Blind Hunger*, was published by Dark Moon Books in spring of 2011, and a horror-themed writing manual co-authored by Araminta will be in print in spring of 2012.

★ ★ ★ ★ ★

When I met Jacob, I thought I'd met the perfect man. He had all the caliber of a Rhett Butler, opening doors for me and sending me flowers at work. All the while, he maintained an understanding of the gender gap, of all the subtleties of my womanhood, of the swaying hands and coy glances of femininity that most men couldn't fathom. Jacob maintained this because Jacob was born biologically female and raised as a girl.

I had met Jacob when he was Stacey. We had collided at a youth group for GLBT teens. Stacey had seemed a little too butchy, somehow missing some significant detail: it was as if she were a cartoon sketch of herself that hadn't yet been colored in. Jacob emerged three years later, out of his teens and well into college. His surfacing was subtle — a mutual friend suddenly stopped talking about hanging out with "Stacey" back home and talked about this new person, "Jacob." In all honesty, I never would have guessed they were the same person.

Then, a party. It always begins with a party, doesn't it? I was home from college for the weekend and called Steve for reprieve from my parents. Steve invited me to a party his friend Jane was throwing, and, although I knew the crowd would be a little younger, I was already out the door.

The party was a classic parents-away-for-the-weekend sneak-a-bash. Beer cans floated in the early autumn pool. Teen siblings sucked on cigarettes, hiding coughs behind the convulsions of faux laughter, as young adults found corners to make-out in. I escaped to an alcove on the deck, surrounded by twilight and trees. In the dark, I pulled my knees up to my chest and silenced the roar of the party with a melody of stars.

"Hey," a voice cut through my solitude. "Can I sit down?"

I looked at the dark silhouette standing in front of me. Short hair, baggy jeans. A voice I didn't recognize — deep and a little gristly, like the glide of a needle over the imperceptible grooves of a record. "Of course," I said.

Taking a seat next to me on the built-in deck bench, he pulled out a cigarette and pressed it to his lips. A second later, the flash of a Zippo lighter illuminated his face. The slightest hint of facial stubble, glasses — my favorite black, square frames — and spiky brown hair.

I didn't recognize him.

"I'm Mina," I said.

"I know," he said. "I'm Jacob." He turned and offered me his hand. We shook hands. We. Shook. Hands. At a party surrounded by popularity contests and experimentation, maturation and premature ejaculation, Jacob and I shook hands like two Wall Street business partners sealing a deal. I knew right then, the way I always knew, that he and I would hook-up. It was that sensation in my abdomen, the burn of foreknowledge, assertion, belief, pre-cognizance — whatever you want to call it, the fact of the matter is, I just knew.

We spent all that night talking, hours slipping past as the moon inched lower in the sky, and never once did he reveal to me how we'd met. He was Jacob. It was as if he had been reborn in some non-Christian, gender-blurring baptism. He was a new man.

I got his number from Steve and called him from college a week later. We spent whole nights on the phone, talking as though our lives fit inside one another like a nut inside a walnut shell, two rulers of infinite space. Since I had started dating women in high school, Jacob was the first man I'd met that sparked a fire in my abdomen. He got it somehow, the way no one gets it, that gender is a choice, that women are subjugated inadvertently by the media, that it is hard to fight against the stereotype that all Women's Studies college feminists are man-hating, hairy-arm-pitted dykes.

I think I must have started realizing that he was different early on, but I never owned it. It wasn't long before I started spending my weekends off from school with him. And then, our first kiss...

"Jacob, you take amazing photographs," I said, gazing at a stack of shiny black and white portraits. "Really amazing," I dropped the pictures on the coffee table and leaned back on the couch. Turning, I propped my head on my hand and smiled at him.

"Thanks."

Slowly, I leaned in, my eyes on his mouth. "You're really quite talented," I began. "Your art, I mean, transcends. You have an eye for image." "You're just flattering me," he said, my mouth now inches from his. He didn't pull back, so I pressed my mouth to his. When our lips collided, I knew. In spite of the forced stubble over his upper lip and around his chin, I could tell. I'd kissed enough boys and girls to know. His lips were soft, smoothed and plumped by the excessive use of ChapStick. The folds around his mouth were plushy soft, and the kiss. . .The kiss was gentle, and delicate, like pressing rose petals against the sensitive skin of the lips, like bubbles bursting and tingling against the skin of the neck. I knew. And now, I was the one who didn't pull back.

It would seem I had caught Jacob at the beginning of his transition. It was so early that, even though he visited his family twice a week, to them, he was still Stacey. Each morning, he strapped his breasts down with an Ace Bandage — this was even before he knew about chest straps. He'd coat his face and neck with foamy shaving cream and shave the baby-fine, feminine hairs of his face just for the ritual — and the hope that all that shaving would inspire new growth. It was even before the legal name change from Stacey to Jacob, let alone before the hormone replacement therapies and the chest surgeries. In fact, I think I may have been his first girlfriend as a F2M. I can't even remember now. I know that as I write this, as the memories spiral through my body, there is this painful nostalgia that breaks my heart. That makes me wish things had turned out differently between us.

And so, as with most adult relationships, we moved ever closer to the monument of sex. At first, it was taboo to speak of it. This monument in the middle of the room, and we had to pretend it wasn't there.

"Turn off the light," Jacob whispered into my ear as he kissed up the aquiline of my neck. I stretched a silent arm toward the lamp and pressed the switch between thumb and forefinger.

As darkness swept around the room, Jacob's mouth found its way to mine, his tongue turning circles around my own. His fingers found the buttons of my blouse and, one by one, slid them open. Slipping his hand beneath the material of my bra, his hand found my breast. I arched my back, grinding my hips into him.

His mouth worked over my bare shoulder as my hands slid down the back of his shirt. He moaned softly as his face slid down the length of my body. In the darkness, wriggling with pleasure, I could not give myself over completely to that throbbing, pulsing moment. I could not focus wholly on his tongue. I could not imagine what was to come because, in the back of my mind, I was racing over imaginary rules and questions. What do I do? Where can I touch him that won't insult him or make him uncomfortable? That won't remind him that his body is a prison as he had described it so many times. How can I give him this same pleasure when the source of it, the root of sex, is a space he rejects? Where do I kiss him? Where do I stroke him? What can I do?

"*I* had spent many nights imagining what it must feel like to be him — to be a whole person trapped inside a body that I could not call my own, that was foreign and hostile to me."

My mind was reeling. I had such reverence for his body — more so than any other partner I had ever had. I could not bear the idea of upsetting him. I had spent many nights imagining what it must feel like to be him — to be a whole person, trapped inside a body that I could not call my own that was foreign and hostile to me. The idea of me touching him the way I'd touched other lovers was, in my mind, rude and thoughtless, and lacking any semblance of compassion. So caught up in this idea was I, that I couldn't bring myself to touch him anywhere but his beautiful face. This was the beginning of the end. After all, there was no manual on how to please a trans man (as far as I knew).

Weeks passed. We slept together a few more times, always him pleasing me and me freezing up with the fear of insult until finally he came to visit me at my apartment in college.

Snuggling in bed together, he pressed his lips to mine and said, "Let's take a shower together." In a flash, my mind rolled over a thousand scenarios: a hand slipping and touching a breast that shouldn't be there. A leg raising just enough that the knee makes contact with a wet vulva that should be a hard penis. I was terrified I would hurt him, but how could I say "no?"

In the bathroom with no window, Jacob turned on the shower and shut off the light. In fumbling darkness, we climbed over the edge of the tub and stood together under the shower. He kissed my body, caressed my hips and ran a hand up my thigh while his mouth warmed my breasts. And I just stood there. I let him touch me and I didn't touch him back. I became a prisoner in my own body.

In retrospect, I should have just told him how terrified I was, afraid that if I let myself go, lost to the folds of sexual pleasure, that I would lose my self-control and would reach for his breasts or strive to touch his clitoris. Because I had been with women and men, I knew the pleasure of both. But I didn't know the pleasure of someone who was not completely either one — or, perhaps someone, who was even more than either one could dream of being.

About a month later, we parted company as lovers and became friends. Whether it was the complications of sex or my inability to explain myself to him, I'm not sure. It could have been my desire for him to be out to everyone, I suppose. I'm not really sure.

Because I was still away at school, he did it over the phone right before I had to go to work. He probably wanted to avoid a messy scene, but I was still youthful and emotional and I wouldn't allow it to be so cavalier. After calling into work, I climbed in my car at eight at night and drove directly to his apartment where I made him face me when he did it. I cried so hard that his face blurred. I tried to reason with him, as though his mind wasn't made up — as though I didn't realize it was all my fault — but it was no use.

I gathered up the things I had left at his apartment weeks before. A tattered teddy bear I had named Little Amsterdam, some photographs, a shirt. Just things. And I walked to the door. As I stood there, the brass doorknob to his apartment solid in my fist, I froze. I couldn't turn it, I couldn't leave and I couldn't turn back to face him.

In a moment of compassion, Jacob placed his hand on the back of mine and gave it a squeeze.

"Everything changes," he said, his free arm wrapping around my shoulder and giving me a squeeze. I turned the knob and stepped into the hallway.

"But remember, change is good."

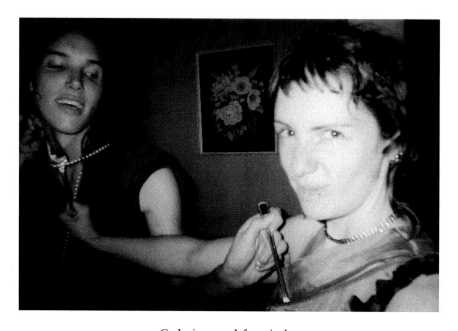

Cadmium and franciszka

Cartography of Us
franciszka voeltz

franciszka [aka: franciszka fierce]: anchor, collector, seer, magician. open-heart surgeon in a sequined mask. mouse/lion. prude/slut. homebody/adventurer. grad school poet riding the waves of change. first-and-a-half generation polish-american wandering potato fields of the old/new world. communicate/commiserate/collaborate: franciszkavoeltz@gmail.com, frantelope.wordpress.com

$\ast$ $\ast$ $\ast$ $\ast$ $\ast$

With the most dazzling love and respect for every genderqueer/trans person mapping this path with me, past, present and future, and to every trans SOFFA reading this: I wish we were in the same room, sharing our stories.

No one tells us how to do this. No one tells us how to create and share community with transgender/genderqueer/gender variant folks as they navigate their way through change. No one tells us what it will look like to be lovers, housemates, friends, collaborators and co-organizers with trans folks. It's a mapless exploration. We draw the terrain as we go. Jagged lines and smooth blue shapes. We document the journey so we may provide some kind of rough reference for others as well as a testimony of our own stories for ourselves.

A Realization

Up until this moment, I never considered the possibility that being someone who loves trans people as a valid part of my identity. (Identity is about who you are within, not about who you date, right? This theory falls apart when I consider queer, pansexual [sexual choice not limited or inhibited by gender], bisexual, lesbian and gay identities.) I identify as a trans ally. But being an ally is not about who I am, right? Being an ally is about the people I want to feel safe, welcomed and included in discussion groups, at dance/play parties, in art shows and in my communities. It's about responding to inappropriate questions about trans people so that trans people might not have to.

It's about the people for whom I offer correct pronouns when others invalidate their chosen gender identity. It's about some of the people I have held when they share stories about being harassed on the bus, in a store or walking down their street. This could never be about me. Could it?

"*But* being an ally is not about who I am, right? Being an ally is about the people I want to feel safe, welcomed and included in discussion groups, at dance/play parties, in art shows and in my communities."

Summer, 2003

Cadmium and I meet in my living room, where my housemates and I interviewed her as a possible new addition. A few weeks later, she moved in. She had been out as trans/genderqueer for about a year.

Me: cisgender woman. (cisgender: not transgender; a gender identity that society considers to match or be appropriate for the sex one was assigned at birth. The prefix cis- means "on this side of" or "not across.")

Cadmium: transwoman/genderqueer on the M to F spectrum. (genderqueer: similar to "gender variant." A term that recognizes gender as a spectrum rather than as a binary.)

Over the next five years, Cadmium would: begin taking hormones, change her pronouns from she to ze back to she again, shift her gender presentation from somewhat masculine to higher and more visible femme/inine and come out as trans to her extended family (she was already out to her parents and siblings).

Over the next five years, I would: claim my queer identity and come out to my immediate family/friends, learn more about trans identities and being a trans ally, move through questioning and ambiguity about my own identity (gender and otherwise) and begin to take on and claim my own low femme identity.

Over the next five years, the two of us would become: good friends, then lovers/dates/primary partners in a three-year open relationship, then ex's with a stretch of time apart and then friends reconnecting.

Although I've had and still have many relationships with trans people as housemates, lovers, friends and collaborators, my relationship with Cadmium is the main source of the map I'm writing for you now.

Two Photographs

There are two moments during my relationship with Cadmium that stand out as some of the most important pieces of my story as a trans person's lover. I carry the moments like creased back-pocket photographs. If you look closely at them, you'll notice Cadmium isn't even in the pictures. Instead, I am in each photo talking with another cisgendered woman who was/is dating a trans woman.

In one moment, I'm standing aside with Maia at a show. It's around the time Cadmium has begun taking hormones. Maia tells me, "If you ever wanna talk about how it was for me when Bee started taking estrogen, give me a call." And I did call her. The map she shared of her journey with Bee ended up looking much different than my journey with Cadmium. But that didn't matter. It was the first time someone offered anything like it. In fact, I didn't even think to seek out stories of what the process would be like for me. I was thinking about how hormones would affect Cadmium. (Would her developing breasts give the folks who harass her that much more ammunition? How would the Estradiol and Spironolactone impact her health? How would her family react?) I also had a few questions about how that process would affect me. (How much would I have to reacquaint myself with the person I knew so well? Would it change our sexual connection?)

As it turns out, Cadmium's physical and emotional responses to the hormones were stretched out over time, which made my adjustment process a smooth one for me. Cadmium and I continued to get it on with the same intensity/frequency as before. Her changing breasts demanded a gentler approach and brought us new hotness. However, the process of injecting hormones itself was emotional, scary and painful for Cadmium and me. Sometimes I was there with her, holding her hand. Sometimes I was there holding the syringe, counting to three out loud before jabbing the needle into flesh.

Another memory comes forth: around three years into my relationship with Cadmium, Emily and I are hugging goodbye in the sun. We met for the first time earlier that day through my dear friend/her new date, Michelle (a trans woman). Emily and Michelle are passing through town briefly. We talk about how loving trans people has meant losing friends/family or losing a depth of connection we once had with friends/family. As we say goodbye, I tell her, "Make sure you are taking care of yourself. Make sure you are getting as much love and support as you are giving." It's as if I'm giving my own self from three years ago that advice. It's something my own self from three years ago desperately needed to hear.

A Little Story (Eclipsings)

I am nine. My mom just bought her first pair of quality walking shoes. She's been walking three miles most mornings for a couple of years now. She has such a hard time spending that much money on herself, that she leaves the shoes in the box on the verge of return at any moment. Months later, she opens the box, unwraps shoes from tissue paper and laces seventy dollars worth of leather onto her feet for a first walk.

Each year, my mom spent at least three times that on back-to-school clothes alone for my two sisters and me.

At some point, her life became a lot less about herself than it was about her children. One of her ways of parenting was to erase herself almost completely out of existence. Instead of her story, she placed our stories. Instead of her needs, she placed ours. Instead of her life having its own significance, she placed it in us.

Along the way, I learned to do the same with lovers and friends. The pattern has often played deeply into relationships with trans folks, with Cadmium in particular. Sometimes I wanted to be her more than I wanted to be myself. It took several years into our relationship to recognize this so articulately. Since then, I've put intention and energy into deconstructing such familiar and damaging ways of forming relationships. Sometimes I succeed at breaking the patterns down. Sometimes they break me/my relationships down.

Spring, 2004

My parents are scheduled to visit me, my home, Cadmium's home in a month or so. Mom and I are on the phone sifting details into place. I spend nearly half an hour introducing the word 'transgender' to her, explaining Cadmium's gender identity and directing her to the book *Trans Liberation* by Leslie Feinberg as a reference. I tell her about my home being Cadmium's home, and how it's important for Cadmium to feel safe and comfortable there. I talk about how using female pronouns for her during the visit is a way to ensure this.

This dialogue would repeat itself many times with friends and family. Not only about Cadmium, but other trans people in my life as well (explaining pronouns 'ze' and 'they,' taking more than a few seconds to answer "boy or girl?" when I'm talking about a new housemate or friend). Each of those conversations taught me a lot about advocating for others. Over time, they also taught me a lot about advocating for myself.

After talking with my mom, I realized how ridiculous it was to put so much effort into telling my parents about my housemate's gender identity when I had never put much effort into telling them about mine. The next time I visited my parents, I came out to them as queer. I was a queer dating a trans person in an open relationship.

Before I came out to my parents, I had some work to do. Historically, much of my identity has been based on what I'm not rather than what I am. I resisted taking on labels of any kind whenever I could. Spending time with Cadmium, who thought a lot about her identity and the words she chose/created to define it with, influenced me. I wanted to be able to do the same. I began questioning my sexuality about 10 years ago. But it took me five years after that to take on the word 'queer.' Once I did, I struggled with feeling not 'queer enough,' not visible as queer or like a spectator in the queer community around me. These struggles have lessened immensely over time (perhaps after my self-induced hazing).

In some ways, it has been easier for me to advocate for my friends, housemates and lovers than it has been advocating for myself. It's easier to be vulnerable with other people's stories rather than my own. It's easier to leave room for people's hurtful responses and questions. It's easier when it involves some, but a lot less risk of losing friends or family.

A Few Things We Know

For as much as I have advocated for Cadmium, she advocated back. We were aware of how dangerous a place the world could be/feel for both of us, me, female-bodied and somewhat femme presenting. And her, question-mark-bodied and highly femme/feminine presenting. We were both aware of a few things. One: the patriarchy hates women. Two: one thing the patriarchy hates more than women is men who deny their male power and privilege in order to become women or another gender.

We face this patriarchy when we are talking with doctors or teachers. We face it when we walk past people on the street. We face it when we interact with cops, landlords and our bosses.

Fall, 2003

I'm working alone at the Back to Back, a worker-owned collective Café.

At midnight, I shut the door behind the last customer and lock it. While mopping along to the dishwasher hum, I look up, startled, to find Victor standing inside the café. I realize the lock must not have been turned all the way. Victor is the shaved-headed, thickly muscled man who asked me to go dancing the other night. In mid-mop, I tell him with my words, my arms, my body, "No. We're closed. No." Although his first language is Spanish and mine English, I know he understands "no" and "cerrado." He continually attempts to verbally engage me, but I maintain my stance and he eventually leaves. After his exit, I'm shaking, but holding it together to finish my job. I'm scared to go back outside to grab the tables and chairs. I'm scared to go back outside to take out the trash and recycling. I have no idea if Victor has walked away or if he's waiting for me around the corner.

He is waiting for me, both when I take out the trash, and as I unlock my bike to ride home. He does this thing that people do in movies. He just appears out of nowhere, all three times.

With my bike between us, his heavy hand clamps on my handlebars at one side and mine on the other. He demands answers to his random assault of questions. "Listen, I'm tired. I have to go." I respond. I liberate my bike from his grip and ride home unsteadily; looking over my shoulder and feeling haunted the whole way.

At home, I tell Cadmium what happened. Maybe I am crying at this point. More likely, I am angry and talking through clenched teeth, knuckles tightened. Cadmium holds space for me, for my fear turning to anger, for my story. She tells me that I can call her next time. And we will ride home together, pedaling side-by-side through the dark. I laugh at the vision of Cadmium showing up in her question-mark-body with her question-mark gender in the face of potential danger and harm. And I feel safe, comforted, heard, supported, understood and validated. This is what it looks like to be an ally to an ally.

Cadmium and I have other allies. This keeps us from exhausting ourselves by relying solely on each other for support. In every relationship, it's essential for me to have multiple resources where I can be held, listened to and given space to process my tangled feelings. Friends, as well as my co-counseling community, are such resources for me throughout my relationship with Cadmium.

A Demand

Although Cadmium and I had each others' backs, I don't always feel that way with other trans folks in my life. My queer community gives a lot of validity to genderqueer/trans identities (on the F2M spectrum in particular). Sometimes that means my community overlooks gender identities that aren't overtly queered or trans. Too many times, I have checked in with folks about their pronoun preferences without being asked about my own. Too many times my gender identity has been assumed. Too many times I have done the same to others.

I want my queer/trans community to recognize that all gender identities are equally valid, complex and important.

"*In* every relationship, it's essential for me to have multiple resources where I can be held, listened to and given space to process my tangled feelings."

A Claiming

Coming into my low-femme identity continues to be a confusing, empowering and emotional process. I have a history of resisting/rejecting femme for reasons including: my internalized sexism, being labeled femme rather than choosing it and my ambiguity about defining femme. Being so close to Cadmium, (a fierce femme) helped to encourage me into my own femme identity as well as intimidate me. The fact that Cadmium's other dates were often femmes intimidated me too. At times, because of that intimidation, I felt like I had to choose femme to keep up. And if I chose femme, I felt like I had to construct it, learn the moves. At the same time, it feels accurate to say that low-femme has always been a part of my gender, even when I was choosing my back-to-school clothes from the boy's section in junior high, even when I was wearing a criss-cross cut-off swimsuit as a bra to press my chest as flat against me as possible, even when I was an honorary member of several boys clubs throughout my history.

Some Algebra

When I held my equation of female socialization and identity to Cadmium's equation of male socialization and transfeminine identity, I struggled with some particularly complicated emotions. Sometimes because of the male privileges she received growing up, I resented the access that Cadmium had to things I didn't.

I resented how her transfeminine identity drew positive attention from cisgender femmes when I myself would struggle with competition or feelings of invisibility with those femmes. I resented her highly expressed sexuality when I had felt so robbed of mine that I was still working to exhume sex and bring it into my language, my movement, my presentation. I resented her accomplishments and the ways she took authority in her life when I was still working through the victim role I had taken on through messages I received about the world being a dangerous and scary place that didn't belong to me.

The basic underlying thought went something like, "How dare you identify as a woman when you never had to struggle through all the damaging shit I did to get there!" (Everything about being an ally told me not to write that last sentence. But everything about offering my experiences as a resource told me to be as honest as possible.)

This, of course, completely overlooks the fact that the process of gendering/gender socialization is painful and damaging for every single person who endures it, regardless of whether they choose to identify with their assigned gender or transition into a different one. It also overlooks the fact that the gender socialization process is complicated by a constellation of so many other factors (class, race, size, ability, religion, region, etc.) that to boil it down to a simple binary process is problematic at best.

It's difficult to decipher whether the things Cadmium had access to were a direct result of growing up with all the privileges that come along with male socialization. Perhaps this access was because of class privileges or because she grew up in less isolation with more progressive parents or because she didn't have 15 years of Catholic conditioning to unshake.

On a good day, I wasn't thinking about who had access to what privileges. On a good day, I was feeling honored and inspired by the fact that Cadmium had indeed dared. On a good day, I was amazed that we both dared to love. We loved with these bodies that have a lifetime of mapping ahead of them. We loved with these bodies that we will spend a lifetime reclaiming.

"Love Me" by Jonas Jaeger © 2012

Cameron and Melanie

Identities:
Evolving Into Myself
Melanie Whitley

Melanie is a political scientist by training. In her free time she enjoys writing children's books, yoga and spending time with her husband (Cameron) and dog (Pal). She is currently working on a children's book about a transgender child.

As virtually anyone who has ever tried to publish knows, the publishing process is an arduous one that often takes years to complete. That has been the case with this anthology and thus when I went to review my submission nearly five years after I wrote it, I was both reminded of forgotten feelings and surprised by how much my own identity and relationship with my F2M partner had changed. When I originally wrote this piece my partner and I had been dating for two years, I was 22 and still developing an adult identity that accommodated my professional and personal lives. That stage of my life was a particularly dramatic one, filled with pondering and self-reflection that took me to my highest highs and lowest lows. It was also a time of extreme instability — my job, education, living arrangements and personal relationships seemed to be in a semi-constant state of flux. All of these external realities played a dramatic role in how I responded to my newly acquired F2M boyfriend and the way that his identity affected mine.

As I revise this today, I am 27, my partner and I have been married for nearly three years and our lives, both as individuals and as a couple, have fallen into the stable patterns that at 22 I would have found dull, but today I find comforting, even joyous. Although I still have a flare for the dramatic, something happened around 25 that calmed much of my dramatic energy and altered the way I look at the world. These changes present an interesting challenge. What I wrote five years ago was, at the time, remarkably candid; yet today, much of it feels trite and like the processing of a young woman who no longer exists. The piece describes feelings I remember having, but it no longer feels true. And so I am stuck in a quandary, how do I revise a piece that describes a fluid process, which time and experience have fundamentally altered? More importantly, how do I do this while honoring the process that has moved me from the past to the present? What follows is my attempt to convey the past in its genuine form while also providing a testament to the transformation that time brings.

When I saw my F2M partner for the first time, and by first I mean the first time I truly saw him, I was taken away by his beauty and depth. I was wildly attracted to his thin body and incredible ambiguity. I was fascinated by his perspective on life and his understanding of gender. But, more than the pleasure of attraction or the interest of new romance, I was scared. Actually, scared doesn't quite describe it, I was panicked. I had, for my entire life, identified as a straight girl; not just any straight girl, but the kind who is attracted to only the most masculine men, who feeds and thrives on established gender norms. That was me, and yet I was undeniably attracted to a pre-operative, early testosterone transgender man who didn't really pass and absolutely did not fit into my understanding of myself or my gendered world.

We began to get to know each other on a religious work-trip during which my numerous day dreams about this man, my future husband, were interrupted by panicked imagery of what I would say to my parents — one of them a fundamentalist Christian, the other liberal but conventional — and what this attraction meant for my own identity. At the time, I couldn't conceive of both dating a transgender person and maintaining my own straight identity. I thought that this attraction meant I would have to identify as a lesbian or bisexual or at the very least queer, and I didn't know if I wanted to take that on. I had had limited exposure to the queer world, and although I delighted in what I had seen as an observer, I wasn't sure that I wanted to become a participant. Further, the prospect of my own queerness lighted an internalized homophobia that I didn't know existed and would not be able to name for nearly five years, though it would haunt me with doubts about the morality and acceptability of my relationship for years to come.

Despite a looming identity crisis, I pursued my partner. There was a part of me, the part that is drawn to drama and underdogs that saw difference as a badge of honor and allowed me to overcome my fears. It's not that I stopped having doubts about the relationship or my identity, but there was something very powerful about the prospect of being part of a group of outsiders. Of understanding that if I took a leap of faith and pursued a person who fell outside of my understanding of gender, there would be others who would have had similar experiences, who would understand and who would fortify me against any condemnation and judgment from the normative world. Our first date was bliss — a prelude to years of happiness — and that bliss pushed me to find comfort and clarity in this new relationship.

In those early days I tried to overcome any doubt and reservations I had by fortifying myself, an integral part of which was identifying a label for myself. Language is powerful, often dictating the way we think and the boundaries we are willing to push. I thought that if I had a word that other people understood, I could clarify to myself and to others who I was, what they could expect from me. Unfortunately there was no word that described my unique position, as a queerly straight woman attracted to masculinity, not simply men. And so I told people what I thought they'd be able to understand. To my dad, who had no understanding of trans issues, I was a lesbian. To my mother, who wanted me to be anything but a lesbian, I was still straight. To my best friends, I wasn't anything exactly — they didn't have a word for me either. This approach did not in the end provide any clarity, any peace. Instead it muddled my own understanding of self and made it difficult for me to move forward in my relationship. I am someone who is deeply affected by others' perceptions and has spent a significant amount of energy trying to fit in. With a different label for each person and none that accurately described me I felt anxious, unable to easily explain to others who I was or what they should expect from me. This problem has only worsened with time. In the beginning, it was obvious that my partner and I were not a typical couple. People thought we were lesbians, or that I was my partner's older sister (he looked like a 12-year-old boy at this point), or any number of other things, but no one assumed that we were simply a straight, normal couple. As a result, when our relationship or interactions were something other than normative, no one was surprised. This was comfortable for me.

But as time has passed and my partner has transitioned, we are no longer perceived as anything but a straight couple. This physical transformation, coupled with a lack of language about my identity, has meant that in order for me to be open about my relationship and identity I have to out my partner and explain our circumstances in detail. I don't do this. The result, however, is that I have struggled with social anxiety about how others will perceive our often non-normative interactions, mannerisms and life. As an educated, self-aware woman, I recognize that such a strong concern with what others think is neither healthy nor particularly mature, but it is one of my life challenges, one that has created problems in my relationship. The wonderful, gentle and often feminine things my partner does, things that made me fall in love with him; have at times become the source of cruel conflict. It has not been uncommon for me to press my partner to be more masculine in public because I fear what others will think, what others will do. If only being transgender was more socially accepted, I think, then we could have a word, we would not have to bend and mold ourselves to fit in; we could just be. While this is true, the effort to fit in has not only been hurtful to the husband I adore, but has also damaged our relationship and created an internal battle for me. My relationship with a transgender person has highlighted a difficult duality in myself; while I am open even excited by difference in others and am the most likely to root for the underdog or try to lift up the oppressed, in my personal life, I am a conformist. This has been a difficult and disheartening realization, one that I am unlikely to have made without a transgender partner. As I have aged, my life has calmed into a happy routine and my relationships with friends and family have stabilized, these concerns have become less prominent and my love for my husband has encouraged me to be his defender instead of his critic. Yet, at the same time, every day I have to work to overcome my social anxieties and accept the difference within my own life, my own relationship. Any success I have had in this process has largely come from two things, age and the acceptance of ambiguity. I no longer seek a one-word identity but have come to an unstable peace simply existing. In fact, I had to chuckle recently when I attended a night of drag queen bingo. The announcer asked the crowd to raise their hand in turn if they were gay, straight or bisexual. I kept my hand down for each category; in the early days I would have raised it for each.

Although my relationship with my F2M partner has challenged my identity, it has largely been filled with joy and, despite my fears, normativity. In our daily lives my partner's transgender status is no longer a point of interest. It is only on rare occasions, like when we are planning a trip to a developing country, that we even discuss it with any depth. We go about our lives doing the things that all couples do — working, laughing, playing and fighting. Like many wives I thank God for giving me such a unique and amazing husband, but I feel like I have so much more to be thankful for than most. My partner is a man like none I've ever met. The way he touches me, talks to me and teases me makes my skin tingle. He challenges my own gender assumptions and pushes my boundaries. I hear people occasionally say that trans people are the best of both worlds. This statement is often interpreted as insensitive or rude, but I think it is very, very accurate. My husband is absolutely a man with a delicious masculinity that I drink up, but he was also a woman and carries with him all of the beautiful parts of femininity that I seek in intimate friendships. This combination creates a marvelously balanced partner who is at once compassionate and empathetic, who is strong and gentle. I have been amazed at the power this balance has to heal.

I am a rape survivor. In my partner I have found the gentle, feminine spirit that has a too-intimate understanding of assault and can thus comfort and hold me in the sacred space of pain and healing with compassion and deep understanding. Keeping us company in this space is the masculine heart of a man that I love, not the men who wounded my soul and caused me deep pain, but a man who has felt my pain, spoken my frustrations and has come willingly to hear my anger, accept my boundaries and love my being. In my relationship, I have experienced a healing that is partly the result of a loving, intimate relationship, but is also the unique feature of a relationship with a trans man.

"My husband is absolutely a man with a delicious masculinity that I drink up, but he was also a woman and carries with him all of the beautiful parts of femininity that I seek in intimate friendships. This combination creates a marvelously balanced partner who is at once compassionate and empathetic, who is strong and gentle. I have been amazed at the power this balance has to heal."

This type of deep understanding and compassion has played a vital role in our relationship, guiding us through both dark and joyous times. It is profound and occasionally surprising, but it is the gift of a transgender person. It is the greatest blessing of my life to have a partner with this beautiful gift, with a unique past, with a life that balances the extremes of masculinity and femininity, and I look forward to each moment I get to spend with my husband and best friend, even when it challenges my own identity.

FAMILY

"My family was lovably bizarre before gender reassignment was even a glimmer on the horizon, so my experience is hardly applicable to any other families ... I recommend this: Have a damn sense of humor about it."

—Jonathan Feakins,
adult son of a trans

Family

According to Buddha, "A family is a place where minds come in contact with one another," however, these points of contact are not inherently straightforward. How we think of ourselves in relation to our family members varies, thus the stories in this section are as diverse as these relationships. Not only does 'family' comprise our most intimate relationships, but it also represents our extended families, step-relatives and relatives due to marriage. This section tackles the issues and joys associated with parenting a transgender child, having a transgender sibling and being raised by a transgender parent. Many of the stories in this section and others cross boundaries. For instance, Pearson, the mother of an adult transgender child, is a political activist and strong ally of the transgender community through her position as the Director of TransYouth Family Allies (TYFA).

The stories are inspirational with raw emotion and a common theme of love. In this section a child of a transgender parent describes his unique family structure (Feakins), and a sibling wrestles with honoring her brother when faced with questions from outsiders (Bryant, Petra Hendrickson). Parents of transgender adults talks about their struggles and joys in coming to terms with the transition of their adult children (Ulrike Hendrickson, Ramsey, Schwartz), while families with young transgender children articulate the unique issues in raising a child in a world that may not understand or be fully supportive (Clark, Jeltsen, Maines, Pearson). What is unique about this section is the love and respect that fills the pages, even when perspectives may not align (Miller).

FAQ

Q. How does my child (brother/sister) really know they are transgender?

A. They know because it is likely they have struggled with their gender identity most of their lives. Remember: no person chooses to be transgender. Did you choose to be male or female? Neither did your child! Think back on your life. How did you know what gender you were? How did you feel comfortable in this gender? What if you sensed that the gender the world thought you were was wrong? How might you feel? It may be hard to imagine, but it is even harder to live. Your child or sibling would probably not come out to you as transgender, unless they were really, really sure.

Q. Could my sister be going through a phase?

A. Some children enjoy playing with gender norms: the little girl who is the father when playing house with her friend and the little boy who wants a Barbie doll. This may be a phase the child goes through, but if it is consistent over a period of time, and the child insists that they are the other sex ("No, Mom, I'm really a boy," when told to act more like a girl), then your sister *may* be transgender.

Q. My child is transgender, did I do something wrong in raising her? Could I have prevented this?

A. Absolutely not! No more than you could have encouraged your other children to be transgender. Most scientists believe that being transgender is biological. The existence of people who cross gender boundaries has existed and still exists in every culture, and even in the animal world. Trying to make your trans girl dress like a boy or your trans boy play with "girl toys," doesn't work and just makes the child want to hide what they enjoy doing rather than expressing it openly. If you seek professional help for you and your child, make sure it is for the purpose of helping her become more who she is, not to change her (Diane Ehrensaft's book *Gender Born Gender Made: Raising Healthy Gender Non-Conforming Children* published in 2011 should be very helpful). If you raise a child who is open, wants to share her personal life with you, and enjoys who she is, then you are a very successful parent.

Q. I miss my son, the one I remember growing up. Should I just pretend that I am happy with his transition?

A. Your trans child (no matter his age) experienced many different emotions as he was transitioning. Your child wants you to be supportive, but probably doesn't expect you to be happy all the time about his decisions, because he isn't always happy either. Sharing your personal feelings with your trans son will help him express his own feelings as well. But remember, his transgender identity may be fragile, so share your feelings, not your judgments.

Q. Will my trans niece ever have a family?

A. Remember: every trans person already has a family unless they have been disowned (unhappily many are). But this question probably means: Will she get married and have children? Yes, indeed, if she chooses to. There are as many ways to have a family, as there are people, because we live in a time of infinite possibilities. Many trans people will have life-long committed relationships, some will get married, others may choose to remain single, but have friends that they perceive as family (or all of the above). Many trans couples have children or decide to adopt. When your niece feels comfortable, she will share her plans for building a family with you. As PFLAG says, all it takes to make a family is love.

Q. I saw a trans person once on Jerry Springer. **Is that how my sister will behave?**

A. Don't worry, if your sister would not have been on *Jerry Springer* before her transition, she won't now. It is also important to know that representations of trans persons in the media are not usually flattering or accurate. Fortunately, this is changing. As an example, Chaz Bono, son of Cher and Sonny Bono and a recent participant on *Dancing With the Stars*, is a good role model.

Q. My brother was very handsome as a man, won't he just be ugly as a woman?

A. Women learn how to apply make-up, style their hair and dress well. Your brother will be learning these things too. He may be embarrassed at first to ask for help, but you can be a valuable resource to help him look the way he has always wanted.

Jonathan

Dana

Loveably Bizarre
Jonathan Feakins

Interviewed by Dana Rudolph

Jonathan shares a bit of his "lovably bizarre" family, talks about his experience as the son of a transgender father, and reminds us of the importance of keeping a sense of humor. Jonathan is a member of COLAGE (Children of Lesbian and Gays Everywhere).

Dana is a lesbian mom living with her spouse of 19 years and their eight-year-old son. She free-lances as a journalist while working as the Online Content Manager for the National SEED Project on Inclusive Curriculum at the Wellesley Center for Women. Previously, she was a vice president at Merrill Lynch, developing marketing and business strategies for several key online initiatives. She was also the first leader of the firm's global LGBT employee network. As a free-lance journalist, she writes the award-winning Mombian blog (mombian.com) as well as a regular Mombian (Lesbian Moms) column for several newspapers, covers LGBT legal and political news as a correspondent for Keen News Service and is a regular contributor for several websites, including The Bilerico Project.

$$\star \quad \star \quad \star \quad \star \quad \star$$

Tell us a little about the family in which you grew up. Who was in it? Anything particular you'd like to share about yourselves?

My family is a witch's brew of geeks, dorks and delinquents. We built secret passages in the basement for fun, and my father fought an eternal battle against right angles. My oldest brother just got married: he walked down the aisle with his wife to 'Where Is My Mind,' by The Pixies, my sister-in-law chucked a bouquet of dead flowers to the tune of 'The Doom Song' from Invader Zim, and then the entire place (a museum) was rocked by Britpop and New Wave until midnight. Because that's the way my people roll. And by the by, my father is a transgender woman.

What has been the most challenging thing you've faced as the child of an LGBT parent? How did you handle it?

My father came out as transgender only when I was 21, months before I was to graduate university: the secret pact between her and my mother was to wait until my two brothers and I were fully grown. Consequentially, the biggest challenge has been just to juggle the split between my parents. They're both the best parents a boy could ever ask for and really quite happy living their separate lives: they endured the divorce with maturity and sensitivity, which is a testament to the strength of both their characters. They still talk all the time. But when they both live on separate sides of the country, plane fare just gets to be a pain after a while.

What, if anything, did your parent(s) do to help you understand their sexual orientation or gender identity, or to help you deal with any issues this raised at school or elsewhere? Any resources (groups, books, movies, Web sites, etc.) you found particularly helpful?

Nothing needed to be done. Before my father came out, she had been borrowing my books on gender theory for two years prior. My brothers and I all had gay and lesbian friends, and I had transgender classmates and professors by the time I was 16. When she finally came out, my initial instinct was to ask whether we could still make the 2:20 showing of X-Men 2. My oldest brother's response was, in fact, 'Well, duh.'

How does having an LGBT parent affect you in your adult life? Or how has the experience of having an LGBT parent shifted in adulthood?

Considering that I use female pronouns for my father — my awesome father, who I inevitably mention in passing conversation, like any other member of my family whom I love — I become the de facto gender-theory ambassador. Conversations occur because of the 'I Love My Trans Dad' button that I place on my pinstripe suit. And for some reason, I find myself speaking on panels about my experience, because people have decided that my opinions are worth listening to. Wacky. Growing up — when my father was a man — all my friends thought that he was smoking hot. 'Shawn's Hot Dad' was a local band, actually. Now that she's a woman, our friends still think the exact same thing. And really, that never gets any less creepy.

What are the ways that having an LGBT parent has made you into who you are today?

My family was lovably bizarre before gender reassignment was even a glimmer on the horizon, so my experience is hardly applicable to any other families this side of the looking glass. So I recommend this: Have a damn sense of humor about it. Humor wins you friends, disarms enemies, forges bonds, relieves stress and helps people forget their troubles. Worrying only does so much, after which it only sours relations, rots potential and undermines dreams. Laughter gets you the rest of the way.

Why did you choose to become involved with COLAGE (People with a Lesbian, Gay, Bisexual, Transgender or Queer Parent)?

I was working in Turkey, and a girl — an American girl, a co-worker — spoke ill of my father: called her a bad father, in fact, because she 'obviously' was so obsessed with her sex change that she 'neglected to raise me well.' One of the most vindictive things I've ever heard uttered by another human being, actually.

How else, if at all, are you involved in your community or in LGBT activism or politics?

I've definitely fallen into transgender activist circles, which as a smack-talking straight boy does make for hilarious stories. Like whenever I take a piss at a transgender conference, I realize that every F2M in 20 feet is staring at me (albeit in the most discreet way possible). And then they come up to me later that evening, half-drunk, yelling, 'You're so convincing!' I tell them it's from 20 years of practice.

Please share a favorite memory of being a COLAGE or having an LGBT parent.

My father's a woman who races cars in her free time, and she constantly embarrasses men by knowing far more about high-performance engines and independent suspension than they do. It's hilarious, every single time.

Originally published in "Mombian: Sustenance for Lesbian Moms," 10/9/07, Family Voices XI.

Heather

The Trouble With Pronouns

Heather Bryant

Heather won the 2009 Southeast Review Narrative Nonfiction Contest. Her short fiction has appeared in *The Southeast Review* and online at www.women-writers.net. She teaches writing at Pace University and leads workshops on transphobia and other topics for COLAGE, a national organization for people with one or more lesbian, gay, bisexual, transgender or queer parent(s).

When I talk about my father, I try to leave off pronouns, because it's easier that way. The pronoun, "she," confuses people who think of all fathers as "he." Saying "He" feels like a lie or a violation of my father's wishes. I find myself defending my father's choices even when she's not there. Some call it the "pronoun game," how you dance around pronouns to avoid seeming different.

Avoiding pronouns is a linguistic circus act in which sentences turn clunky and heavy with nouns. "My dad," I say, and even that's a lie because she took the name "Robyn," and that's what I've called her for 24 years. I say, "Robyn," I say "she," but even twenty-four years later, I don't believe it in my bones.

Sometimes when I see her, I'm an amateur visual archaeologist, digging through layers of smooth skin and shoulder-length hair in search of a curly-haired man with spindly legs and salt-and-pepper hair. To bring him back now, I would have to be a magician, one of those wand-wielding fairies from stories.

This is what I know about my father:

Her name was David. Once upon a time, she had curly dark salt-and-pepper hair, stork-thin legs and dark coils of leg hair. Sometimes the body doesn't cooperate. It gives us things we don't want: too much hair or not enough, a flat chest or heavy breasts, long legs that turn pants into highwaters or legs that swim in slacks and shorts.

In her case, she was head-to-toe mis-matched. She looked in the mirror and saw a stranger. *David*, a man who whistled and wore skinny jeans, sneakers and crisp white button-down shirts. That's who I knew from age zero to ten.

David. Dad. A man in a hurry who liked things just-so. Hush-hush with plastic-wrapped books and the Mont Blanc pen poised and full of ink. Too much sun and David started to melt, sheets of skin peeling off in layers, pale skin underneath. After shaving, he used to stick bits of tissue on his face that looked like tiny daisies with red middles.

I hardly knew "David." We had a short decade together and during that time, he was often away with his lovers in far-flung parts of the globe. Pancake-maker, book-tote, legal pad propped on a lap desk, legs crossed over his knee. He used a cigarette holder when he smoked and drank bitter coffee from a mug. All I have are photographs or slivers of memory.

"*W*hen I talk about my father, I try to leave off pronouns, because it's easier that way. The pronoun, 'she,' confuses people who think of all fathers as 'he.'"

We traveled in a pack of three: *mom-sister-me.* Visiting David in London, San Francisco, downtown New York, across the country by train, car or plane. Back-and-forth. Coast-to-coast. I didn't know why we decided to move thousands of miles from home out-of-the-blue. I didn't overhear the phone conversation between my parents when my Dad said, *"This is what I plan to do."* Switch bodies like an amphibian moving from water to land. Like the *Little Mermaid* tale. Two lovers and 3,000 miles apart, my parents decided to move back in together in a house my Dad found in Berkeley.

All I knew was that I would have my own room. This seemed like a good enough reason to move. I could choose all the colors: pink, pink and pink. We packed cardboard boxes full of books, plates wrapped in paper and the boombox my sister and I shared for playing Genesis and Huey Lewis and the News cassette tapes. "HCB's room," we wrote in permanent marker on the side or "SAB's room" on the boxes for my sister's room. The things we still shared went into a common box. All of it got loaded on the big green and yellow Mayflower truck. The movers listened to the Beastie Boys, "What'cha Want" while they loaded the boxes.

Outside my window in Berkeley, a lemon tree grew. That's what I wrote about in letters to my friends. I sent letters on the redlined stationary with my name printed on one side: the same stationary I used to write fan letters to Ricky Schroeder, George Michael and the lead singer of A-ha. I told my friends about the lemon tree. I didn't write, *"Today my dad went for electrolysis and came back with a bright-red face."*

I didn't write, *"This weekend, my dad wore a long skirt for the first time, and outside no one blinked or looked twice."*

A scarf around her neck to hide the Adam's apple, and we were ready to go to the bookstores on Telegraph or the candy store in Rockridge, Sweet Dreams.

People are sometimes surprised that we kept the change a secret in the Bay Area where they picture men in ass-less chaps co-existing peacefully with women strutting with peacock-stiff mohawks. But our Bay Area was a car-pool-station-wagon-private-school place. We visited the Castro, but we didn't live there. In the all-girls private schools where my sister and I lined up in crisp ironed uniforms, no one else's father was crossing over from man to woman. Not one. Unless that family, too, was silent. A hidden family like mine.

No one told me I had to keep it a secret, but somehow I knew. I went for a long stretch without inviting friends for play dates or sleepovers. We lived across the Bay from my school, so it made sense that I would go to my friends' houses. One of my friend's fathers spent so much time in his study or at work, we hardly ever saw him. Usually, her mother made us sandwiches or snacks, cutting the crusts off of peanut butter and jelly. Her mother had a short no-nonsense haircut. She shooed us to my friend's room to play, which was the main goal of the sleepover: hours and hours of "Let's pretend."

When my father told us the new name she'd chosen, we were sitting in the kitchen in our house in Berkeley. Rah-bin.

A name neither he nor she.

The first thing I wanted to know when I learned her new name was this: *What if I slipped and said "Dad" in public out of habit, if I called it out across a book-store when she was browsing titles across the way? Would she turn away or pretend not to hear me? Would she correct me in a chiding tone? Would she answer back like nothing happened?*

One of my father's ex-boyfriends, Donnie, took me to the Father-Daugh-ter dinner dance at my school while she stayed at home. The theme of the dance was the 1950s. We'd practiced songs in music class: "Alley-Oop" and "Lipstick on Your Collar," songs that were supposed to remind our fathers of their teenage years. I wore a white top and skirt with black polka dots that night. Donnie wore a skinny black tie with a white cardigan. We took pictures before the dance, standing in front of the white wall in the dining room, hold-ing up the placemats I'd made in art class. "Donnie and the Doo-Rites," his placemat said in letters cut out of pink and black construction paper.

At the dance, the sixth-grade girls formed a ring around Donnie on the dance floor. He didn't like sitting with the fathers in charcoal and navy suits talking about bear hunting at tables set with white table cloths and separate glasses for water and wine. One of my friends spun away from Donnie on the dance floor.

"Is he *you-know?*" she said, making a waving motion with her hand.

"No," I said. "No," and shook my head. I looked up at Donnie, wondering if his white cardigan was too baggy or if his laugh was too high-pitched. The goal I'd set for the night was to blend in, to look like everyone else, chameleons in a room full of three-piece suits.

After we sang "Lipstick on Your Collar" on the staircase in the school's main hall, each girl ran down the stairs to her father, waiting in the crowd of men with bemused expressions in response to our a cappella performance. Mine was across the Bay. If I'd brought her here, she would stand out like a cardinal in the red blazer she liked to wear. An easy target, unlike the lumbering bears the men tried to find between crisscrossed twigs and trees, leaves rustling underfoot.

"*The* goal I'd set for the night was to blend in, to look like everyone else, chameleons in a room full of three-piece suits."

In 1986, Renee Richards, the famous tennis star who transitioned back when it was as likely as landing on the moon, published a book called *Second Serve*, about her experience transitioning. Robyn showed me the book one day. I peered at the book jacket photo of a striking blonde woman. She showed me the before and after photos. I filed the knowledge away with my growing awareness of the world. *This is what is possible.* Some things I knew were impossible: human flight, living underwater, the *Dukes of Hazzard* car tricks. People hired stuntmen or built machines to do the impossible: airplanes, scuba gear, clever edits so that Bo and Luke landed safely, daredevils who risked lifting ton-heavy cars off the ground. Fathers jumping the gap from man to woman was a new one to me, but at the time I took it in like the world just got slightly bigger.

"This is my dad," I used to say, and I didn't know then that the phrase would become as rare as the multi-syllabic words I liked to sound out on the pages of thick books or on movie screens.

Supercalifragilisticexpialidocious.

I thought everyone's father liked to watch Julie Andrews float on umbrellas and spin on hilltops in Austria. When I told a friend I learned about make-up from my Dad, she looked at me like I was confused or needed a vocabulary lesson. I didn't know it was strange until I said it out loud.

There is nothing gender neutral about the word "Dad." I say it and think scratchy face, Adam's apple bobbing in the throat, undershirt, boxers, hairy toes, cigarettes, coffee, V-neck sweaters, sneakers, chunky watch, thick-framed glasses. I think of our neighbor Will with his big glasses and bowl cut hair. "Dad" meant skinny jeans and sneakers, navy-blue jackets and neckties.

Practice the words until you know them by heart.

The electrolysis took months to finish. Hair is stubborn and cyclical under the skin. It keeps growing back so she has to go back for round after round of electrolysis, each time returning with a reddened face, tender skin and tales of pain under the zap of the aesthetician's wand. Each hair is zapped out, killed dead at the roots.

She and my mom drove to and from Trinidad, Colorado, from green to desert and back. When she came back from surgery, she had no voice. Just like in the *Little Mermaid* story. An anesthesiologist botched the job, damaged her tracheal tube while inserting the tube at the hospital. She was left with a whisper.

She hunched on the couch, recovering from surgery. She didn't want to be "my Dad" anymore. And the word, "Robyn," didn't belong to me. This person with softness instead of muscle, smooth hands, long hair. I could understand what happened and say it out loud, but on some deeper level, I didn't understand.

Why did I feel like someone was missing from my life? Maybe because that is the story we told, over and over. To family, friends, teachers, coaches and everyone we met. Our parents are divorced. Our father is not around any more. Back then, she introduced me as her niece. Her name was Robyn. Aunt Robyn. It didn't have the same possessive quality of "dad," the same stamp of our relationship. "Dad" was easy, shorthand, mine. No one told me that by saying the word "Aunt" over and over again, it would become true, replacing the old close language of parent and child.

Our family therapy sessions were designed to urge acceptance. All the fat books on the therapist's shelves, the brown leather couch where my sister and I sat side-by-side, the big desk where she sat, none of this would tell me where I could find my father again.

I try to borrow other peoples' memories. Recently, one of our neighbors in Berkeley told me that she met David for the first time when he was out on a walk in the Berkeley hills with my sister and me. I have no memory of that walk, though. I try to bring it back: eucalyptus-laced fog, pine trees by the road, the curving turns of the asphalt as it laced through the hills.

If I had to give advice, I would say this:

Move to some planet where everyone already knows what it means to be both father and woman, to start out as a boy and leap into the league of ladies. Build a house on that planet and stay there for as long as you can. Even if the weather is Arctic and you have to make an igloo to stay warm. Even if the planet is so close to the sun, your skin burns to a crisp. You won't ever have to explain your father's existence to all the curious people who want to know more. You can introduce your dad as your dad and not have to choose between parent or Aunt or "family friend." You can use "Dad" and "she" in the same sentence. Or maybe on this planet, there would be no "she" or "he," "dad" or "mom," "his" or "hers."

The prefix "trans-" comes from the Latin for "crossing over." It's not something that's complete and done once. It's ongoing, a continuous crossing. Each day I invent a new story about my father. This reminds me that I'm part of that crossing, too.

"no barbies" from the daily shots of the
"complex — learning to divide collection"
by dylan scholinski © 2012

Ruthie and Meg

Pink China
Meg Whitlock Clark

Meg lived in China and California before settling in Pennsylvania. When she's not juggling household needs, she likes to paint and write. After having three birth sons, she and her husband adopted an eight-year-old from China. They assumed they were adopting a boy. That's what they get for assuming! Meg is now pleased as punch to have a daughter. (Note: although we fully accept our daughter is a girl, we use the male pronoun to refer to her during the phase we all thought she was a boy.)

In the first picture we saw of the boy we decided to adopt there he stood wearing a red shirt holding a pink stuffed animal. "It's a meepit!" the twin boys shouted. They were in a phase where they loved their small pink creatures that looked like guinea pigs on two legs. Wasn't it cool their soon to be brother liked them too? I knew that when I lived in China, boys didn't wear red, but maybe things had changed. Later we were sent updated photos. In one, he looks adoringly up at the camera, a small pink address book with Disney's Cinderella pressed to his cheek. Worriedly, I started asking around on online adoption groups. Was this a phase? People poured in their anecdotes, how so and so's son wore his sister's skirts; somebody else's son loved to try on his mother's high heels, another had a son who hoarded Polly Pocket dolls, then grew out of them. Things would change, I was told, and especially once he joined a household of three brothers.

Eventually we were able to send presents and even communicate by email. We sent neutral or traditional boy items: a stuffed duck and monkey, a super hero wallet, animal stickers, a navy long-sleeved tee with a soccer ball on it. Curiously we never heard any enthusiasm or gratitude for our gifts. Weren't children in orphanages excited by presents? One day, after we'd started using the webcam, I showed off my new skirt. "Can I have one?" he asked enthusiastically. Ummm. Through the months we repeatedly asked what names he liked and he never responded. We offered suggestions. Right before we flew to China to adopt him, I'd asked him if he wanted to go by his Chinese name, or Rudy, a name we'd picked out for him. He blurted out, "I don't want to be called Rudy and I don't want *my Chinese name*, I want to be called Ruthie!" At the time we ignored his request and went with Rudy.

At this point I suggested to Hubby we pick an androgynous name, just in case. He blew up. He would claim ownership of our new child by choosing one of his favorite names, "Rudy." And Rudy was not a girl. Not long after we received a final report of our child's habits, abilities and preferences. "He likes holding a doll while sleeping." "His favorite toy is Barbie doll." "He likes pretending to be girls." One of our reasons for adoption (perhaps ill-advised) was to balance out the family, have a similarly aged brother for our little guy, since his older brothers were twins. What if *he* were a *she*? What if he didn't like any of the same things Ted did?

"*I* want to be called Ruthie!"

In China, at the adoption office, our new son edged in, turned around, ran into the hall and purchased ice cream pops for everyone in the room. Then he sat shyly with his foster mom. He wore a muscle tee and on his shoulder was a temporary butterfly tattoo. His English was limited. He did however know some terms from movies. He'd point to Ted, and say "You're Jasmine, I'm Ariel!" To Steve he'd say, "You're Cinderella, I'm Belle!" In this way he mentioned most of the Disney princesses. Oh boy. It was tortuously hot so we chose to go swimming in the hotel pool. We had to buy goggles. He of course wanted the pink ones. Even then we cringed. It was not in our parenting philosophy to say no, but we deeply wanted to. Pink goggles it was.

Before we parted, his foster mom made us promise not to buy him a new Barbie. She'd taken his away prior to saying goodbye. While we waited for all the official documents in Guangzhou, every evening he'd sit at the restaurant and tears would well up and slip down his cheeks. Trying to console him, we bought him a new doll. I knew in my heart, if he really was transgender, the best thing we could do for him is let him arrive in America as a girl. Then he'd never have to socially transition. I leaned over, and in Chinese inquired, "Some people feel like they are born in the wrong body. They may have a boy's body, but they know they are girls. Do you think this is you, or do you just like girly things?" "I just like girly things." Okay. For now.

Originally published in "Open Salon," 12/8/10

Ruthie's First Day at School as Ruthie

Meg Whitlock Clark

Advice to those starting a social transition midyear without switching schools: have a sibling get a new haircut on the same day! My first grade twin boys Connor and Carl had surfer long hair. Last week Carl got a buzz and people are still reacting to it. I learned this and other things on Ruthie's first day of school as a girl.

Ten days ago TransYouth Family Allies (TYFA) had sent a rep to train a select group of teachers and staff to deal with the ramifications of a child starting out the school year as a boy and switching mid-year. The trainer reported that everyone felt much better after the workshop. But it was the principal who really surprised me. Picture this: medium height man wearing tight tucked-in polo shirts emphasizing his buff physique and sporting a thin mustache groomed straight on the upper edge. He has some difficulty looking people in the eye and seems ill at ease when greeting people around the school. I've occasionally complained about his seeming inaccessibly and awkward manner. When this very same man told me that Ruthie should start wearing a dress as soon as possible I was blown away. He said that if Ruthie had to travel all the way from China at age eight in order to find a family that would finally see her for the girl she truly is, then he would go to any length to make sure she need not suffer another day under his auspices. He is now eager to train the entire school and down the line the counselors from the whole district as well. If nothing else, having a transgender daughter has taught me to expect the unexpected.

But let's return to the morning of Ruthie's first day at school as *Ruthie*. Connor — one of my fifth graders — hugs me goodbye and takes off on his bike. Although a bike is faster he leaves for school before us to avoid the crowded sidewalks. I, on the other hand, dawdle going out the door. The other three play catch on the lawn, backpacks lined up on the porch glider. I am blessed with children who hate to be late. But I don't want to be early because

Ruthie is wearing a skirt to school today for the first time, and I don't want her to linger unnecessarily before the crowds of ogling children.

It is a humid spring day; the flowering cherries and crabapples have reached their peak. The vibrantly colored tulips amass in more diligent people's gardens. En route my other fifth grader Carl walks a little in front. I grab Ted's hand on my right, Ruthie's on my left. Ted's hand is cool and loose as always. Ruthie's is a furnace — also, as always. Come summer I will usually refuse to hold her hand, I am extremely temperature sensitive and feel great discomfort by a hot touch when I am overheated. This morning is probably only in the sixties but it's muggy and we're warm from walking. I hold on tight.

I find myself bracing before any interaction, peering into peoples' eyes to see what they are really thinking about us. We pass the house of the twins' friend and I tense. He and his mom are in the driveway. "Hey, Carl, nice haircut!" the mom calls. They are a new family and I have only met them to say "hi." I honestly don't know if she knows the story of Rudy/Ruthie. We keep walking.

We pass the first crossing guard, Bob, who greets us. Bob crossed us in the fall on Ruthie's first day at school in America, when she sported a very close-shaven crew cut and wore boy's clothing (does anyone else have problems with pronouns when writing about pre-transition days? I'll use "she" because, really, she's always been a girl, we just didn't know it.) Bob had broken his arm over Christmas so has missed most of the gradual change from boys clothing, to pink shirts to today wearing a skirt. He doesn't know our names, though, so I don't know if he assumes Ruthie is a girl or a boy. We keep walking.

We approach a dad that works with my husband. He waves hello and calls, "Nice hair cut, Carl!" I'm beginning to let down my guard. The second crossing guard is a long-term sub, but she was absent last week. She has no reason to believe Ruthie isn't a girl and we pass with only one comment: "You got your hair cut!" I'm really regretting not having Carl's haircut just yesterday so that he could be even *more* of a foil to draw attention away from Ruthie.

A friend and her daughter walk across the lawn. She smiles and holds up one index finger, raising her eyebrows. "Is this the first day as Ruthie?" she's asking with her gestures. I nod and gulp. As we get closer she tells Ruthie she likes her dress. Ruthie ducks her head and mumbles thank you. I can feel her pulling back on my hand, dragging her steps. Now we are cutting towards the front entrance. I really don't notice anybody staring but I don't see a lot of third graders either.

We walk in and I wave to the secretary through the glass windows. She smiles but a little uncertainly. I think she's nervous about fielding phone calls from irate parents who didn't like the letter that went home on transgender children. The gym teacher always stands in the hall and welcomes the students. Was his grin a little off? Not sure. Ruthie reports that somebody is laughing at her. I reassure her that people will have to get used to her dresses, it might take them a while to understand. But I don't look to see who's laughing. The halls are crowded, and she's worn her pink t-shirt and white pearl-buttoned cardigan before. So in the crowd not everyone will notice her skirt.

At the top of the stairs stand the fifth grade teachers, all young, unmarried and very kind. A few months ago I had called two of them to talk about Ruthie because the twins were in their classes. I was relieved at their support. Last week they attended TYFA's training and saw the *20/20* special on transgender children, *My Secret Self*. Now, one of them complements Ruthie on her skirt, and they all give us encouraging smiles.

Down the hall stands Ruthie's teacher. She's young and sweet but firm with her class about diversity and accepting differences. She has managed a classroom so far that has all been behind Ruthie; she has never gotten teased there, only amongst the wider school population. For them, only the name and the skirt will be different. They are all used to nail polish and stick-on earrings and drawings of princesses. Still, Ruthie hangs back reluctantly, trying to hide behind me. Seeing her so shy to go in, my eyes immediately well up with tears. All of a sudden I feel like we're at pre-school, and it's the first time I'm leaving my baby at school. I bend to give her a quick hug then rise to greet the guidance counselor. We confirm that Ruthie wishes to leave the room when the counselor gives her introduction of transgender issues and the name change.

As I walk back down the hall the tears are falling faster. The cluster of fifth grade teachers all smile sympathetically, then one says, "Now stop that or I'm going to start crying." And then she does.

So begins Ruthie's first day at school as Ruthie. Later we'll leave early for a dentist appointment so we'll miss the after school mayhem and perhaps some unwelcome attention. For today.

Originally published in "Open Salon," 2/28/11.

Petra and A

Finding a New Normal
Petra Hendrickson

Petra is currently a graduate student in political science. She studies civil wars and coups. While she spent much of her childhood trying to be different from her sister, she now enjoys having so much in common with her and is so grateful for the relationship with her sister that she almost can't remember what it was like to have an older brother.

The summer before my junior year of high school, my brother told me he was really my sister. I think I surprised her with my "ok." At that exact moment, though, I didn't fully comprehend what it would mean to have a trans sister. The biggest thing is that it had to be kept a secret. All the teachers in my high school knew me as my brother's little sister, and the conservativeness of the town, and my desire to keep a low profile for the rest of my high school career, precluded setting the record straight.

I think part of me was in denial, because even though I knew it was no longer the case, I still frequently referred to my brother. To an extent this couldn't be helped, because everyone knew I had a brother and were curious as to how he was doing in college. Because I couldn't correct them, I stayed in the brother state of mind and began to pretend that nothing had changed. I think part of it may have also been shame, though I regret this now. I lived in fear that I would be found out, that someone would find out about what my family had become.

When I didn't refer to my brother directly, I tried to use the more neutral "sibling," carefully avoiding any use of pronouns. This was the first effort I made to publicly (though obviously covertly) take account of the change my family was undergoing. I had a gender neutral sibling for most of my senior year of high school and into my freshman year of college, hoping that no one who didn't know would ask me if my sibling was a brother or a sister, unsure of what my answer would be. I hate to lie and am not very good at it, but I genuinely wasn't sure what the "honest" answer was at the time. Everything felt so muddled, so confused.

It wasn't until my freshman year of college that I told anyone the truth. One of my professors had gone to graduate school where my sister was currently attending, and their two departments had shared a building. I had spoken before of my brother, and my professor, with whom I was very close, wondered if she had ever seen him. As she scrolled through the graduate students of my sister's department, my professor asked his name, and I had no choice but to admit to her, and really to myself, that my brother was, in fact, my sister.

That incident proved to be a watershed of sorts. While it still felt slightly dishonest to say I had a sister without including any caveats, I could at least acknowledge and accept the fact that I no longer had a brother and now had a sister. Part of me wonders if this transition would have been easier if I had had a better relationship with my sister at the time this was all taking place. My sister and I are four years apart. While we were quite close as children and frequently played together, this age difference proved nearly insurmountable after she hit puberty, probably because she was already aware of the fact that she didn't feel like a male. The gap between us continued to grow when she went to college, and by the time she informed me of her transition, I was more or less indifferent toward her. Her breaks from school were a tense time, wrought with arguments and cold shoulders. I felt she was intruding on the place that had more or less become mine and mine alone, since I was the one who was at home all the time. With her transition, though, things between us have changed. Perhaps it was my going to college, catching up to her in terms of life experiences and becoming a fully mature adult that changed things, but I feel like fences were beginning to be mended even before I went off to school. Even then, though, it was an awkward process, as we grew accustomed to the changes that we had undergone as a family, and as we struggled to find a new normal, where we were no longer essentially enemies and where we could trust and confide in one another the way we did when we were children.

It was a slow process, and it wasn't until I was mostly done with college that I could say we had fully mended our relationship and could act as if things had always been the way they were now. I'm still careful, though; I told my first boyfriend about my sister and had decided beforehand that if he wasn't okay with the situation, I would not continue to date him. It's important to me that my partners accept my sister as a woman. Since I have started graduate school myself, I feel comfortable just saying I have a sister without feeling like I am withholding information. I will still use her as a litmus test for future partners, but it's no longer something I feel any kind of shame about. If a partner can't accept my sister for whom she is, I have no interest in dating that person. My sister and I are quite close now, and I feel like I'm closer to my sister than I probably ever would have been with my brother. After all, I had spent most of my life trying to distinguish myself from my brother. Where he took German, I took Spanish. Where he took art, I played in the band. Since gaining a sister, though, I have learned to acknowledge our differences while at the same time embracing our many similarities.

"While it still felt slightly dishonest to say I had a sister without including any caveats, I could at least acknowledge and accept the fact that I no longer had a brother and now had a sister."

My mom has been much more accepting of the change than my father, who even today slips up with pronouns and even names. That first Christmas, my mom and I had to go find a new stocking for my sister, since her old one would clearly no longer do. There was a great deal of uncertainty, both because our stockings had always been handmade, and there was simply not enough time to make a new stocking that year, and because we were not sure which spelling variant of her name she had chosen, and so our quest was put on hold until we could find out for sure. Everything seemed so uncertain that first Christmas: were her general interests still the same? How much had changed, exactly? Would she like what we had gotten her? Were the gifts somehow too male-centric? Everything ended up being okay, and all the worrying was for naught, but the preceding uncertainty tainted the holiday as we all walked on eggshells, self-consciously trying to avoid offending my sister or making her feel unwelcome by doing things we had always considered normal, but which we were no longer sure were acceptable.

I think that for me the biggest transition I had to deal with was my standing with my extended family. My brother had been my grandparents' favorite, another male heir to the well-respected family name. I, resembling my mother, who was not particularly well-received in the family, made me more of an afterthought for them. That changed with my sister's transition, though. My grandfather no longer accepted her as part of the family, and my tides turned as a result. I went from outcast to favorite. Everything I did and became was a significant accomplishment to be praised and hailed. My sister's college graduation barely registered a blip on the radar (my grandmother did manage to smuggle a card to my father to give to my sister), while mine was heralded with a great deal of fanfare. Both grandparents attended my college graduation; only my immediate family had attended my sister's. As my grandfather's mental state declined, we slowly started reintroducing my sister into the family, first as my friend (at least that's what we told my grandfather), and then without explanation when he declined further. With his death, my sister has been mostly reintegrated into the family. My grandmother is thrilled to see her when she comes home and has vowed to attend both of our grad school graduations. The rest of the extended family is a slightly different story: it's been a decade since anyone last had contact with her, and to an extent that can't be repaired, although at Christmas, when everyone gathered to spend time with my grandmother, all the cousins did their best to act as if no abnormal amount of time had passed. I think my sister appreciated the gesture, but I don't know that she feels as close to them as she once did.

I'm glad my immediate family has been accepting of my sister. While I would have been accepting of her, even if it took a significant amount of time, it's much less exhausting to have a family that is just as supportive as I am. We can celebrate each other's accomplishments and weather the setbacks together, united, as a family. While it has taken me several years to become as comfortable with the situation as I am now, I am happy with the new normal I have found and embrace the fact that I have a big sister.

2.05.12 — from the daily shots of the
"complex — learning to divide collection"
by dylan scholinski © 2012

"Mask of a Thousand Sorrows" by Melanie Whitney © 2012

Great thinkers throughout history have identified the importance of masks in human society. This picture honors the masks we often wear and the ones we hide our sorrows behind.

My New Daughter

Ulrike Hendrickson

Ulrike currently resides in Southwestern Ohio. She spent 20 years in the Air Force and has lived both in Europe and Asia, as well as many areas of the United States, throughout her life. She currently works in the Information Technology field, which (unfortunately) still appears to be male-centric and unrepentant in its lack of gender diversity. Ulrike's children will be anonymous in this piece. She refers to them as C (her biological son before transition), A (her transgender daughter after transition), and P (her biological daughter).

It was the year between my oldest child's sophomore and junior year of college. C, my biological son, came to me to tell me that there was something I had to know. His father and I had divorced two years previously, so my child was opening up to us individually. His father had already been told the news and I was next. He was coming out as transgender and wanted me to continue to be part of his life. My only son would now become my second daughter, A (my transgender daughter's chosen name). My initial response, which I tried not to show, was fear — for her and for what challenges she would face in the future. I asked, "So, aren't you still my child?" We (my trans-girl, my biological girl, and I) had a quick cry and carried on for the rest of the day. Later, my new daughter told me that the LGBT group on campus had voted me the mother of the year, jokingly, based on my reaction.

I struggled with the knowledge — knowing that the transgender are the least understood of the LGBT quartet — and that the road ahead could be dangerous and lonely. Luckily, A has not been alone, and although the way has not always been easy for her or on us, we have gotten through it.

Early during my transition into the mother of two daughters, the hardest part was the change in pronouns. He now became a "she," and in the early days, I often slipped. Calling by proper names was easier, for less thinking was involved. While I still slip once-in-a-while, this is a rare thing; so rare, in fact, that I have to stop and think when referring to A to people who know her only as C and are not privy to the private workings of our family. We have told trusted friends, but since I live in a very conservative city and state, the knowledge is not yet available for public consumption. This has caused me some distress, for I am not able to brag about A's educational accomplishments as freely as her sister's, and I fear that outsiders think there is a rift in our family because of this. I am extremely proud of A's many attributes and accomplishments, including her post-grad work toward a Ph.D. in Sociology.

A had legally changed her name while at University, so her BA would be in the proper name. She was inducted into the Mortar Board Honor Society, for both her academic excellence and her work toward acceptance of LGBT people and causes, and she was accepted by her co-workers in the Grounds Department, where she worked at a campus job to gain some spending money. Grad school followed, where A still is today.

My entry into LGBT culture was aided by a PBS show that (luckily) was airing in our area (albeit at one AM on Sundays) called *In the Life*. By letting me see how others were coping with their life choices and changes, I saw that my daughter would be able to live a fulfilled life. We discussed some of the episodes, and the topics brought out by the show. Less effective to my education were several fiction books I read at the time. One, whose name I cannot remember (A says the name is [Julie Peter's] *Luna*), was too scary to contemplate, with the transgender child running away and being hurt. [Chris Bohjalian's] *Trans-sister Radio* was less frightening and did allow for full integration into society. I have not seen the film, although I understand it is quite good. *The Education of Max Bickford*, which was aired around the same time, was exciting for the portrayal of a normal family with a transgender relative and how the children and friends of the family dealt with the change, especially the former wife of the transgender person. Somehow, these acknowledgements on a larger social scale made me feel not so alone.

As A expanded her circle, I was introduced to lesbian culture as well, as she sought female partners. I moved from having a straight son to having a lesbian daughter. This was all so new to me, for while I had lesbian co-workers and friends, I never sought entry into this world. Actually, A's preference for other women eased some of my fears, for I've always felt (irrationally, I'm sure) that women on the whole are less threatened by the "other" and would be less likely to perpetrate violence than men. Some of these feelings may be part of my upbringing in the warrior culture of American society — first as a military dependent child in the US Army, and then because I had not learned my lessons, as a member of the US Air Force. For example, my first experience with transgender issues occurred in the United States, in Hawaii, where a young man I worked with was being court-marshaled for assaulting a *ka-toi* sex worker in Honolulu. Assaulting a *ka-toi* was treated the same as assaulting a woman and prosecuted as a felony. (Note: I believe *ka-toi* is a Thai [or Americanized version] word for female impersonator.) However, there hasn't been much in the civilian world to make me change my mind about male-perpetuated violence! Women still seem more tolerant than men about such things.

"*So*, life continues .... My daughters and I stay in close contact. We celebrate each other's triumphs ... and defeats .... We remain close."

Of course, some of the women I was introduced to were more accepting of my ignorance than others. As I was learning more of this world, I became worried that A might have difficultly finding partners who would be accepting of her. One of her partners, whom I will refer to as X, seemed more brusque and dominating than the others. This was early in the process, and I made the mistake of trying to talk to A alone. I wondered whether A would be a receiver of pleasure as well as a provider of pleasure during sex. I was not seeking explicit details of the how, but rather assurances that A would have a fully realized sexual identity. X found me naïve and humorous, that I should worry about such a trivial (in her eyes) matter. Trying to explain what I was asking only made it worse, even though X had not been invited into the conversation and had butted in. I was upset that this woman (X) would not even let me talk with my daughter one-on-one, without interference or input. To my relief, if not A's, X went to grad school in another state, and I have not seen her since.

We told both sets of grandparents around this time, and my father was more accepting than I had expected. Perhaps the years had mellowed him, and as an old warrior (Army), he had seen enough to understand that not all can be as we want, and the best we can hope for is love from our family. A's paternal grandfather, on the other hand, was a complete shock. He was an MD, and we felt that if anyone could understand the many facets of humanity, he would. Initially, he appeared okay, with the news. A few weeks later, he did a u-turn, and A was banished from family functions. A's paternal grandmother went along with her husband, although she did keep contact through A's father. My mother had passed away prior to A's coming out, so we will never know how she would've reacted.

So, life continues. We, my daughters (A and P) and I stay in close contact. We celebrate each other's triumphs (passing comps, good grades, getting rid of a bad thesis advisor) and defeats (loss of a significant other, friends behaving badly and disappointments at work). We remain close, and as they grow and mature, one of the things I denied them as children has come about. P used to complain that I was mean and wasn't her friend. At the time, I told her that my job was not to be her friend, but to be her mother. Mothering did not include letting her do everything she wanted, nor did it involve liking me. My job was to keep her safe and to set the boundaries that would give her room to experiment and grow, but not endanger her. Both A and P have grown into accomplished women, and I am proud to call them both daughters and friends.

"Ghost Leaf" by Hillary Brenneman © 2012

"Untitled" by Troy Jones © 2012

Our Twins
Melissa Jeltsen

Tom and Ryan were born identical twins to Dennis and Cecelia; Ryan has now transitioned to live as Sylvia. All names have been changed to maintain confidentiality. Melissa is a journalist who wrote this story as well as one in the Friends section, "My Best Guy Friend is now My Best Girl Friend."

Although born identical twins with matching DNA, Tom and Ryan were two immensely different children. As toddlers, Tom entertained himself with toy trucks while Ryan fawned over his girl cousin's Barbies and Little Mermaid dolls. Photo after photo of them at that age show Ryan with a t-shirt wrapped around his head, mimicking long, flowing hair. At age 4, he asked his mom, Cecelia, a heartbreaking question: "When do I get to be a girl?" A few months later, while assisting his dad, Dennis, with a plumbing job, he told him that he hated his own penis. Dennis choked up. "I cried and he cried, and then his brother came in and we all hugged and cried," he says.

When he was six, his parents sought professional advice. A local psychiatrist diagnosed Ryan with gender identity disorder (GID) or transgenderism, a rare condition in which a biological male or female feels a strong identification with the opposite sex and is extremely uncomfortable with his or her own gender. Like Ryan, many transgender youth express disgust with their genitals from a young age, and some even believe they'll grow up to become the opposite sex. These feelings can cause significant psychological distress, and, not surprisingly, depression, anxiety and the desire to self-harm when they become teens. Statistics on the number of transgender children are hard to estimate. In adults, where the prevalence is approximately one in 500 to one in 1,000 — an elusive figure due to lack of national registries — diagnoses of GID have tripled since the 1960s. This increase is likely due to more people coming out as transgender because of growing cultural acceptance, not an increase in prevalence.

Ryan is now 12 and goes by the name Sylvia. In skinny jeans and metallic ballet flats, painted nails and pigtails, she comes off as an energetic tween girl. She's the more gregarious of the twins, but her bubbly disposition also serves as a protective facade: since that first therapy visit at age six, Sylvia has been in counseling to help her cope with anxiety and depression. In a world where everything is divvied up according to gender, there's little room for a kid who falls somewhere in the middle.

It was easy to fit in when she was younger, but elementary school brought new challenges. She grew her hair long and asked to wear dresses and skirts. When her parents tried to discourage her, Sylvia rebelled by acting out in school and at home. One day she told a teacher she wanted to die. "It was terribly hard on her, to be told repeatedly that everything she thought and felt was wrong," says Cecelia. "We finally decided to just let her be whoever she wanted to be."

"Some afternoons, she stared at herself in the mirror in bewilderment. 'I'd look at myself from the neck up, and I'd be okay with it, but then I'd look from the neck down, and I'd feel like I was one of those mismatch puzzles,' she says."

In fifth grade, after the long summer, Ryan came back to school as Sylvia. Although she was nervous on her first day with her new name, Sylvia found the majority of her classmates warm and welcoming. "Some of my friends asked me why I had waited so long," she says. That year, Sylvia excelled academically and was voted class vice-president. At the same time, she was being seen by Norman Spack, MD, an endocrinologist at Children's Hospital Boston and a leading expert in GID in children and adolescents and evaluating psychologist Laura Edwards-Leeper, Ph.D. Spack, along with urologist David Diamond, MD, had helped launch the interdisciplinary Gender Management Service (GeMS) Clinic at Children's — the first pediatric academic program in the Western Hemisphere to evaluate and medically treat young transgender people.

Sylvia's parents immersed themselves in transgender research before coming to Children's. "We were learning everything we could," says Cecelia. Their biggest concern was what would happen when Sylvia hit puberty. She was petrified of developing "whiskers," and was increasingly embarrassed about her body. Some afternoons, she stared at herself in the mirror in bewilderment. "I'd look at myself from the neck up, and I'd be okay with it, but then I'd look from the neck down, and I'd feel like I was one of those mismatch puzzles," she says.

Her parents knew if Sylvia went through puberty and into adulthood as a male, she was likely destined for a life of expensive surgeries to attempt to reverse the masculine attributes and transition into a female body. But their hopes rose when they heard of another option that could help Sylvia avoid some of the irreversible physical changes, like a deepened voice, facial bone structure, a beard and broad shoulders, which would forever define her as a genetic male.

Halting Puberty

Puberty is embarrassing and awkward enough, but for transgender kids, it's the body's ultimate betrayal. "This is the only big change in the body that they remember, and they feel it's all going terribly wrong," says Spack, adding that transgender youth have one of the highest suicide rates among teens in the country.

But what if you could halt puberty and stop the permanent changes from occurring? While it remains controversial, puberty suppression has been the standard treatment for transgender kids in the Netherlands since the 1990s. Since 2007, Children's has been one of a handful of hospitals in North America to offer this treatment. Before any medical intervention takes place, psychologist Edwards-Leeper administers a rigorous series of psychological tests, forming a complete history of the child's gender identity development. "The testing protocol we use is modeled after the Dutch clinic, which has been successfully treating and researching transgender youth for many years," she says. Those who meet the stringent criteria for treatment are given monthly injections or a temporarily implanted drug to block their sex hormones. It's fully reversible at any point; if they want to go through puberty as their biological sex, they can stop taking the drugs.

So far, the GeMS clinic has treated 17 patients with pubertal suppressors. "For the appropriate patients, we've found that the use of this therapy not only prevents severe psychological distress, but allows these young adolescents a chance to begin to blossom into their true selves," says Edwards-Leeper. Spack scoffs at critics who accuse the clinic of fooling with nature. "I don't think of transgender people as 'changing genders,'" he says. "Almost every one of our patients felt that they were born with the wrong body. They're not changing genders, they are affirming the gender they always felt they had." Puberty-suppressing therapy should be seen as a method that gives families and medical teams more time to think about what to do, according to Spack. "We no longer have to rush to beat the patient's biological clock," he says. It was the perfect choice for Sylvia. At age 11, at the first signs of puberty, she started taking the pubertal suppressors.

The Future

On a recent afternoon, Sylvia and Tom ride their bikes in circles in front of their house, soaking up the summer heat. When they stand side-by-side, they're no longer identical. After a year on the puberty-suppressing medication, Sylvia only needs to look at her brother to see the path she avoided. She's willowy, he's stocky. He has wispy new facial hair, while her face is clear. Tom, who says he always felt like his twin was a girl, isn't surprised by the twists their lives have taken so far. "I do wonder what it would be like to have a brother," he says, smiling at Sylvia mischievously, "But I guess a sister cuts it."

Sylvia can't delay puberty indefinitely, and in a few years, she'll need to make a decision. She may choose to stop the pubertal suppressors and go through puberty as her biological sex. But it is hard to imagine. It's more probable that, at age 16, after undergoing additional rigorous medical evaluation, she will decide to physically transition to the female she has always felt she was. If so, she can start taking hormone therapy under Spack's supervision and will develop breasts and hips. When she's 18, she can have feminizing genitoplastic surgery at an adult hospital if she desires. If she does go through with the full transition to a female gender, Sylvia — with a narrow frame, womanly curves and feminine voice — will be indistinguishable from a genetic female. But for now, the family is taking it one day at a time, encouraging Sylvia to enjoy her life as a kid while she can.

Of course, there have been some bumps in the road. After Sylvia faced painful bullying from a particular student in sixth grade, the family uprooted and made a fresh start in a new town. "We're a normal family raising kids; Sylvia just happens to have this medical condition and not cancer or heart disease," says Cecelia. "Why everyone gets so upset about it, I can't understand."

But the family is more cautious now. At her new school, Sylvia easily passes as a genetic female, and none of her classmates know she is transgender. Hiding her true identity isn't ideal, but at least while she's in middle school, it's the route she's decided to take. "It makes me feel like I'm not being completely honest, but my honesty got me in a lot of trouble a few years ago," she says. Seventh grade isn't easy: when the other girls aren't fixating on the minute differences that set them apart — whose nose is bigger, who's taller, who has freckles — they're gossiping about boys. "Boys, boys, boys, it's all these girls think about," says Sylvia. "It's a little hard to find someone to talk to right now."

While her parents are nervous about the coming years, especially high school, they're upbeat about Sylvia's opportunity to live an adult life unrestrained by her appearance. "She will get past this and become a productive member of society," says Cecelia. "We're giving her the resources to become whoever she is." Though it took Sylvia's dad, Dennis, some time to adjust, he's now one of her biggest advocates and works to educate other parents about transgender youth. "The key is, you have to be courageous enough to do this while these kids are young," he says. "It's so much harder later on. You've got to be brave so you can give them a chance."

Originally published in "Thriving, Children's Hospital Boston's Pediatric Health Blog."

Nicole and Wayne

Transgender Remembrance Day
Wayne Maines

Wayne is the proud father of Nicole and Jonas Maines and has recently started to write short stories about his families' journey and his experiences discovering the joys that come from listening and learning from his young children. The American Civil Liberties Union of Maine presented the 2011 Roger Baldwin Award to Wayne, Kelly, Nicole and Jonas Maines for their extraordinary efforts toward ending discrimination against transgender Mainers. His family story was recently featured in the *Boston Globe*. Wayne is the Director of Safety and Environmental Management at The University of Maine in Orono, Maine.

$\star$ $\star$ $\star$ $\star$ $\star$

Today is Transgender Remembrance Day [held each November to memorialize murdered trans people]. A few years ago, if you asked me what this day represents, I would have said I didn't even know what transgender means, never mind that there's a whole day dedicated to the memory of transgender people who've been victimized by hate crimes. I may have been unaware of these issues back then, but I'm a different person now. Since opening up about my daughter Nicole's experiences as a transgender tween [http://childrenshospitalblog.org/childrens-gives-transgender-tween-new-hope/], my eyes have been opened to many issues concerning the transgender community; some good, some not.

The other night I had one of those "not so good" moments. As I was tucking Nicole in for bed, she took my hand and told me she had something to tell me. "Daddy, I'm working on a project for Transgender Remembrance Day," she said. "Did you know people are being murdered and raped because they're transgender?"

I didn't know what to say. How can I look at my sweet child and tell her there are people in this world who might want to hurt her, simply because of the gender she identifies with? Any time I find myself at a loss for words when talking to my kids, I think about how my wife Kelly would react. As the foundation of our family, she always seems to know exactly what to do and say. Channeling my inner Kelly, I hugged my daughter and told her she has parents who will love, support and protect her, no matter what.

But as we held each other, I knew I had to tell her more. I had to communicate that despite the fact that my love for her knows no bounds, it's not a force field that can shield her from the evils in this world. I told her that as much as we loved her and would do everything to keep her safe, there may be times that her mother or I couldn't be there for her. I reminded her that she needs to always be aware of her surroundings, to stay close to friends and her brother if she feels uncomfortable and to call me any time she felt threatened. It was a very sad moment, knowing my innocent young kids have to shoulder such unique responsibilities that most children their age couldn't begin to fathom.

"As I was tucking Nicole in for bed, she took my hand and told me she had something to tell me. 'Daddy, I'm working on a project for Transgender Remembrance Day,' she said. 'Did you know people are being murdered and raped because they're transgender?'"

I remember thinking, as I often do, that no dad should have to have this conversation with his young child. No dad should have to discuss hate, fear, evil, rape or murder when they are tucking their baby in. In the past when these topics would come up I might have been tempted to repeat the message my parents told me when I was young. "Don't worry sweetie, everything is going to be ok." But we live in a different time, and I can't make that promise. It's a sad reality, but a reality my family must face; denying the truth isn't going to protect anyone.

But when my children and I talk about these tough issues, I choose to focus on the positives instead of the negative. Sadly, there are ignorant people out there who do despicable things, but there are also wonderful people who love unconditionally. For every hate monger lurking in the shadows there is a role model of acceptance, ready to inspire. People like our friends at Gay & Lesbian Advocates & Defenders (GLAD). The GLAD people we know are amazingly smart and strong and give me hope that Nicole has a bright future ahead of her. It may be a different future than I originally envisioned, but if she works hard and stays safe, I truly believe she will help change the world for the better. Having that level of faith in your own child is an amazing feeling, and I refuse to let the ignorance of others tarnish the pride I feel.

After Nicole and I finished our conversation, we hugged and kissed goodnight. As I turned off the lights and walked out of the room, I felt sad and angry at the same time. I was sad that my daughter had to grow up so fast and angry that there is so much work to be done to protect her, and the thousands like her. It may be a daunting task, but it's work worth doing. And one day, thanks to people like my daughter, my wife, the good people of GLAD and Dr. Norm Spack at Children's Hospital Boston, maybe we'll live in a world where no one knows about Transgender Remembrance Day; not unaware of it the way I once was, but unaware of it because a solemn reminder of the dangers faced by transgender people won't be needed anymore.

But that's enough talking, time to get to work.

Originally published in "Thriving, Children's Hospital Boston's Pediatric Health Blog."

Mark and Rafi

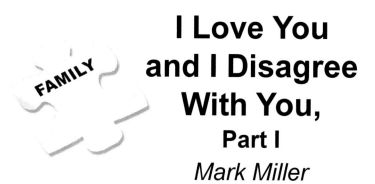

I Love You and I Disagree With You,
Part I
Mark Miller

Editors' Note: Mark wrote his essay when we first began our anthology and subsequently passed away before its completion. Mark asked to remain anonymous, and we have respected his request. Mark's transgender stepson, referred to as S in this piece with feminine pronouns, was asked to give permission for the piece to be included and chose to write the second part of this piece as a male, using his new name, Rafi. Rafi drew this picture of Mark and himself together.

*   *   *   *   *

S is my stepdaughter. I can't remember when she first announced that she was going to change her gender, but it must have been about six months ago. S is in her mid-20's and lives in a different area of the country, so the initial impact of this announcement was diluted. I can't even remember where I first heard about it, and I'm not even sure whether her mother told me first or S told me first.

Here is a little background about myself. As I said above, I'm married to S's mother, but S is my stepdaughter. Her mother was my second wife; we did not have children together. I have three children (two boys and one girl) from my first marriage; my wife has one son and S from her first marriage. S's biological father is deceased; he died when he was middle-aged.

Some more information about my background and present circumstances may provide a greater understanding of my reaction to S's decision. I'm middle-aged; all of the children, except for one, are independently living on their own, including S. My youngest, P, still participates in the shared custody agreement between his mother and myself. He is a teenager, though not for much longer.

Several other important pieces of information are needed to understand my reaction to S's decision to change her gender. First, my wife and I are observant Jews. My wife was not raised in what one would call an "observant" home, and her parents had scant Jewish education. Although they clearly identified themselves as Jews, they did *not* raise my wife to be a "religiously observant" Jew [one who practices the Biblical laws and observes Jewish Holy Days, like Passover], although she became one after various life experiences. She also felt that raising her children in an "observant" Jewish environment would be the best approach for them, and probably the first major decision along this path was to send the children, including S, to Jewish schools. S enjoyed those schools very much and attended religious Jewish schools at a young age, continuing her attendance even post-high school. When my wife and I met, my wife had already made these major decisions; marrying me had little or no effect on those decisions (her children were already teenagers when we met).

Although my religious path was somewhat different than my wife's, I too had ended up on the same road as she chose. While I had attended Jewish day schools from K-12 and was raised in a fairly observant Jewish home, I began to have serious questions, and ultimately reservations, about being an observant Jew. When I turned 21, I officially became a "non-practicing" Jew. While I remained proud of my Jewish identity, I gave up my observance of most Jewish daily rules and commandments. Sparked by a move to a new city, and new questions about the meaning of life, approximately seven years later, I began my return to Jewish observance. This return to Jewish observance was slow and difficult. But, I met a number of people along the way who were interested and capable of answering my questions. I continued to become more observant in a Jewish fashion, ultimately becoming comfortable in my commitment to a very traditional Jewish lifestyle.

The second most important piece of information about me is that I have incurable cancer. Diagnosed over 2 ½ years ago with Stage 4 cancer, the doctors informed me immediately that there was no cure, and that I would only live a few years. After the diagnosis, they requested that I stay in the hospital for surgery. I survived the surgery, and one month later, they began chemotherapy. Currently, I am being treated with chemotherapy on a weekly basis; aside from a few short breaks, I have not stopped chemotherapy in 2 ½ years. Chemotherapy will only stop when I can no longer stand the treatment. Without chemotherapy, I cannot fight the tumors. The only questions are how long I can continue chemotherapy and how long until the tumors kill me, once the chemotherapy stops.

The third most important thing to know about me is that I have a Ph.D. in the social sciences and teach at a local college. I conduct research and teach topics like cultural diversity, stereotyping and prejudice in the classroom and therefore thinking in different ways comes naturally to me. My wife and I very much care about making the world a better place to live and are committed to a life of sharing kindness and charity with others.

Now that you know some of the crucial things about me, I will explain my reaction to S's decision. Some things are right and some things are wrong. I don't believe that anyone would disagree that there are correct actions, and there are incorrect actions. We may disagree, however, on what actions are right and what actions are wrong. Sometimes our value system is called an ethical system or a system of commandments, but the vast majority of people would agree that there is "right" and there is "wrong." So, how does one develop a system of right or wrong? There are various approaches to this, but my experience is that most people learn "right" and "wrong" from their families. They may also learn this from their religion. As an observant Jew, I believe that there is a system of right and wrong that has been handed down through Jewish tradition for over 2,500 years. I study this system and have religious authorities to ask questions, if I am not sure. As I wrote above, I questioned the system as a young adult and worked through my difficulties over a period of years.

"*I* must acknowledge that I don't really understand S's decision to change her gender. I assume that she feels more comfortable in her new gender, but I don't understand why. She has lost friends and family as a result, and I feel sad about that. Without my set of religious principles and laws, I have no rational reason for believing her choice is wrong."

Well, what about from the transgender person's perspective? How do I look at S? I love S, and she is one of our family. I also disagree with her profoundly. According to traditional Jewish belief, everyone deals with a personal struggle between the temptation to do the "right" thing and their temptation to do the "wrong" thing. In my opinion, everyone has a weakness — someone might be tempted to steal, someone else might be tempted to act haughty and yet a third person may be tempted to be cruel to animals. That is why people sometimes do the wrong thing. No one, according to the Jewish faith, is perfect; that is, I believe, the human condition. To put it in contemporary terms, I would argue that S has made the wrong choice. Our Creator grants human beings free will, and it is her choice to change her gender. But, human beings still make the wrong choices sometimes.

I must acknowledge that I don't really understand S's decision to change her gender. I assume that she feels more comfortable in her new gender, but I don't understand why. She has lost friends and family as a result, and I feel sad about that. Without my set of religious principles and laws, I have no rational reason for believing her choice is wrong. Yet, according to Jewish tradition, one should not change his or her gender. Perhaps there are rational reasons for not changing one's gender; I don't know. What I do believe is that G-d [some Jews do not spell out the name of the deity, out of respect] has provided us with a set of principles and a manner of conduct that should guide us in all of our decisions. We may not understand all of these principles, or even like them all of the time, but they are the best system for us. Of course, I can only speak for my family and friends. I believe that they should follow these commandments. I am sad when they cannot. Of course, I realize that I am not perfect either, and they may be disappointed in me sometimes, too.

It is said that one should not judge another human being until one is in his or her shoes. I agree. I don't "judge" others, including my children, but I believe that we should have opinions about "right" and "wrong." Our Creator is the ultimate judge, so I don't need to serve in that role. I have talked with my other children and shared that while I don't agree with S, I still love her.

S and I are in telephone contact and talk about once every 10 - 12 days. She came to visit me in person once since her gender change, and we had a pleasant time talking and sharing our thoughts. I generally find her interesting to talk with and have in fact sought out conversation with her, particularly when I feel troubled or upset by something.

In sum, I love S. I still disagree with her decision to change her gender. I feel sad that she will lose contact with some members of the family and certain friends. I hope that one day she will change her decision.

I Love You and I Disagree With You,
Part II
Rafi Daugherty

Rafi is a 29-year-old trans guy currently living in Denver, Colorado. He has also lived in St. Louis, Missouri; Brooklyn, New York and Tel Aviv, Israel. Rafi was raised as an Orthodox Jew and that is the basis for much of his life experience. He transitioned from female to male in 2007 and has become a voice for TransJews wherever possible. Rafi earned his BA in psychology and sociology from Hunter College and has an MA in Crisis and Trauma Studies from Tel Aviv University. He has worked with special needs children and adults as well as homeless New York City and Israeli youth. He currently works for Keshet, a national organization that works for the full inclusion of LGBT Jews in Jewish life. He is actively involved in the Jewish community in Colorado and hopes to become a foster parent in the near future.

$$\star \quad \star \quad \star \quad \star \quad \star$$

When I first looked over the essay that my stepfather wrote for this book, I was somewhat taken aback and fairly disappointed. He wrote this essay from a very religious point of view in an almost dry and non-compassionate way. He also used female pronouns for me and referred to me as his "stepdaughter." Let me explain why this was so shocking.

When "Mark" married my mother, I was 16. We had a decent relationship from the beginning and often, he was the voice of reason in my teen years. Sometimes he would help my mother in dealing with me, and sometimes he would help me in dealing with my mother. He was always fair and kind. We would stay up late having philosophical discussions. (At that time, I was much more religious than he was!) At a certain point in our relationship, he started giving me the traditional blessing that a father gives to his daughter on Friday evenings (I had a very complicated relationship with my biological father who died in 2002). When I moved out of the house, he would call me every Friday afternoon and give me this blessing. When I was living in their house, my gender never came up as an issue. To me, no matter how uncomfortable it was, G-d made me female, and there was nothing I could do about that. I always dressed and acted more masculine compared to my female peers (I only attended school with other girls and had to wear skirts), but no one really thought much of it.

When I was 24, I had been in New York about three years on my own at that point. I had come out as "bi" [bisexual] a couple years before and had "butched up" to the point of being mistaken for male on a somewhat regular basis. After a lot of soul searching and therapy, I came out to myself as transgender, as a man. I knew that my mother would not take this well at all. My stepfather had been diagnosed with incurable cancer a year and a half before, and my mother was having a hard enough time dealing with that. My brother had three children at the time; I knew I would be forfeiting my relationship with those children whom I cared about dearly. I wanted to hold off telling them as long as possible.

"When my mother cut all contact with me, my stepfather continued speaking to me weekly and continued being loving and gracious to me."

My stepfather came to New York in the Spring of 2007 to visit myself and my stepsister. It was a Friday evening, and we were chatting with my good friend who is a gay Jewish male — also from an Orthodox background. My friend unknowingly "outed" me as trans to my stepfather who proceeded to ask me a lot of questions about my decision. At the end of it all, he basically said, "I love you and I disagree with you," hence the title of his essay. He walked me to the subway and before I got on, he gave me a huge hug. Mind you, we had never had physical contact before due to our religious beliefs. I was startled and exclaimed, "Is this because you think I'm a boy now??!" He said, "No, it's just because I love you."

Although he and I had some discussions about my decision after that point, he was very respectful and tried his utmost to use my chosen name and pronoun when speaking to me. He was receptive to articles that I would e-mail to him about my situation. He managed to keep my "secret" from my mother for about four months before he finally told her what was going on. She had an idea that something was up. When my mother cut all contact with me, my stepfather continued speaking to me weekly and continued being loving and gracious to me.

One day, out of the blue, he asked me if I would like him to start giving me the blessing that a Jewish father typically gives to his son. I was so shocked; I never would have asked that of him, thinking that he would consider this using G-d's name in vain. My eyes welled up with tears and my heart was full of gratitude that he cared enough to offer that blessing to me.

When he started getting more ill, I went to visit him in my hometown, and we spent a day together. We did not tell my mother I was there until after I left because it would have upset her so much. We started saying "I love you," after we spoke as his time was drawing near. He would often call me because he was sad or lonely, and we would chat.

When the treatments stopped working, we knew it was only a matter of time, and we talked openly about how he felt about death and dying. He had become more religious since he got sick and felt very strongly that there was a G-d who would take care of him after death. He felt he had lived an honest and respectable life and was grateful for that. Three months before his death, my boyfriend and I drove four hours each way to visit him in Baltimore where he had a treatment study done. We only talked for a little while, but we were both silently aware that this was going to be our last visit. He told me how proud he was of me and told me to be good to my mother, to give her time. Before we left, my boyfriend photographed us with our arms around each other. I will cherish that picture for the rest of my life. Because my stepfather wished to remain anonymous, I couldn't post the photo; instead I drew a version of it to be published here.

He and I talked about me coming to his funeral. He told me, "I'll be dead anyway, we have to do what's best for your mom." My mom had no wish for me to be there so I did not attend. When I learned of his death, I mourned with my boyfriend in my apartment. I had some people come to visit me. I had lost the one parent that I had left at the time. It was terribly painful. He wrote me a letter that my mother sent me after he passed. He left me a small trust to continue my education or for emergencies. He wrote at the end of his sweet letter, "I will love you forever." So will I, Poppa M., so will I.

Kim

Difference Isn't Wrong... It Just Is

Embracing Families with Transgender and Gender Variant Children

Kim Pearson

Kim is one of the nation's most sought after and experienced educators on the topic of gender diversity in children. Whether it is a discussion with a school principal or guidance counselor, an in-service for a group of educators, a workshop for medical professionals or a presentation at a national conference, Kim has an innate ability to create an atmosphere where participants feel safe to share their fears and concerns. Her extraordinary success at bringing meaningful understanding to her audience is rooted in her ability to accurately identify and speak to the level of awareness unique to each individual. Drawing from her personal journey as the mother of a transgender child, her professional connections with leading experts in the field and her vast experience as a transition facilitator, Kim empowers families, educators and others by providing the tools for success. She is executive Director/Co-Founder of TransYouth Family Allies (TYFA), National Board President, PFLAG-Transgender Network and President/Co-Founder of PFLAG, Lake Havasu City, AZ.

✳   ✳   ✳   ✳   ✳

In the GLBT movement, most of us are familiar with the capital "T" representing transgender folks, but there is also a lower case "t" beginning to emerge as a bright and shining star of education and advocacy in our community. The lower case 't' represents the trans and gender variant children in our community and the families who love and support them.

Due to the flurry of recent media attention, these children have been thrust into the public eye. Unless you are personally acquainted with one of these children/families, how much do you really know about their lives and experiences? How accurate is the information you may have? What is transgender? Transgender is a very broad umbrella term, which represents many things to many people. For this article we are going to use it to refer to children who do not identify with the gender they were assigned at birth. This would include children who were assigned female at birth but self-identify as male, children who were assigned male at birth but self-identify as female and children who, regardless of their birth assignment, self-identify as either, neither or somewhere in between. The either, neither or in between children are those whose gender identity or expression differ from expectations for their assigned birth sex, and they are often referred to as gender variant, genderqueer or gender questioning. Not all children will identify with our socially constructed binary gender system [assumes that there are two and only two genders] and will continue to be gender variant into adulthood.

"*Sexual* orientation is about whom you find attractive. Gender identity is your internal sense of masculinity or femininity (not always congruent with biological or assigned sex). Gender identity is who you are, not who you find attractive."

As executive director of TransYouth Family Allies, Inc. (TYFA), I share the story of raising my pre-school gender variant child with audiences all over the country. It goes something like this: When my child was four, I was under the impression that I had a daughter who strenuously resisted gender typical dress, toys and activities, would not wear dresses, sported a flat top haircut, dressed in boy's jeans, tees, shoes and hats, played baseball (not softball), basketball, army men and most other "typically" male activities. My child even cut off eyelashes, offended by folks saying how pretty they were. The explanation was, "I can be 'cute,' but definitely NOT 'pretty.'" This was truly a gender variant child.

We define gender variant individuals as those whose gender identity or expression differs from expectations for their physical sex characteristics or assigned birth sex. Unlike my child, who did not verbally express his male gender identity until he was 14, many children are clear about having a cross gender identity from as early as two years of age. In [Edward Schor's] book *Caring For Your School Aged Child: 5-12*, the American Academy of Pediatrics states: "A child's awareness of being a boy or a girl starts in the first year of life. It often begins by 8 to 10 months of age, when youngsters typically discover their genitals. Then, between one and two years old, children become conscious of physical differences between boys and girls; before their third birthday they are easily able to label themselves as either a boy or a girl as they acquire a strong concept of self. By age four, children's gender identity is stable, and they know they will always be a boy or a girl."

Try to imagine yourself as the parent of a two-year-old son who says to you, "Mom, why do you keep buying me trucks? Don't you know I am a girl and I like Barbie dolls?" What does a parent do with that type of information coming from a two-year-old? How do you react? As parents, we are called upon to make difficult decisions every day. Many of us base those decisions on the big picture. What will be best for my child and family in the long run? If you have a child who tells or shows you through his/her actions and reactions that s/he doesn't identify with their assigned birth sex, it becomes necessary to consider the negative effects of denying your child's gender expression, whether you agree or not. This does not refer to children who are "pretending," "play acting" or simply trying out different gender roles or activities. These are children who consistently, persistently and acutely identify with the gender opposite of their birth sex — children who, over the course of months leading into years, express this cross-gender identification to their parent(s). These children, if not given the opportunity to express their gender identity, may be so distressed that they resort to self-harm or even suicide.

In the early stages it is not uncommon for a parent to think that their child may be gay or lesbian, which may or may not be the case. Sexual orientation and gender identity are not the same thing. Sexual orientation is about whom you find attractive. Gender identity is your internal sense of masculinity or femininity (not always congruent with biological or assigned sex). Gender identity is who you are, not who you find attractive. Transgender people have the same sexual orientations that other people have.

There are many ways in which a child expresses gender variance. At what point does a parent know that they need to DO something about it? The parents of gender variant children, their teachers and even healthcare professionals that TYFA works with often begin by asking if a child can be taught "appropriate" gender behavior. Pressuring a child to conform to normative standards may result in changed external behaviors; however, it isn't likely to change their sense of who they are. Forcing gender conformity has been shown to cause depression, anxiety, malaise, poor school performance and even suicidal ideation. According to the GLSEN (Gay, Lesbian and Straight Education Network), 2005 National School Climate Survey, which surveyed 1,732 students, ages 13-20, 26.1% had experienced physical harassment at school due to their gender expression and 11.8% had been physically assaulted due to their gender expression. The average GPA for transgender students frequently physically harassed was 1/2 grade lower than students experiencing less harassment (2.6 vs. 3.1).

Once families find acceptance of their child's gender identity, there are many questions they may need answered: How and what should we tell our family, friends, school, etc? What does transition mean, and how can we be sure our child is ready? What about the changes of puberty?

How do we bolster our child's self-esteem? Telling your family and friends the truth is a good place to start. It might go something like this: "My child has a medical condition which manifests itself as incongruence between their sense of who they are and their physical anatomy." If the child's gender variance is obvious to others, the sooner the topic is addressed, the better. Being up front opens the door for providing education, and education is the key to understanding and acceptance. People tend to fear what they do not understand. Experience has shown us that being matter of fact, positive and upbeat really helps. The attitude and level of confidence a parent displays often sets the tone for how others handle the information. If the information is presented as being problematic, painful, difficult and dangerous, people are likely to respond negatively. Alternatively, if you state the expectation that your child's future will be happy, successful and bright, then they will likely respond positively. How, when and to whom you disclose this information is a highly individual and personal decision. Your family, schools and other organizations are not likely to be familiar with your child's condition and cannot do their job of providing a safe and nurturing environment without some help. If you feel well-informed and confident that you can educate others, then you should. Parents of gender variant children and youth who are acutely distressed by the incongruence of their gender identity and their social gender role (i.e. how they dress, name, pronouns, etc.) may choose to transition that child. Simply put, this means letting the child live in the gender they identify with at home, at school and in all areas of their life. Parents and others may ask, "How can we be certain that transition is the right thing to do?" Are we ever really certain of anything when making parental decisions? Sometimes the worry is that children will later change their mind. If this happens, you simply revert to their previous gender presentation. With young children there are no medical procedures or medications to take, therefore everything is totally reversible.

"Forcing gender conformity has been shown to cause depression, anxiety, malaise, poor school performance and even suicidal ideation."

There may be some discomfort with the fluidity of this type of reversal, but however uncomfortable or embarrassing it may be for the adults involved, it is far more difficult for the children. They need support and validation of who they are. Many families choose to live "in stealth" and do not see the need to divulge their child's medical information after transition. Some choose to only tell those who "need to know," such as physicians, teachers, etc. Others may tell everyone in order to minimize the risk of exposure. In the end, it is up to you and your child and what you feel comfortable with disclosing. With adolescents the transition process may be more involved. There are medical intervention options a family may wish to pursue. Modern medicine has made it possible to delay the development of the secondary sexual characteristics brought on by puberty, because these changes are often devastating for gender variant children. The medications are called GnRh analogues (puberty inhibitors) and are prescribed by an endocrinologist. The effects of these medications are reversible if the child changes their mind. However, if a child has consistently presented as gender variant from childhood through adolescence, the odds that they will change their mind are practically nonexistent.

Not all children express that they are transgender in time to delay puberty. If puberty has already begun, there may be ways to help minimize the discomfort, such as stopping menstruation. An endocrinologist can help parents make informed decisions about such treatments. Where is my family with this journey now? Well, our suicidal, gender variant, teen "daughter" is now living a happy and fulfilling life as a young man. My husband and I made many difficult decisions along the way, but the most important decision we ever made was to love our child unconditionally. In 18 months we have transitioned from having a child on the brink of dropping out of middle school — a child who wouldn't speak to anyone outside of our immediate family (not even to order food at a restaurant) and was literally disappearing before our eyes, to a child who is happy, outgoing and excelling at school. Our son is now a youth advocate who travels all over the country speaking to youth, communities of faith, schools, colleges, universities, pretty much anyone who will listen. The message is always the same: affirming a child's gender identity expression is one of the most significant things you can do for a gender variant child. Being supportive and paving the way for that child's acceptance at school and in other social situations speaks louder than words. Difference isn't wrong...it just is.

"Field" by Dominic Perri © 2012

Miles' Tattoo

~ And the day came when the risk to remain
tight in a bud was more painful than
the risk it took to blossom. ~
Anais Nin

Once a Daughter, Now a Son

Kathy Ramsey

Kathy lives in Seattle with her husband of 31 years and two furry canine kids. They have been blessed with the privilege of raising two wonderful sons.

$$\star \quad \star \quad \star \quad \star \quad \star$$

My daughter, now my son, Miles, age 26, told us two years ago he was transitioning to be the male he always should have been. It was very difficult for my husband and I to understand, but we love him and he is our kid no matter what age or gender. I actually found an online transgender parents support group TransKidsFamily (TKF) the very night he told us. It saved my sanity and provided much needed support, compassion and information over the last two years. It is an incredible family to be welcomed into.

A month or two after he told us he was transitioning, we got to a very angry and uncommunicative place, and I was really feeling pushed away. I realized I was only giving him negative reactions to everything, so I wrote 'Things I Know.' I felt I had to let him know that I was actually trying to accept his decision, but he had to try to understand me, too. It was honest and raw, but straight from my heart. Regular emails had all but stopped between us, and conversations were uncomfortable and short. It made a big difference to him when he read it. We were able to communicate much better after he understood my feelings, and that went a long way towards our healing and acceptance.

After I first wrote it, I would re-read it all the time to remind myself of what I had to keep in sight. It was kind of a commitment to Miles that I would try, that's all he could ask me to do, and all I could do.

It has been shared with TKF, Seattle PFLAG, at the Gender Spectrum Conference 2009 and was published, in part, in the *Huffington Post* in 2012. It was humbling to see how many people were touched by my letter to my son.

I updated it a year into my son's journey, and it really shows what a difference a year can make. The first lines (italicized) are from the original letter; the words following (bolded) are the 'year later' additions.

✭ ✭ ✭ ✭ ✭

To Miles: "Things I Know, What a Difference
a Year Makes." © 2012

*I know this is a process of stages. Grief is the first, acceptance the middle,
celebration is the last.*

**I am now celebrating the wonderful joyful man that
you have become.**

*I know I have to be able to see the 'firsts' and accept them as they happen,
not with distress, but with open-mindedness.*

**There aren't any 'firsts' anymore, I am blessed to be
able to watch you continually grow.**

*I know I can move forward through my grief and sorrow, and eventually
find a sense of peace, seeing my child truly happy.*

**There isn't any more sorrow, if I ever had any
doubts about your choice to live as male, as you always felt you should, they are gone. I see a more confident, strong, giving man than my 'daughter' had
ever been, it is amazing!**

*I know that you have found yourself, once and for all, and I am glad for
that.*

**You knew your truth and had the passion and re-
solve to move towards your life as you knew it
should be.**

*I know my 'days' of sadness are changing to 'moments' and it is okay that
I will still have some.*

**I don't have many moments of sadness about your
transition anymore. It has allowed you to be your
true authentic self, and I can only be as happy about
that as you are.**

*I know as you become more comfortable with the changes in your body, so
will I.*

How funny that now I look at you and see my son.

All of the changes, inside and out are all parts of you (of course, you running around without a shirt on, showing off your manly chest makes it easy to see!).

I know someday, very soon, everything will seem that it was meant to be and I can put it all in perspective.
That day is here. My perspective just had to learn to keep up with you.

I know I must move forward and support you with acceptance and joy for your happiness and contentment.
You taught me there was no use in looking backwards, that there is no other direction but forward.

I know I don't have to 'erase' the past. All the memories are mine to keep. I can have them and the new ones to come, together in my heart, they'll all fit.
You have already shown me that the new ones are astonishing in their joy and brilliancy.

I know I am waiting to hear "I love you, Mom," when you understand how hard I am trying.
I know you knew and appreciated my efforts. Hearing your love and appreciation for our support and acceptance means so much. Now it is as effortless for me to support you, as it seems to be for you to tell me you love me.

I know I have been thinking really hard about how brave you are and how difficult it must be for you to be true to yourself.
You are the most courageous person I know. I am in awe of your undeniable determination.

I know I will get through this because I love you more than you can ever know, I want only for you to be happy and at peace with yourself. I am blessed to have you in my life no matter what.
You were patient enough to allow me my worries

and confusion, and you are loving enough to share with me the tranquility and joy you now possess.

I know that I care deeply enough for you that communication can't be stifled by my discomfort, even if I am struggling.
You allowed my awkward attempts at understanding until I could stop struggling and start believing.

I know that I am proud that you feel you were raised with the strength to be able to do this rather than cower and hide in a life of unhappiness.
I was able to learn by your example and discover that I had that same strength within myself.

I know now this isn't a loss, I will still know you, my child, with every smile and hug I get.
The person I raised will always be here. Looking different on the outside made no difference to the wonderfulness that you are.

I know 'practicing' a new name and pronouns will be hard for me, but for now, you are 'M', my child.
Somehow Miles fits you far better than your birth name ever did, because being Miles is your truth. Miles is happy and comfortable in his own skin, my daughter never was.

I know that your peace is worth far more than my sorrow.
I see the peace and stillness in you now and know that my 'sorrow' was really just selfishness. For that, I am sorry.

I know I can embrace not only physical changes taking place, but the changes in your self-esteem and confidence as well.
I embrace your transition with much joy and wonder. Outer appearances didn't really change who you are, they just allowed you to become your genuine self.

I know I have not lost my child. I have found him.

I didn't 'find' him, you were there all along, I just needed you to show me.

I know I have to trust your judgment in terms of what you need to be whole and what you need in order to live your life with authenticity.

I was able to have faith in you, because you showed me how much you had it in yourself.

I know when you realize the full support I am offering, then you will be able to embrace the fullness of your past, including those pink dresses and pretty bows.

You acknowledge that who you are today is made up of everything you have experienced, and I am proud to have those old memories, and I am ready to celebrate the new ones too.

I know I am extremely grateful for how I have grown because of what my children have taught me.

I learned so much in the past year, about you and about myself, how to trust, to accept, to understand and to love — unconditionally.

I know that if I educate myself and love my child, it isn't all that hard.

Loving you and trusting in you is never hard. Loving me and trusting in me is.

I know you aren't the only one who is transitioning; I am transitioning right along with you. Because I love you, I know there will come a point when I will be settled with your identity.

Your identity has always been there, now your outer appearance matches the inside. I don't need to be settled with your identity, because you are.

I know I don't have to pretend to understand everything, but I do need to ask questions, and try as much as possible to do a lot of listening when you answer them.

I loved you enough to listen and learn, and to accept your choice, and in doing that I was able to understand.

I know responding to you from my heart is sometimes painful for you, but I need to be honest and help you to understand me, too.
You accepted with patience my initial confusion, and your willingness to give me time to realize this was real and true for you, showed your incredible compassion.

I know coming to know 'M' will become such a gift, a way to a fuller understanding of the beloved child I have always embraced and will always cherish.
Your transition was a gift — to yourself, to me and to everyone who knows and loves you. You will always be my beloved, cherished child, no matter how old you are.

"I love you, no matter what!"

Hindsight is amazing, isn't it? When I could finally put together the 'puzzle pieces' about a year and a half ago, I did a little head smack and thought 'Gosh, I should have known.' I can look back now and point fingers at the activities she liked, sports, etc. and say 'Look, see? Was she masculine?' but to me, her feeling 'gender different' was not obvious at age 10 or 11, she was just our daughter. But the funny part is, she didn't exactly know either, until age 23. I honestly do not remember her ever verbalizing it to me that she was a boy or wanted to be a boy when she was small. I had no idea why at age seven or so, I heard 'I don't like it, take it off' when I wanted to put my little girl in pretty dresses. I had no clue why my daughter would rather jam a baseball hat on her mop of curly hair instead of combing it in her impatience to go outside to play when she was eight or nine. I only knew that my straight 'A' daughter excelled at school, passing most male peers with pride when it came to academics.

She loved softball, basketball and swimming and did all of them better than most of the guys she knew. I never missed a game, cheering the whole time as she slid into third base in the mud. I had a daughter and however she acted was what my daughter was. She was our female child, whether she was in pink bows or digging in the dirt. She did 'act' girly for quite a long time when she was little. I don't think I made her pick out pretty hair bows or pink lacy skirts, or paint her room pink or turquoise. These were things she chose, but again, in hindsight, was it because Mama wanted it for her? But as she got older, I gave her the freedom to wear the blue jeans instead of dresses, and not comb her hair, just jam a hat on and call it good, and go play rough and tumble with the boys. It didn't make her masculine or not my girl, it just made her my daughter. In his letter to us telling us he was transgender, Miles said,

> *I've always known I was somehow gender-different, ever since I was very small, but did not know why or what it meant. I always felt like one of the guys. It's just the way I am, and I make no apologies for being this way. I cannot change this fact about me any more than I can change the fact that I have brown eyes and am right handed. I like who I am, and I know I am a better person for being able to accept this and choose to be true to myself and live as male. This was something I had to work out on my own. I had to get to a point where I was okay with me being this way. I had to get to a point where I knew this wasn't something that was going away. I had to get to a point where people calling me "girl" made me cringe on the inside and the thought of not being able to be who I feel I really am was almost suffocating. It is a waste of time wondering about the what-ifs and the maybes and why or how this happened, why didn't I come to you sooner, why couldn't you see it, what could you have done to help me, these are all useless questions that in the end don't matter at all. None of that matters, except this is the way I am. It doesn't matter how I got here or when, I'm here now, and I am happier for having arrived.*

I think that said it all for me...He was strong enough to be honest with himself and me, and our lives changed forever. Now I look at myself in the mirror and see a woman who helped raise a child who is strong enough to move out of a life of unhappiness into one of new possibilities. And I am so proud of both of us.

Eli and Kate

What Do I Say?

Kate Rood

Kate lives in Portland, Oregon. An alumna of Smith College, Kate is an avid letter writer and thrift store shopper. Her other loves include her wonderful boyfriend, her labradoodle Pasco, the color green and all things ginger. Kate currently works at Evanta, a company that facilitates corporate leadership conferences. This article and the next tell of Kate's journey with Eli through his transition from F2M.

When Emma calls to say she is going to start living as a man when she begins her new job in New York, my first thought is that she is too far away. I wish she were sitting next to me, and we were rid of all the miles separating us.

It is July of 2005, and I am home in Oregon. Emma has recently moved to New York City and is barely surviving a failed sublet experience and a period of unemployment that is interrupted by a brief stint of employment at a falafel restaurant and ends when she secures a job in a library at Columbia University. I have had to loan her $1,000 from my summer internship stipend so she can try and pay the broker's fee for an apartment in south Harlem. My mom and I are both relieved that she is about to make the promising professional upgrade from falafel slinger to library assistant.

The call comes as my mom and I are watching television. My mom is lying back in her recliner, and I'm perched on its overstuffed arm with my arm around her shoulder. She talks to Emma first. We've muted the sound of our show, so I absorb my mother's responses as I continue to watch a frenetically paced interior design makeover of a kitchen on the screen.

"It's okay honey…What are you so worried about?…Yes, it's okay…." Now my mom is nudging my ribcage with her elbow, motioning for me to turn the television off. She keeps one hand on my leg while the other holds the phone. She's using her special mom voice, a deep rich tone that soothes like a cup of warm tea. "I love you…That sounds like a good plan, honey… Just tell them what you just told me…Yes, they will like you just as much as they did in the interview…Okay, I love you so much, here's sister-bear." She hands the phone to me.

"Hey sis." Her voice sounds distant, probably because she's calling a land-line from her cell phone. At least the reception isn't choppy. This isn't the kind of conversation you want interrupted by a dropped call. "So, I think when I start my job at Columbia, I'm going to go to work as a man. I want them to use male pronouns, and I am going to tell them that my name is Eli."

"Eli." I repeat.

"Yeah, I like Eli. I'm 99 percent sure about it. I know I want to keep the E. It might be easier for the family too. Like when cousin Amanda decided to be Amanda, not Amy, that wasn't too hard."

"Yeah. We'll see." I want to reassure her, but we both know this is not going to be like the summer Amanda decided she wanted to lose her nickname.

"It's supposed to be the first step, you know, living full time as a man." She sounds much more nervous than she needs to be. Doesn't she know I am prepared for this?

I have spent the last three years trying to learn more about gender identity, preparing myself, with a twin's intuition, for this phone call, made shortly be-fore our 20th birthday. Having just completed my sophomore year at Smith College, I had befriended many of the politically active transgender men on campus during my first two years. I had also spent those first two years at Smith trying to make friends, best friends, who might make me feel the way I felt when I was with my twin. I picked a women's college in part to try and replicate the space I'd grown up in — a house of women, just my mom, my sister and me. I was in college looking for a best friend who might be there for me like Emma was before she left me in high school while she went to college early.

At Smith, I advocated for gender-neutral pronouns in our school consti-tution and lobbied the college for safe, gender-neutral restrooms on campus. I worked hard to respect what seemed to be Emma's growing unease with her female identity. I introduced her to friends as Em, honoring the more ambiguous nickname she had started using. I defaulted to calling her my twin more often than my sister. It had already been over a year since she started signing her e-mails and letters just E.

So when she calls, I do not have to waste words being surprised or con-fused or upset. I tell her I love her. I tell her that her new supervisors at Co-lumbia will surely understand — it's a liberal place, and she will be working for the School of Social Work, after all. I tell her that I wish to hell she was not so far away. I say, it's okay, several times.

I hang up the phone, and immediately I want to call her back. I have ques-tions, but I sense she does not have the answers yet. Emma's decision is about to move beyond our family, beyond my intellectual engagement with understanding the restrictions of the gender binary [which assumes two, and only two, genders], and beyond my vague understanding that if she wanted to, my sister could live as a man. A commitment from me, that I would wholeheartedly respect her male identity, was only one step in my sister's movement towards living as a man. Emma would now be Eli, and she would now be he. I wanted to savor the intimacy of this decision, but the situation did not allow for the private reflection I wanted. Many other people were about to get involved.

After that first phone call, it went unspoken that my mom and I would start the task of gently introducing Eli to our — to his — friends and family. And so I wish I had asked him the question, what do I say? What do I say when the people who don't yet truly know Eli ask about you? And ask they did.

"What is your sister up to these days?"

"Where is Emma?"

"How is Emma?"

"Did Emma get that job in New York?"

"Is your sister coming home to visit this summer?"

What do I say?

Eli, with his undeniable charisma, kind heart and keen mind, had touched the lives of many people. Now these people, not all of them, but many of them, needed to be updated. The person they knew as their wonderful friend/classmate/relative/neighbor was still their wonderful friend/classmate/relative/neighbor. He just would like to be called Eli and referred to with male pronouns now.

Eli's decision immediately divided my relationships, from my most intimate to my most casual, into complex categories based on how each person knows my brother.

Category 1- People who knew Emma and now embrace Eli fully.

Category 2- People who knew Emma and now know Eli, but are reluctant about it.

Category 3- People who only know Eli.

Category 4- People who still only know Emma.

During the first year of Eli's transition, I was in Oregon executing a unique "study abroad" plan, which involved spending my junior year at Oregon State University. I was living with more independence than ever before. I had my own apartment with my boyfriend of several years. I was growing up, and I was constantly meeting new people with whom I could start totally fresh. I sought out these uncomplicated conversations to the point where I was practically using the line, "Hi, my name is Kate and I have a twin brother named Eli" to introduce myself, relishing each new friend's easy acceptance of this truth.

The more my identity as a grown, straight woman solidified, the more I felt I had to prove my place in the transgender community by being the perfect ally. I had plenty of opportunities to earn my stripes because at Oregon State I was spending more time with friends from high school who did not have the luxury of being steeped for the past two years in the rich political and activist culture of an elite women's college. Their understanding of transgender issues was almost non-existent. And their recollection of Eli was still inexorably tied to memories of when they last really knew him — as Emma, the slightly odd smart-girl who came out as a lesbian in the high school newspaper and then left for college two years before everyone else. I became more and more adept at explaining that the girl they remembered was growing into a wonderful young man, my brother.

My speech went something like this. "Yes, my sister is my brother now. He identifies as a transgender man and is transitioning so that people will correctly recognize his male identity. He goes by the name Eli now," short and to the point.

Language commits many acts of subterfuge. It can betray what the eyes see and the heart knows. Even though our friends and family knew they needed to confirm Eli's identity by using male pronouns and respecting his name change, they had trouble using the right words in this new context. People were prone to keep thinking of Eli as a woman because he was transitioning in New York, thousands of miles away from all of us in Oregon. Even though I shared general updates about his hormone therapy with friends and family, and they could hear his voice changing on the phone — it was getting lower and happier — they were trying to keep up with his physical and emotional transition from the other side of a continent.

I was blazing the trail for Eli so that things would be easier when he came home to visit. I didn't mind doing this legwork, and he was constantly thanking me for taking on what he thought of as a burden. It was hard work, but it made me feel important. My overachieving, straight-A personality was operating at full speed. I wanted to be involved and to be a model of support. Most significantly, I wanted to be needed by my twin.

Gradually I discovered that the most tactful technique for guiding the well-intentioned friend or relative was to rephrase their words, using the correct name and pronoun as many times as possible.

If they said, "When is Emma coming back to visit Portland?" I would say, "*Eli* is coming home in December. *He* should get here a few days before Christmas, and *he* can stay through New Year's Day."

If they slipped up and said, "Eli would like that restaurant, she loves good sushi," I would say, "Yes, I think *he* would love that restaurant. *He* has always loved good sushi, and *he* can't get enough of it."

"My speech went something like this. 'Yes, my sister is my brother now. He identifies as a transgender man and is transitioning so that people will correctly recognize his male identity. He goes by the name Eli now,' short and to the point."

Like a psychologist teaching apes to use sign language, I tried to retrain them in their use of language. But there were still endless situations in which I was left wondering, what do I say?

The first Christmas after Eli started transitioning, we both returned to Portland for a week. In between family commitments, we found time to have dinner together at Norm's Garden, our favorite Chinese restaurant. Housed in a building that used to be a fast food joint, Norm's Garden boasts booth style seating and a remarkable assortment of teal and mauve décor. There is always one table, near the cash register, piled high with a mountain of string beans waiting to be trimmed. The waitresses work on this project between runs to the kitchen and the customers.

Our usual waitress, the matriarch of the family who runs the place, recognized me and started making small talk as she poured our tea. The china cups at Norm's are marked by unique patterns of tiny surface deep cracks, little capillary veins stained brown with tea.

"Oh! You! How come we never see you here anymore?" she accused gently.

"My mom moved to an apartment across the river," I replied. Eli gulped some tea.

"Ah ha. But you are here now. We are still worth the trip," she declared.

"Of course," I said, proceeding with the socially required flattery. "There aren't sautéed string beans like yours anywhere else in the city." This satisfied her, and she took our order. Minutes later, food in hand, she returned.

"Where is your sister? I remember your twin, she is our number one doughnut fan." She was referring to the tasty little dessert rolls, fried and dunked in white sugar, which are Eli's favorite thing on the menu. Eli smiled and tried to make eye contact with her, but she looked right past him.

"She is living in New York now," I managed to say, hoping with each word that I was not hurting him.

She nodded, her hand on her hip. "Ah. Very good. Good Chinese food there."

After she walked away, I looked up at Eli and was pleased to see him smiling. "What should I have said?" I asked.

"I don't know. You could have said I was studying penguins in Antarctica." I laughed. Penguins were his favorite animals when we were growing up. He had the collection of penguin stuff and I had the panda bear stuff. That's how it often went with our childhood toys, complementary, but not identical.

"Really," he continued. "It's okay to take the easy way out sometimes. You don't have to make sure that everyone who has *ever* known me knows Eli."

I felt reassured; I had his permission to lie sometimes. I could let strangers think my twin was still in the world as Emma, and it would not make me disloyal. When it was important to let someone know, I could educate, explain, justify and defend. Or I could just say my sister was indisposed at the moment, studying penguins in Antarctica.

When the waitress came to clear our plates, Eli spoke up.

"Can we have an order of the doughnuts, please?" His voice sounded noticeably lower, but it was still early enough in his transition that he consciously manufactured a deeper tone when he spoke.

"One order or two?" She was looking right at Eli now.

"Two!" We said in unison.

My senior year of college, a full year and a half into Eli's transition, I find myself walking next to an acquaintance from a political science seminar. She is plugged into the queer community at Smith, so she knows I am involved with transgender advocacy on campus. She starts reminiscing about the presentation I made three years prior on the need for gender-neutral pronouns in the student government constitution. She starts to remember the details of my speech.

"Hey. Don't you have a twin? Wasn't she transgender?"

What do I say? Here we go.

"Yes, my sister is my brother now."

She's lighting a cigarette as we walk and as soon as she releases that first desperate exhalation of smoke, she replies, "Yeah. A lot of the lesbians I used to date are men now. I guess they want to be trendy."

I shift my book bag to my other shoulder. "Okay, see you later. I have to check my mailbox," is all I can muster in response.

What do I say? Nothing. I let her get away with it. She has reduced Eli, his fundamental being, to a trend, something people do as a response to social pressures. I walk away, feeling like shit.

A year later, I encounter the same woman at a mutual friend's birthday party at a champagne bar in Gramercy.

Eli is with me, and before I can introduce him, she looks at me and asks with provocative inflection, "So. How's your twin?"

I touch Eli's elbow, lifting his arm towards hers, which she is already extending in handshake. "This is my brother. This is Eli."

"Ooooh. Nice to meet you. I'm sorry I didn't know it was you."

"You went to Smith?" Eli raises his eyebrow and puts a chill in his voice.

"Yep. Same year as Kate," she replies. But her voice is trailing off. She has caught sight of some friend across the room and is already pivoting away from us.

Later she corners me by the bar and digs herself in a deeper hole.

"I'm sorry. I didn't know that was him. He looks great. He's the most convincing one I've ever seen. I mean, he really looks good!"

What do I say? I wish it was loud enough in the bar to pretend I haven't heard her, but it's not.

"Thanks. We've actually got to get going. It was nice to see you." I have failed him again.

Thanks? I should have told her there is nothing to be *convinced of.* My brother is not Pinocchio, trying to be a real boy. He is a man, and not just because you think he looks like a man ought to. Something — etiquette, discomfort, social pressure — keeps me from confronting everyone who shocks or saddens me with their lack of empathy for Eli. So I carry these little betrayals with me, walking that line between educating people or perpetuating their ignorance. My sister? Yeah, she's studying penguins in Antarctica.

How long will it take the rest of the world to catch up? It's like everyone else is stumbling through, making an ugly mess out of what seems so easy to me. I want to say to the confused: I have a brother. Everyone used to think he was my sister but we're setting the record straight. I have a brother. I try to be patient while they think it through, but it's hard. Some are oblivious. Some are bigoted. A very few do the required emotional and cognitive work with grace and intelligence. They reflect, ask respectful questions and then change the label on the file marked "Emma," stored in the frontal lobes of their brain, without much fuss.

"Bird of Paradise" by Hillary Brenneman © 2012

Sympathy Pains
Kate Rood

FAMILY

Frank was the first dog I had ever met with a taste for Altoid mints. As I sat with Eli and my mom in the waiting room of Dr. Brownstein's office in San Francisco, I watched the office assistant open her drawer every five minutes to slip the chubby dachshund another curiously strong mint. I found out later that Frank's mint habit was supported by many of Dr. Brownstein's loyal patients who, for years after their surgeries, continued to send tins of Altoids to San Francisco for Frank.

We were in San Francisco, a year into Eli's transition, for him to have gender confirming chest surgery (aka, top surgery). After a year of therapy and testosterone injections, Eli had decided this was the next step for him. He spent months doing research on the internet and carefully comparing the reputations and results of the handful of surgeons in the country who specialize in gender confirming surgery. There were a million factors to consider, from the type of procedure he should choose to how he would pay for it. In addition to being located on the west coast, which would allow Eli to more easily spend some of his recovery time at home in Portland, Dr. Brownstein was renowned in the transgender community for his consistently excellent results.

Dr. Brownstein's waiting room was full of other patients. Most of them were accompanied by friends or partners and appeared to be in their early twenties. Some held hands, others read, played games on their cell phones or looked at their feet. One-by-one they got up to go see the doctor, and I could tell that they were all binding their breasts, because they hunched their shoulders instinctively and their chests had the same tight, thick look as Eli's did. I recognized something in the eyes of those who did make eye contact. Their faces ached to be seen, and their eyes held a quiet vulnerability that I used to see in Eli. I saw fear, too, fear and determination.

Two days after Eli's initial appointment, we arrived in pre-dawn fog at the private surgery center where Dr. Brownstein operates. After Eli and my mom completed a clipboard of endless paperwork, they took Eli back to prep him for surgery. A few minutes before the scheduled surgery time, my mom and I were finally allowed into the nurses' station to see Eli. Immediately, a peppy male nurse started to chirp his way through his usual script.

"Are you going to be on your best behavior for us?" he asked Eli, smiling as he rapped his pen on the chart he was holding. I raised an eyebrow at my mom and I saw she was grinning too. We were both remembering when Eli — then Emma — had taken a groggy, half-serious swing at an anesthesiologist right before going in for minor heart surgery when he was 13. The doctor had teased Emma that her good grades must have been the result of cheating, and Emma had said "I don't cheat," before throwing her arm in the direction of the doctor. His first question having gone unanswered, the nurse tried again.

"And who do we have here?" He spoke in a tone more appropriate for a reluctant toddler at their first dentist appointment than for a 20-year-old about to have a double incision mastectomy with nipple grafts.

"This is my mom, Joanna, and my twin sister, Kate." Silence.

"Twins? Wow. That's a first for us." The peppy nurse paused again and looked back and forth at us the way people do when they don't see the resemblance. "Twins," he repeated, and then yelled down the hall. "Hey, we've got a twin today!"

A second nurse approached and started putting white compression stockings on Eli's legs to protect against blood clots during surgery. When she was finished she patted Eli on his nylon-covered leg. "Your family's here. That's nice, real nice." And then turning towards my mom, she said, "We don't get to meet many family members. Good for you."

As my mom asked the nurse about how long the surgery would take, I thought back to Eli's pre-op appointment at Dr. Brownstein's office. I enjoyed the praise of these nurses, but it was disheartening to know that we stood out because so many people fail to support their transgender family members. I tried to remember the tired faces I'd seen in the waiting room. How many of them had parents or siblings who disapproved of their decision to transition? How many brothers or sisters had Dr. Brownstein shaken hands with before striding off to build their siblings a new male chest? The nurse had confirmed that I was certainly the first twin sister.

Five hours after they whisked Eli back to surgery, he was out and ready to be discharged. As Eli was loaded into a wheelchair, one of the nurses pulled me aside.

"He's going to be pretty nauseous for the next day or two, especially tonight as the anesthesia wears off. I'm going to give you some disposable alcohol wipes. It's my secret tool for fighting nausea. Hold it under his nose if he starts feeling sick."

"That actually works?"

"Yes, every time. I'll give you a handful of them."

"Okay, thanks,"

Still faint with relief, my mom and I tried to absorb all the post-operative care instructions. "Make sure he sleeps on his back. He'll probably need the Percocet for the first two or three days, then try switching him over to Ibuprofen. He shouldn't lift his arms above his head, so make sure he keeps wearing only button-up shirts." Someone handed me a stapled packet of information with emergency contact phone numbers and suggestions for how to keep Eli comfortable over the next week.

We had just gathered our coats and bags and were wheeling Eli out of the building when I started feeling sick. The physical release of an unhealthy dose of worry chased with relief struck hard. And it must have shown on my face, because the nurse who was helping us get Eli into the cab suddenly turned her attention to me.

"Hey, you okay sweetie?"

"I don't know. I'm feeling pretty dizzy." I sat down on the curb.

"Here, use one of these." She started unwrapping one of the alcohol wipes that were supposed to be for Eli. "Remember what I said about using them for your brother? Take one now. Breathe it in. Keep breathing."

Sympathy pains between twins are well documented, but before that day I had never experienced anything that could be described as a physical response to pain Eli endured. Aside from the nervous tears I shed, my thirteen-year-old body did not respond when Eli had surgery to correct the minor heart arrhythmia — supraventricular tachycardia — that he had as a young adult. I felt no physical pain when Eli contracted Lyme disease and then a painful staph infection the summer he worked in an organic garden after his sophomore year of college. There was no psychic connection between the two of us when he dislocated his kneecap playing basketball his senior year of college. I knew nothing of it until he called to say he was at the hospital getting x-rays. But when I stood next to that nurse in San Francisco, listening to her describe how to care for my twin, who had just had his breasts removed, I experienced devastating nausea and an attack of whole-body weakness like nothing I had ever felt.

When I try to remember details of the first hours after Eli's surgery, my memory recalls only the harsh scent of rubbing alcohol. I can't remember what Eli said when he first woke up, or whether my mom cried, or whether his chest looked any flatter under the layers of bandages. What I remember is still feeling scared, even though the surgery was over, and there had been no complications. Eli's transition was manifesting in his body, but I felt it too, as if my body was doing whatever it could think of to absorb some of the shock that Eli was experiencing. I had worried myself sick, and now I was torn between hugging him because he was okay and punching him for putting me through this.

During the week we spent in San Francisco for Eli's recovery, I had several jobs. I carried gallon-sized jugs of bottled water from RiteAid up the steep San Francisco hills to our hotel room. I went to Chinatown in search of my mom's favorite roast duck dish. I made long-distance calls to update friends and family. And I emptied the drains that were inserted into Eli's chest to help release the bloody fluid that accumulated at the incision sites. Twice a day, we went through the routine of checking the drains and tracking their output.

"20 CCs on the left, 15 on the right. You're draining like a champ," I would report as I squeezed the contents of the bulb-shaped reservoir into a tiny measuring cup. The nurse at the surgery center showed me how to empty the drains, but I usually made several attempts at re-sealing them after each emptying because I wanted to make sure I was doing it right. If there wasn't enough pressure and suction, the liquid wouldn't drain correctly, and it would slow Eli's healing. I recorded the output results on a medical chart before carrying the cups to the bathroom to rinse.

As I laid out the little hospital measuring cups on a generic hotel washcloth to dry, I felt acutely the unfairness of Eli's transition. While some twenty-year-old guys I knew were getting new cars for graduation presents, our mother was taking out a second lease on her Honda Civic so that Eli could get the double-mastectomy that he knew would help people recognize his true male identity. While other young men were planning their first forays into adulthood, Eli, with the help of testosterone injections and a new chest, was taking baby steps into the male puberty he had missed the first time around.

Because I shared almost everything with Eli, from the intimacy of our mother's womb to the mundane details of every family vacation, it was very hard to accept that Eli was enduring challenge after challenge that I would never have to face. Purely by luck, I am happy with the gender I was assigned at birth, and I will continue to go through life with the privileges that come with being a straight, white, pretty, healthy woman. I dutifully rinsed the bloody discharge from my brother's chest, because it was the least I could do.

A few days into our trip, my laptop had a meltdown. I had brought it with us so we could watch DVDs in the hotel room. When I tried to turn it on that night, I got nothing but a blue screen with a truly ominous error message in the top left hand corner. I lost it immediately.

"Shit, shit, shit. Something's going on with my computer. Shit." Eli and my mom stopped reading and looked up at me. Before I knew what was happening, I was crying and pressing Ctrl+Alt+Del like a madwoman. "My papers! All my photos!"

"I'm sure it's fine," Eli said from across the room.

"Yeah, right. Look at the screen." By now I was more upset that I was crying about a computer than I was about actually having to face the problem. I started gulping for air, trying to stifle the tears.

"You don't have to get so upset, it's okay," my mom added.

"No, it's not! All my papers and photos and music are on here," I repeated.

Eli rose from the bed and walked slowly over, gingerly protecting his chest. "It might just be overheated. Let's turn it off and turn it back on."

"I tried that, the power button isn't even working. Everything is frozen."

"You just have to hold it down longer. Here, see." He leaned on the button for a good fifteen seconds and let go. The computer hiccupped and the screen went black. "Let's just give it a second. I'm sure it's fine." I slouched in the chair, crossed my arms and started jiggling my leg. I was embarrassed. In the midst of recovery from life changing surgery, my brother still acted with remarkable composure.

When the computer turned on with no sign of its rebellion from moments earlier, I felt sheepish and muttered a quick thank you before retreating to the bathroom to wash my face. Since we were little, I have always relied on Eli's instincts and poise to augment my planning and emotion. Now, his ability to calm and comfort me seemed stronger than ever before; it was less than 48 hours after his surgery, and I wondered what was coming next. Eli had the opportunity to reinvent himself, to keep just the best parts of himself and mold the rest into a man he could be proud to be. There's nothing like watching someone else make big decisions to make you re-evaluate where you are in your own life. Was I brave enough to make my own changes, improve myself? Would I stay anxious and unmoored while he grew up?

Eli's surgery was taking place barely one month after the end of a four-year relationship with my first love. I was headed into my senior year of college, single and without much of a plan. In a way, the timing was perfect: rather than examine what I should do with my life, I could be a passenger on Eli's journey. I could get nauseous when he got nauseous. I could wait for him to calm me down instead of figuring out my own strategies for dealing with life's challenges, big and small.

Academic twin studies, conducted by psychologists across the country, strive to explain the close relationships observed between twin pairs. Identical twins, it is argued, form closer bonds than fraternal twins because they are predisposed by evolutionary biology to want to protect and advance their own genes, genes that their identical twins share. Indeed, much of this research focuses on identical twins. Fraternal twins are used as a control population to illustrate that it's the shared genetic blueprint of identical twins that creates their unique bond and demonstrably similar personalities. Whether it's exploring the phenomenon of identical twins that are reared apart and then reunited, or observing twin pairs who seem to share secret languages, society has always been fascinated with twins for what they reveal about human connection.

Although we may not be identical, Eli and I share a closeness that challenges the findings of these peer-reviewed studies. I see myself reflected in the mythology of twins more than the science of twins. Across time and culture, literature and mythology have explored the deep solidarity of twins. Castor and Pollux, the well-known twin brothers in Greek mythology are so connected that Pollux willingly gives up half of immortality when Castor dies so that they can share half the year in the underworld together. Twins Apollo and Artemis complement each other as god of the sun and goddess of the moon. Shakespeare, who fathered twins himself, featured twins in several of his comedies, exploring themes of identity and kinship. In *The Comedy of Errors*, the character of Antipholus of Syracuse is separated from his twin brother. He immediately feels the impact of this distance on his own sense of self, declaring, "I to the world am like a drop of water/That in the ocean seeks another drop."

Being a part of this cultural mythology and tradition is intoxicating. My life is more significant because it is connected so naturally and undeniably to Eli's. We own each other's successes and failures in a way that most non-twin siblings do not. That we've had to assert our identity as twins with extra gusto because we do not look alike has only strengthened my identity as a twin. Even when people believed we were two little girls and we wore matching dresses, people were always saying, "You can't be twins! You don't even look alike." The initial disbelief and then shocked fascination from strangers was always part of the fun.

Our last day in San Francisco, a full week after Eli's surgery, we went back to Dr. Brownstein's office to get Eli's stitches taken out. It was an unceremonious appointment. A new set of anxious individuals shared the waiting room with us. Frank was fed at least another dozen Altoids. I was expecting some kind of big reveal, or confetti and balloons and a banner with "You Made It Through This" spelled in glitter letters draped across the office. Instead, Dr. Brownstein removed the stitches in a backroom and then sent Eli out to us with a fresh batch of sterile gauze and first-aid tape.

"Dr. Brownstein says things look good," Eli reported.

"Okay. Is that it?" My mom also seemed surprised by how smoothly everything was going. "And you're okay? You're feeling okay?"

"Yeah, I feel great."

"It looks like you're in good hands," the office manager chimed in. "You're going to feel tender for a while still. And remember, no heavy lifting. Some guys want to jump right back into the weights, and I always make sure and tell 'em they have to wait at least six weeks. Okay? Six weeks. Just call us here if you have any questions. Have a safe trip home." Her voiced trailed off as she reached to answer the phone.

After the appointment, my mom treated us to brunch at the posh Fairmont hotel, a landmark of the Nob Hill neighborhood in San Francisco. Complete with manicured hedges, the impressive façade of the Fairmont faces the corner of Mason Street and California Street, just a few blocks away from the more modest Grosvenor Suites where we'd spent the past week. We were celebrating, and the spread of food did not disappoint. I reveled in the luxury of the tiny individual bottles of Tabasco sauce and maple syrup, and I picked the most decadent toppings at the waffle station — fresh blackberries and crushed macadamia nuts. Over mini-croissants, fruit salad and Earl Grey Tea in real china cups, Eli continued to heal.

"*So* while I have gained a twin who finally knows himself, and I feel closer to Eli in many ways than I ever have before, I first had to reconcile with the finality of his transition, and the reality that it resulted in a loss that I can barely articulate..."

Happy and full, we linked arms as we walked back to our hotel to pack our bags. Having expressed his irrational fear that his newly relocated nipples might fall off, Eli continued to walk in a slow, guarded fashion, his hand resting gingerly over the top button of his cardigan sweater. Our stroll had just brought us to the cable car stop by our hotel when we saw them: the most exquisite pair of identical twin sisters. They appeared to be in their late seventies and sported immaculately styled and identical hairdos, thickly applied make-up and old-fashioned stockings. They were wearing matching red skirt suits with matching leopard print fur hats, and they couldn't have been more than five feet tall. We followed them into our hotel and caught up to them just before they turned down the hall.

"I just love your hats," my mom ventured.

"Thank you, so do we," they replied together. Then, arm-in-arm, they gave a little wave to us and opened the door to their room.

"Wow. Aren't they something?" my mom said. Wow, indeed, I thought. It seemed beyond coincidence that we were staying in the same hotel with such an eccentric pair for this trip, a trip that was ushering the reality of my ever having had a sister further into the realm of memory.

A few weeks after returning from San Francisco, I found myself thinking about the identical sisters. I went to the bookshelf in the living room and pulled out a well-worn copy of [Abbe and Gill's] *Twins on Twins*, a book of photographs and essays that someone gave to my mom during her pregnancy. I flipped through a few pages and there they were: Vivian and Marian Brown, the iconic identical twins we had seen in San Francisco. Although taken roughly 20 years before, the pictures in the book captured perfectly the energy of this pair that I had seen shuffling the streets of San Francisco, taking in the cool Bay breezes and breathing not air, but devotion to each other.

The article described Vivian and Marian's habits, from the careful sharing of their paychecks to the challenge of storing their collection of over 100 matching hats. The article traced Vivian and Marian's ascension to twin superstardom and celebrated their various achievements, such as winning the distinction of 'most identical' at several international twin conventions. Towards the end of the article was a line that struck me. While attributed to Vivian, the quote reads as though it were meant to be spoken in unison. I saw Vivian and Marian in my mind — their matching red dresses like two halves of the same heart — as I read the words out loud to myself.

"We think twins are the only way to be."

Vivian and Marian comforted me in the way that bittersweet emotion sometimes can. They were perfect and beautiful, and their unity magnified the fact that Eli and I were now no longer sisters. Despite the long list of things that made us unique to each other — that Eli is queer, that we took our own unique paths to different colleges, that I am a morning person and he is a night owl — when we were sisters, I still felt that we had enough in common to keep alive the notion that we were complementary halves of one person, one woman. So while I have gained a twin who finally knows himself, and I feel closer to Eli in many ways than I ever have before, I first had to reconcile with the finality of his transition, and the reality that it resulted in a loss that I can barely articulate, but that was triggered by seeing Vivian and Marian Brown — Eli and I will never be able to live the same life. Eli changed his gender, and I did not change mine.

"Portrait #21" by Autumn Yamamoto © 2012

"Coming Home" by Melanie Whitney © 2012

The Colorado sky is one of my favorite things in the entire world. At night, it is alight with millions of spectacular stars. When I go back to Colorado the shape and color of the house I return to is not so important as that spectacular sky; it is a sign that I am home.

Forrest Isaac Gump

Shelley Schwartz

Shelley is a mother/sister and friend/ally of the GLBT community. She is married with two kids, and they have a dog named Mo. Shelley is involved in many organizations for social and political change. She taught special education in the NYC schools and presently work with autistic children.

✷　✷　✷　✷　✷

Isaac "is like a box of chocolates, you never know what you are going to get,"
—Forrest Gump from the movie *Forrest Gump*

I don't like dresses.
I want to dress like a boy.
I don't like ballet.
I like soccer.
I want to climb a tree!

I am Bisexual.
I am Genderqueer.
I am Queer.
I am Transgender.
I am Male.

I pierced the top of my ear.
I pierced my eyebrow.

I cut my hair.
I shaved my head.

I shop only in the men's department.
I use the men's bathroom.

I wear a suit — I wear a tie.
I am taking male hormones.
I will have a man's body.

I changed my name.
I changed my driver's license.

That was a lot of chocolates to digest. There was no book I could look at — no one to tell me what it was like or what it would be like through all of these changes. This was a journey that we would experience on our own. I found our family was not alone, yet others were silent. This silence needs to be broken, and we must move towards respect, acceptance and understanding.

To introduce myself, I am a mother/sister and friend/ally of the GLBT community. Since I was 10 years old I knew my brother was gay, yet I did not have the words for it. The world was harsh for gay people 50 years ago. My brother lived through the AIDS Crisis. I watched him suffer through a disease that ravaged his community, watching as his friends pass away one by one. Then his time came and I held him when he took his last breath on this earth. When my child first came out, seven years after my brother had passed away, a lot of painful memories came flooding back. I was afraid for my child. I didn't want my child to suffer as I had watched my brother suffer for all those years. People are fearful of what they do not know or understand. I have had to learn to deal with my own prejudices, fears and questions. One important thing I have learned along my journey is to LOVE and not JUDGE.

Isaac first came out to us as bisexual. Next it was genderqueer, then queer. Then Isaac came out as transgender. Our lives were turned upside down, and I never thought I would stop crying. Yet, I have watched myself transform my hopes and dreams for my daughter to my son. Love has bound our family together.

Placing love in front of judgment is a difficult task. My first instincts were to question. Question to find out what I did not know. I read internet articles, talked to people, went to therapy, read all the books in Borders on trans issues and got onto the trans family yahoo list serve. I also spoke with Isaac a lot, even though at times that was difficult, especially in the beginning. As a mother, I didn't know how to digest this, I tried to first intellectualize it but that didn't work. So then I tried to digest his coming out as transgender spiritually. I talked to Rabbis; I went to a LGBT Temple. Then I realized that what was going to help me was being connected to and embracing my child and my family no matter what. It didn't matter what any Rabbi or person or book said, what mattered was love.

My biggest job after I could stop crying was to piece out what I was feeling. I had to address my fears and all of my questions.

MOURNING for my lost daughter and all of what went along with that. My sadness for no longer having a daughter — what I imagined for the wedding, grandchildren.

My FEAR of how friends and family will react. Prejudice and rejection.

IGNORANCE — people looking at this as a medical condition or worse a mental illness. Thinking, is this normal? Will Isaac ever have a successful life?

All of this has played out and I see how happy Isaac is living life as a man. I still have to say this is difficult for me to understand, and I am wrapping my mind around it. I am not completely wrapped yet. When I look back on Isaac's life I know he always walked to the beat of his own drum. Every day is a new challenge for me. I stumble across clothes, pictures and things or people that remind me of a daughter not a son. That is difficult. The power of prejudice is strong — overtly, covertly and subtly. Hopefully, as we open up to the world, the world will open up to transgender people.

Isaac is thriving and doing well. That is what is important.

Isaac is important to me and our family — not only for what he is — but for what he has taught us. The gift of understanding life differently. The gift of being closer as a family and a relationship based on honesty. We need to remember and honor those who have survived and those who haven't. As we move along, we need to be inspired by their courage and never take that for granted. Isaac has enormous courage to do what is right for himself and the world.

"What I learned … was that Gwen was not the only one who transitioned, but she was the only one recognized for it. While she was discovering her true self, others were forced to join her journey.

—Katherine Baker,
friend of a trans woman

FRIENDS

Friends

American journalist, Edna Buchanan (1939) is credited with saying, "Friends are the family we choose for ourselves." For many of us, friends serve as vital extensions of our biological families. For others, friends have taken the place of our biological family. Regardless of how we think about 'friendship,' this type of relationship, like all relationships poses unique challenges. Sometimes friends are the first people transgender individuals confide in, hoping that friendship bonds will sustain them when they come out to their family members and significant others.

This section highlights the complexity of friendship. The transitional journey friends take as they come to terms with the transgender status of a loved one is often unique, but shares moments of uncertainty, confusion, self-questioning and even joy. Some friends are able to ask challenging questions or engage in self-motivated learning (LoSasso), while others assist in finding ways to help their own family members understand their friend's transition (Baker). Often friends must recognize that friendships will change, even if only in appearance as a loved one transitions (Held). Furthermore, the transition of a good friend (and significant others and family members as well) may call one's own gender identity in to question (Hipps) and test other relationships (Jeltsen). In this section, the joys of trans friendships are celebrated in stories and in performances (Dark), and it is through these experiences that friends become allies and allies become friends.

FAQ

Q. All my trans friend does is talk about himself? Why doesn't he ever ask what is going on with me?

A. Your trans friend is mostly concerned with himself while transitioning. So many things are happening in his body that he *may* become very self-absorbed. Be patient: this too shall pass.

Q. Why did my trans friend wait so long to tell me? Or conversely, why did she tell me before she told her family?

A. Trans people (like all of us) have different personalities. Some of them need to get it "right" in their own mind, before they share it with another person; others need to share it in order to understand themselves better. She may tell you in order to test how her family will respond when they are told, or she may feel that she needs to be accepted by her family before she can tell you. Either way, what your trans friend wants is to be listened to when she is ready to share and to be accepted for her decision.

Q. My trans friend has really struggled emotionally with his transition. Should he see a psychologist?

A. Your friend may benefit from talking with a therapist at various points in his transition; you might need to see someone professionally as well, if you are struggling with his decision. If your friend is transitioning through surgery, then he has to see a psychologist in order to proceed with gender re-assignment surgery. Even so, your friend may just need a good friend to share his emotions with, but if you are concerned that it is more than that, recommending getting help is always a good thing to do.

Q. My trans friend is having gender re-assignment surgery. I don't know what to ask her?

A. Some trans people are comfortable sharing the surgical procedures they are having; others are not. There are lots of books you can read to find out more information, but this is the bottom line: F2M (female-to-male) trans people may have top surgery, removing their breasts, and some may have bottom surgery, the construction of a penis and testicular implants. M2F (male-to-female) may have top surgery: breast implants and/or bottom surgery, removing the penis and constructing a vagina. Hormone replacement therapy is also a part of this process. Your friend, and all trans people, must make her own decisions about whether to have surgery or not and how much to have. Gender re-assignment surgery and taking hormones must be an individual process, because there are many factors to consider, like age, physical health and many other issues. Listening to her as she makes these decisions, if she wants to share, will help her.

Q. Should I ask my friend if he is transgender?

A. Probably not! You may be wrong! But if you are right, he will come out to you if he wants to. In the meantime, become an ally of the transgender community. There are lots of things you can do to support all transgender people and to make our society a safer place for them (see the list of resources at the end of the book).

Q. My friend just told me he is transgender, and I am so honored that he chose me to tell. How can I be supportive?

A. When a transgender person comes out to you, first always tell them that you will continue to value your friendship no matter what. If your friendship is based on mutual trust and honest sharing, then you will know what he needs. However, it is always best to ask, "What do you need from me?"

Katie

Quick Friends
Katherine LoSasso

Interviewed by Cameron T. Whitley

Katie was born and raised in the west. She studied visual communications in college but now works for the Department of Homeland Security. In her spare time she can be found teaching herself to knit or spending time with her animals and those she loves. The names of people referred to in this article have been changed.

Can you tell us a little about your friendship with a transgender person?

I met Julie in high school at a college prep program. We became quick friends, sharing a number of the same interests. It has been well over 10 years since we met. A number of years ago my Julie approached me saying that she was going to transition from female to male and that she identified as transgender. Soon my friend would start going by a different name (James) and he would begin taking testosterone.

How did you react when your friend came out to you as transgender?

Inside I was shocked because I just couldn't understand what was going on inside my friend's head or how my friend felt, but on the outside I was supportive and inquisitive. I never considered abandoning my friend, as we had known each other for so long.

What were your first reactions?

My very first thought was "What is his mom saying/thinking/feeling?" but personally, I really wanted to gain understanding and remember asking a lot of questions. I think because he was so comfortable with who he was becoming, I was also able to be comfortable with his decision to transition.

How did you work through your initial reactions?

I worked through them with my friend initially. I asked questions and received great answers from him, leading me to more research and better understanding.

Did you experience a time of grief or loss of the relationship that you once had with your friend?

For a split second I felt some grief because I didn't know how to respond, and I didn't want to put him into a weird position and make him feel like I needed any explanations. It seemed like a big change, for him and for me. I wondered if he would be different, if his personality would change and if we would remain friends. But my friend and I have a pretty awesome friendship and with him being so open and helpful, I think our friendship grew even stronger. Plus, I can see that he is happier now. You know when you don't talk to a friend for a really long time but months or years down the road you get together for dinner or lunch and you can pick right up from the last time you spoke like it was only minutes ago?! That's our friendship.

How did you find support to deal with your friend who was transitioning? Did you confide in anyone? How did they react? Did religion play any part in your reaction or in how others reacted to your situation (coming to terms with the transition of a friend)?

My friend was essentially my support group, although I really didn't need anything more! He was so understanding and patient with my questions. His transition had nothing to do with religion for me. I was taught that God loves all, regardless. He brought me to his church one time before he started his transition, and it opened my eyes to the truth that God DOES love all.

Are there questions that you wish you could've asked your friend, but you didn't want to offend him?

YES! Man, when I first met up with him after he started his transition, there were a million and one questions flying through my head, and I had no idea where to start. Part of me didn't want to offend him in any way, and the other part was my ignorance of the entire subject. I'm sure that my friend picked up on my mental state and was very open and calm which helped me open up to him! We had a good conversation and since then it hasn't been a big issue.

Since your friend has come out, how has your relationship with this person changed?

If anything, I believe our friendship has grown. James is happier, and he still has the same personality and interests that he had when we met so many years ago. Of course, we have both grown and changed, but the same person I had met all those years ago is still who James is. As I mentioned earlier, we don't talk very much (living in different states doesn't help either), BUT we're able to communicate with ease when we do reconnect! I love James dearly!

What have you learned about the transgender community since your friend came out? Have you encountered more transgender persons and how have these encounters been?

I haven't really learned more about the transgender community, but I have had encounters with some people who are starting their transitions or just finishing. Those encounters were not difficult. It's not that I don't want to learn more, but I have been able to process my emotions and thoughts with James, and he is the same person that he has always been except he is happier now since he transitioned to be male. I can see that. I didn't lose anything when he transitioned, but I did gain a better friend

Did you engage in self-education? Did you read books, check websites? What was helpful and what was unhelpful?

When James first came out to me, he was a wealth of information and knowledge. He introduced me to some of his friends (who were just as amazing at answering questions for me); he showed me some of his research books; he also recommended a web site or two. I was intrigued and did a little more research on my own, but all the info I found reiterated exactly what James had already told me. I came across some unhelpful information on the internet from people that are closed-minded and don't understand. You can usually tell those sites right from the get-go and as frustrating as they are, you can usually ignore them and get to helpful, truthful information.

If you could say anything to someone out there who has a close friend who just came out or who is in the process of transitioning, what would you tell them?

James is who he has always been. The things I love about James have not disappeared; in fact, through his transition our friendship has gotten stronger.

"Untitled" by Jonas Jaeger © 2012

Educating My Family: Trans-Etiquette and Allyship

Katherine Baker

Katherine was featured in the documentary *TransGeneration*. She is an avid writer working on a fiction manuscript, which she hopes to publish in the next couple of years. While she currently resides in Colorado, she has spent time in Seattle and hopes to return to the west coast in the near future.

★ ★ ★ ★ ★

You have to understand that my family can't help being conservative. They all reside in a small rural town west of Denver, Colorado. Their interactions with difference or diverse perspectives are limited by their geography, not by their ability to understand. They are nice people, but just a bit...sheltered. When I announced I liked girls, in that special way that has more to it than friendship, it threw them for a loop, but they coped. I was in high school at the time and with frequent discussions and education on my part, they slowly came to terms with my identity.

After high school I went off to college in Boulder, Colorado. Boulder was much different from my rural community. I encountered people from all over the world and quickly found a group of friends who shared similar worldly perspectives. In this group, I met a woman who I will refer to as Gwen. Gwen and I became good friends. What was unique about Gwen was that she had been born into a male body. Honestly, I never really thought about Gwen's male past. To me, she was always a woman.

Before my family met Gwen, I felt the need to tell them about her past. She was just starting to transition, and I was afraid that they would use the wrong pronoun (he/his/him), since she did not completely pass as female. When I tried to explain that my new best friend at college was trans, the response was "She's a what?" Then came the he, she or it discussion. Those of us familiar with trans folks all know the one. Somehow pronouns seemed to be a hard thing for my family to grasp, especially my grandmother, whose introductions of people always become five paragraphs long as she explains how she knows them, who their family is, what they do professionally, etc. Somehow the moniker of "Katie's friend" didn't quite cover this particular friend's significance, and "Katie's friend, the transsexual" just seemed rude. Since, at the time, they were trying to convince me that "You are more than your sexuality, don't just hang out with gay people," it was hard to find a box to put Gwen in without mentioning that *one* little thing that makes Gwen uniquely different. So we had the proper pronoun discussion, wherein they kept slipping into "it," while I adamantly (and rather militantly, to be honest) insisted on "she." In the end, I won, and they just shook their heads and complained that they didn't understand. To me, it all seemed so simple. Gwen was a girl accidentally born into the wrong body. The concept of gender fluidity and a discussion of how transgender people also have a sexual orientation would come later.

Still, once I'd told them what "trans" meant, they'd slip back into calling Gwen a he. It was frustrating to say the least, but I knew they had good intentions, but it would be a long learning curve. My grandfather was the most difficult. To him sex, gender and sexuality all bled together, more so than other members of my family. When I tried to explain Gwen's past to my grandfather he quickly asked, using the correct pronoun, "Well, does she like girls or boys?" At first I was thrown by this question. What did he want, an answer? How would understanding Gwen's attraction support an understanding of her past as a boy? Being true to Gwen, I chose to answer, "Both." After all, Gwen is bisexual. She is attracted to both men and women, and this fact has nothing to do with her gender identity. "Doesn't that mean he's just gay" was the very next question. I tell you what, explaining the difference between gender identity and sexuality to a Bible-thumping 70-year-old is work. First to be overcome was the "bisexual" hurdle. They'd finally gotten the concept of "gay" and "straight," but someone who liked both, men and women must be just wishy-washy or greedy. Gender identity vs. sexuality brought in discussions of intersex, transsexuals, transgender (which even my spellcheck doesn't understand), and the difference between what's in your pants and what you do with it. Sadly, grandpa is still stuck on this second question. Perhaps, his opinion has not changed much, but he has been forced to encounter sex, gender and sexuality in ways that are not easily defined, in ways that have made him think.

But what happens when confusion arises as the trans person negotiates his or her own identity? What do I mean by this? Well, let me give you an example. My parents, who are bemused but learning, were recently introduced to a friend of mine who had taken over my half of the lease for the summer. Very shy, my friend, who I'll call "Kelly" for the duration of this piece due to privacy concerns, introduced herself as Kelly to my mother, and used her birth male name "Keith" to introduce herself to my father. At the time, Kelly was not presenting full-time as female. She was in an androgynous stage trying to figure out her next step in the transition process. To my parents, who had never encountered someone who was considering transitioning, but who was not fully confident in whom she wanted to be, provided a unique challenge. They didn't know what to make of her when comparing notes later. They wanted to be respectful, but they were confused. They lacked the language to discuss her process or the perspective to understand how someone might introduce herself using two distinctly different gendered names. They briefly discussed it amongst themselves in the car ride home, and then they called me.

When my parents left, Kelly was beating herself up psychologically; embarrassed at the two different names and gender attachments she had given my parents. Intimidated by men, Kelly had slipped and given my father her old male name. It was a coping mechanism, something she had done many times in the past to avoid being ridiculed or humiliated. I was attentive to her embarrassment, insisting that she should not be so hard on herself and that my parents would understand. When I talked with my parents and explained the transition process further they began to understand.

Gwen, unlike Kelly, had been easy, out and proud about her status, even participating in a documentary on trans college students. As Gwen's best friend, I was fortunate to participate in her transitional process and to be a part of the filming. Although I learned a lot about the transitional process for a transgender person, I also witnessed the process that the various members around Gwen were forced to encounter. Her parents had to grieve the loss of their only male child, while celebrating the development of their newly recognized daughter. Extended family members also shared in this process, as did Gwen's friends and family members. What I learned most through my involvement with the film was that Gwen was not the only one who transitioned, but she was the only one who was recognized for it. While she was discovering her true self, others were forced to join her journey. Confusion, frustration or misunderstanding about her journey was often depicted as transphobia. While in reality, it was not transphobia, but a journey her loved ones were forced to experience alone, by hiding their own fears and frustrations in order to be supportive.

$$\star \quad \star \quad \star \quad \star \quad \star$$

My family, perhaps like most, seems to overlook the many contradictions and complexities in culture regarding sex, gender and sexual orientation. For instance, they are perfectly comfortable saying, "You know, so-and-so, who's married to what's-her-face?" defining someone by their relationship to someone else. Yet they are constantly telling me that I should not define myself by my sexuality, or my relationship to someone else. I know this is because I am not straight. In this statement, they are negating my sexual orientation as equally valid to that of straight women. My relationship is something that should remain secretive. Gender identity seems to be an even harder concept to grasp. What they do not see, or have had little contact with, is an entire culture being built on the common ground of shared (and often traumatic) experiences and identities regarding sex, gender and sexuality. There are support groups, conferences and internet resources, binding us together and creating a joint fund of memory in a transient world which does not want to acknowledge those who transcend [gender] binaries. I feel fortunate to have seen the array of individuals that reside in this marginal space, from my transgender friends to those who dress and perform in drag.

$$\star \quad \star \quad \star \quad \star \quad \star$$

For my family, sex and gender are complimentary, equivalent or assumed to be correlated. Women are feminine and men are masculine. A woman may be masculine and a male may be feminine, but this usually signals something about their sexuality. With my help they have begun to understand something about gender complexity, but mostly in a limited way, biological women transitioning to be men (transsexual men) and biological men transitioning to be women (transsexual women). Usually I identify as queer rather than as a lesbian. To me, this term not only signifies whom I am attracted to, but also how I see the world. Those who I have been attracted to may fall into the male or female category, or they may exist outside or between these two polar opposites. For me sex, gender and sexuality extend beyond two opposing options, male/female, masculine/feminine and gay/straight. The concept of the in-between spaces, a third, fourth, fifth gender, help some people to understand gender complexity better, but my family not so much. This brings us right back to the he, she or it debate.

From the conversations I have had with my family about gender, I have often been asked what pronouns to use for someone who does not visually fit into one of the two socially acceptable genders? In my experience, those who walk the line between these two categories are firmly aware of their divergence. I have conveyed this message to my family and other many times:

if you are not sure which pronoun to use, ask! Not only does asking demonstrate a compassionate understanding, but it also signifies a safe space for a transgender person. It is a moment of shared understanding and respect. While some may take offense to this question, I have found that most are relieved to have someone ask instead of assuming and making an inaccurate assumption. Assumptions based on outward appearance may just not be accurate. By helping my family and others to understand, I have been an ally to Kelly and Gwen.

"*Assumptions* based on outward appearance may just not be accurate."

Kimberly

Revealing Ourselves
Kimberly Dark

Kimberly is a writer, mother, performer and professor. She is the author of five award-winning solo performance scripts and her poetry and prose appear in a number of publications. For more than 10 years, Kimberly has inspired audiences in fancy theatres, esteemed universities and fabulous festivals. She tours widely in North America and Europe — anywhere an audience loves a well-told story. Kimberly's shows have twice been named on *Curve* magazine's top-10 performances of the year, and in 2010, Campus Pride named her as one of 25 "Best of the Best" speakers and performers on college campuses.

★　★　★　★　★

The following story, "Revealing Ourselves," is the centerpiece in a solo performance called *Dykeotomy*. This story is central in a few ways: it's told mid-way through the show; it's also the longest single story in a show marked by audience interaction and briefer vignettes. And so far, it's the story that most often prompts people to contact me to discuss their own lives. As with most of my stories, I'm one of the main characters and apparently, I've said things here that upset some and deeply validate others.

I know performance artists who dislike personal contact from audience members. I've come to appreciate that part of what I'm doing on stage is bearing witness for individuals and views that our culture would rather keep hidden. It's not that I want to become a therapist for individual audience members; indeed, I set boundaries to avoid that. And yet, I use my body and my voice to cast a story into a room, and I want to be responsible for what I've done.

At a time in human history, and in a culture where trans people are maligned and stigmatized, it's difficult to be an ally who questions, who argues, who engages in direct and vulnerable discussion. My urge, like so many queer people, is to protect and advocate for my trans friends and lovers. In the bigger picture, that's not always authentic, nor helpful. Some of what unfolds in *Dykeotomy* is my romantic dismay at the changes being undertaken by some of my friends and lovers as they transition from female to male. This is often a fragile and difficult process. Indeed, it is rarely as linear as the language suggests. Of course, I stand up again and again for individual's rights to take those journeys in whatever ways they believe feel best for them. And in tandem, I believe it's healthy to interrogate our culture. It's healthy for all of us to interrogate our cultures. There's no escaping that M2F and F2M transitions have become part of our cultural landscape. Though genderqueer people often feel separate from the dominant culture, our very understandings of gender and sexuality are embedded in that culture. As a person whose primary attraction is to non-gender-normative, biological women, this is my business too. I am an intimate. I am family.

"*T*hough genderqueer people often feel separate from the dominant culture, our very understandings of gender and sexuality are embedded in that culture."

Dykeotomy is a comedy, primarily. In my peculiar world of pop-scholarship and life-as-performance, disjunctions of culture are funny. As with most comedy, there is also substance to the humor. Two things seem clear to me regarding the decision to transition one's gender medically (using hormones or surgery). First, the propensity to see the medical "solution" to the way a healthy body can "feel not right" is cultural. That tendency is itself influenced by the currently dominant cultural trend to medicalize most experiences. Pharmaceutical companies and doctors have marketed into existence many "disorders" of daily living. We hear things like: "Ask your doctor about the little purple pill." "Take a drug to get back to work and family quickly." "Get well quickly and get on with your life," These statements infer that your "real" life is something other than the one you're "feeling." Let me be clear: I'm not anti-medicine. I have been known to accept a prescription with gratitude, although I think it is important to pay attention to the patterns of what I regularly consume. Medical options dominate North American and European thinking in ways that preclude non-medical feelings of "wellness." I'm not the first to point out that culture invents "problems." If gender variance weren't a problem, perhaps it wouldn't need a solution — or at least not a medical one.

The second thing that I believe bears further discussion is that the LGBT (or as I like to say GLBT, so at least we can have it for lunch) rights movement has been based largely on identity. It goes like this: I am a lesbian, and I assert that my desire to have sex with women is paramount to living happily. You shouldn't suggest that I might be just as happy with a man. Of course I wouldn't; I'm a lesbian. So, based on this limited identity, my butch-dyke lover who becomes a man should need to move on and date straight women. Right? And yet, a lot of heterosexual trans men date within and are embraced by the "lesbian" community. (Cultural and personal reasons abound — and I'm sure some of them will be addressed in this book.) I'm not saying there's a thing wrong with that, but it has painted some of us into the corner of not being able to assert either preference/orientation or fluidity with any credibility. How do I reject a trans man's come on when we are bonded through experience and desire in so many ways? How do I accept a trans man's come on and remain true to that which feels like a biological urge to mate with estrogen-based life forms? And how does it all play out in the bedroom and in the political struggle for human rights? After seeing *Dykeotomy*, one audience member wrote to me to say that, if we were to think differently, we could arrange sexual orientation based on some factor other than sex. It might be body type, or height or family history. Sex and gender might not be as relevant to attraction if we didn't believe them to be important.

We have to keep talking about these things, and the way I add to the mix, is through the performance of everyday interactions. The tremendous opportunity in these cultural disjunctions is that lines are blurred, and people's real lived experiences become the means toward greater love and compassion — maybe even for ourselves. I tell stories like this one, on stage and in print, exactly because I love a complicated world, one in which I can love you and still debate the details.

Revealing Ourselves

I spoke with my previous lover this morning and something in our reconnection brought up tears. She is dating someone new now, four months after we said farewell as lovers. I want her to be dating if this makes her happy, and yet, she does not seem happy. She misses me and she says she is still working to know her own life.

She told me she misses me and that somehow this new woman is not the same — well, why would she be? I thought, but then as she spoke on — figuring it out through conversation as people do — I began to follow her thinking. This new woman is a feminine woman, but somehow not the same kind of femme as I am. Feminine isn't enough, apparently. Their interactions are not the same. My lover said she missed the way I treat her like a man, interact with her as a man, especially romantically. I could tell she still had difficulty saying that she likes to be treated like a man, romantically. I know what she means here — I've known women who are still recovering from the queer-hating parts of early feminism. When we were first together, I really didn't realize that she did not accept the masculine part of herself. She seemed so strong and sure, so I just projected my assumptions about butch dykes onto her. It took me a little while to find out that she didn't like what I saw in her. She couldn't believe how much I love the man I see in her, along with the woman. I love them both, though most often it's the man with whom I make love. My acceptance of her masculinity was initially painful for her. But now she says that acceptance has changed her life, lifted a weight from her.

"It's like a brick off my chest," she said.

So, after we hung up, I was crying and thinking about how difficult the woman/man fixation can be. How we can become convinced to withhold love even from ourselves. And how the very idea of gender surgery, the cutting, the pain, makes me feel so much grief sometimes. I know quite a few who have done it. Personally, I have never felt that I was born in the wrong body, though I've often felt my body was born in the wrong culture. Who knows if this is why I love deviant bodies, deviant minds, where does deviance live really? Surely, just in the culture itself.

My grief is for all of us, as we are trying to find our way, looking for the touch, the glance that helps us know ourselves, love ourselves. We are looking for the best of ourselves in others, the lovable things that make us know that we can come home, that we can make home unfailingly. Each person is searching for connection, I think, through conversation, through sex, through contact. Perhaps being queer makes the quest for connection all the more urgent. We call attention to ourselves by being different. We call attention to difference. We call attention to the fear that lives in all of us.

From my previous lover, my mind moves toward another close friend. He is one I love tremendously, one who has scars on his chest, his belly, from the process of becoming not a woman anymore. He is not a woman anymore, though these surgeries seemed so irrelevant to my understanding of his maleness, and I hurt somehow knowing that his road to comfort was not paved, including the jagged terrain of altered skin and organs. I have known quite a few people who have re-assigned their genders through surgery, hormones. Usually it's reassignment from one to another, this to that. I have known only a few who opt for a more permanent ambiguity. Ah, what would life be like if we could each embrace our internal ambiguities?

I sometimes think I'm an expert at embracing ambiguity, but the bigger challenges of my life reveal my frailties, to be sure. By coincidence, this close friend was going through his gender transition at the same time that I had been diagnosed with large, uterine tumors. Hysterectomy was recommended. I was not satisfied with this recommendation. It was a year of physical invasions for my friend and me. He began taking male hormones, grew more body and facial hair. In my body, a tumor the size of an orange became the size of a large cantaloupe within a year. He received a double mastectomy and my body bled so much I sometimes lost consciousness. He happily scheduled a hysterectomy; I vehemently refused one.

At times, I expressed frustration at his choices — dangerous surgeries, expensive therapies — and for what? Because he wanted to be perceived differently? He wanted surgery to help him feel differently? He wasn't comfortable being two things at once, wanted everything legal. Outside of socially constructed meaning, gender pronouns, it's just anatomy. Grow up! I thought sometimes. At one moment or another every woman wishes she'd been born with a different body that would receive different social rewards. It's a matter of maturity to stop focusing on the exterior, I thought. Of course, my difficulties were maturing into large ripe fruit on my interior. And how would I "grow up" about that?

My friend expressed irritation about my choices — refusal of medical advice, "selfish life-endangerment," he called it. I felt I would be somehow a failure if I didn't find the keys to all my life's issues in time to keep my uterus. There was a lesson in there and I wanted to learn it. I was an anatomy purist — I wanted to keep everything I came in with. Limitations and all, apparently.

One night, he visited me at home to have a talk, to dissuade my stubbornness. My hands in his, worried face looking into mine, he said, "My God, Kimberly, just let them take it out! Don't you know there's no part of you a doctor can remove that will make you any less of a woman?" And I felt his pain. His gender pain.

"Yeah," I said. "That's what I've been telling you, too. There's nothing a doctor can do to make you any more of a man, either." And we looked into each other's eyes, felt each other's hands and experienced connection. At least I did. A few years later, he does not remember this conversation that was so important to me. We are different people, after all.

He said he wished he could give me his uterus — the one he didn't want — but that wasn't possible. We each had one removed, same surgeon, same year. Mine is buried in my backyard under a great jacaranda tree and a small hibiscus. And I have made peace with my body; he has made peace with his. We both feel whole, until whatever comes next, I suppose.

And thus life continues. Back out into the world where we see and are seen, where we touch others' lives and are touched. We take our bodies out into the world and inside, where we reveal them to each other, slowly, carefully. We reveal ourselves to ourselves. Little by little.

Makenna

The Three Musketeers
Makenna Held

Makenna is a faculty member at Mercer University, where she teaches courses in social enterprise and development. She also is the director of Bridge Beyond, an organization dedicated to grassroots action in developing countries. She lives in Macon, Georgia with her wife.

I have never been the conventional type; in fact my whole life I have been breaking the moulds that people have placed me in. I did everything I was told not to do and did it with passion.

Boys kissed me, and unlike most little girls, I hit them (I thought it was a fair exchange). I wanted to do ballet, but only in boys' clothes. I loved pink, but only when it was covered in mud. I loved playing with dolls, yet I was always cross-dressing Ken and Barbie. I was not particularly boyish, but I certainly wasn't girly either. I was just me, and I was damned proud of it.

My whole life my identity has been in limbo. As I grew up, I realized that these previous behaviors were actually explainable. I was different. But it was an exciting kind of different, the kind where I got butterflies in my stomach whenever a pretty girl caught my eye. After 17 years of silence on the matter, I gave in and confessed my feelings to my family.

I approached my mother just two weeks before my senior year in high school and exclaimed, "Mom, I'm a lesbian." Her utter shock was expressed clearly as she burst into tears; her good homegrown Christian girl had joined the dark side. To say the least, she was displeased. "But…bububububu…" She stammered between hissy fits of tears. I sighed and said, "I am never going to be with boys, it's just not me." I was damned steadfast on the matter. She hated the idea, and was a mope for a full year. I didn't care; I brought my first Butch Girl home a few weeks later.

My Butch. She was a powerful force, and one that I knew shouldn't be reckoned with. She had a penchant for leaving heartbreak in her wake with a twinge of her lips, that hint of a smile. I knew I was doomed. I was a young newly-out lesbian in love, and there was no turning back. My best friend at the time was remotely jealous, she also saw My Butch as a gorgeous specimen as well, but I had won her over somehow. We dated; I was a femme in heaven. But lo and behold, it ended. We fought and what ensued was, of course, high-heaven *drah*-ma. In the thick of it my best friend became My Butch's best friend too. My Butch was no longer mine, and I was no longer a femme. (In rebellion of this breakup I cut my hair, donned boys' clothes; not a femme, not a butch, but somewhere in the dissonance of the two extremes.)

I had to share My Butch and My Best Friend, but the three of us were pretty unstoppable most days; I couldn't complain. The three of us were sharp-witted, powerful, shorthaired lesbians fighting for revolution in a remarkably closed-minded liberal town — hot damn, did we do a good job — but it wasn't enough. Escapes to the "liberal" east coast were planned the minute our high school diplomas, hot off the presses, hit our hands. We mailed out applications and prayed to be one of the select few to be allowed into the elite intellectual world of the east-coast-liberal-arts-education. Acceptance letters to colleges were received, Women's Colleges. We all had made it to the Massachusetts Pioneer Valley Five College Consortium — My Butch and I at Smith, My Best Friend at Holyoke.

Upon arrival to Smith College, I met my first slew of men. Men at a woman's college were curious, but nothing to raise my eyebrows at. Remember, I wasn't the conventional type, and few things phased me. They became my fast friends, and I was nonplussed by their uses of "he" "him" and "men" in self-reference. By god to me they were men, men with deep throaty voices and belly laughs to match, and I loved them for it. Nothing had changed from my childhood days. If these boys tried to kiss me, I recoiled, god-damned-bonafide lesbian that I was.

One year of Smith College passed, My Butch had moved home to Colorado, and I no longer needed her; I was a butch girl in my own right. I had donned my masculine appearance and clothing as my act of persistent, quiet revolution. I was content to be at Smith, with my best friend a few moments away. My Best Friend, My Butch and I remained pretty powerful. Even across great distance.

We were powerful girls!

One day, my best friend and I were at lunch. Shooting the breeze and enjoying the sights that Smith College had to offer. Two butch lesbians on the prowl.

My best friend spoke first. "Makenna?"

"Yeah?"

"I have been thinking a lot about gender and stuff lately, and well…you know. Umm…Mak, I don't know how to say this, I think I am a boy. I'm trans."

You could have heard a pin drop. The shock on my face probably gutted him. Her. *Oh god! It can't be true.* Not her, not My Best Friend.

I knew it was inevitable, I knew it would happen, that someday I would have a friend transition who I was close to, and here it was, clear as day. There was nothing to do but suck it up and acknowledge the truth. I puffed up my chest and mustered a "Congratulations. I am here for you," And from that moment on, I was indeed.

The Three girl Musketeers were now two girls and a boy. We were powerful. We were strong. We were fighting a good fight. I remained unfazed.

The initial shock wore off quickly. And a few months later I received a phone call from My Butch in Colorado. "Hi, Makenna. How is Smith?"

I smiled; it was always good to hear her voice. We made small talk and what not. She said hi to My Best Friend who always wandered into my dorm at the best times, HE said hi to her. He. He. Him. He. His. I reminded myself over and over. It was still not always easy.

He returned the receiver into my hands, and I placed it to my ear. "Hey babe. What's shaking? How is your relationship going on the home front?" I said.

She responded tentatively, "Well, it would be fine except that she isn't so happy about some recent decisions of mine. Umm…Makenna. I'm changing my name."

"*My* mind soon became a fine-tuned machine regarding the aspects of using new pronouns, as it seemed there was a switch at least once a week with someone."

No shock there for me. I had known Serenity, Current, Hill and Dirt. People get bored and change their names. After my moments of revelry and contentment that the issue was smaller than I had thought, she continued…

"I don't mean that in the way you might be thinking. It's not like Current, it's like you know…I am changing pronouns too, I'm transitioning." HE said.

My thoughts stuttered. He. Him. His. HIM HIM HIM.

Again blindsided, I did my best to disguise my surprise. "Congratulations. I am here for you." "I miss your mac and cheese," HE said.

I hung up.

My Butch, my first love, was never going to grow into the woman I thought she would. Instead HE would grow up to be a man.

We WERE three strong powerful girls. And then there was one. I was a strong and powerful girl. I had two best friends who were now boys. *What the f**k did that mean for me?* I panicked.

We had always been so similar, the three of us. Three Musketeers. Three peas in a pod. Pick your metaphor for togetherness, and you'd be damned not to apply it to us. Now, I was no longer the same as them. Fears consumed me. I was afraid I wasn't trans enough to be their friend anymore. What did it mean that my first girlfriend was actually a boy?

When my mother found out about my two cohorts, she froze. "Makenna, if you ever tell me you are trans that will just be too much." I told her not to worry; she still did. I worried, too. After My Butch came out to me as trans, so did nearly every other close friend of mine. My subconscious screamed, "What the hell did it all mean?"

My mind soon became a fine tuned-machine regarding the aspects of using new pronouns, as it seemed there was a switch at least once a week with someone. New names were just as easy too; in fact old names were hardly remembered. Each time someone changed pronouns or names, I jotted it down in a book, as if I was remembering my old friends' identities and replacing them with new ones. I had to purge their old preferred pronouns and names concretely from my often-thick skull.

I rarely slipped up, and I was open to whatever pronouns my friends hoped for. I fought hard for trans rights at Smith. I was a friend and ally to the trans community. Yet, each new friend who came out brought a new wave of panic deep within me. As if something was stirring, yelling at me to realize my own identity.

Am I different like them too? Am I trans? Did I misconstrue my lesbian identity for that of a deeper gender dysphoria?

I had always been boyish and dreamed about marrying women in white dresses, while I was dressed in a black dapper tuxedo. I had massive penis envy as a child. Hell, I have it now.

"OH GOD I MUST BE A BOY TOO!" My new identity screamed inside of me, dying to come out. I think I then understood why med students diagnose themselves with every problem in the DSM-IV. Fear that they have been living a lie of some sort, or that all of their past problems could be figured out with just an identification, a word that says "THIS IS WHAT IS

WRONG WITH ME!"

My parents just eventually assumed I would come out of the closet as trans, and honestly, so did I. I figured it was just a matter of time, as if some mythological realization just hadn't happened yet. I explained all of this to my newly-out friends, who responded with giggles, "You are too girly!" and mimicked my previously uttered words of affirmation, "We're here for you if you make that decision."

But that massive realization never came, and I never had the desire to change my name. And I certainly never wanted to start using new pronouns.

We Three Musketeers now live far apart and separate lives. We are still powerful. We grew up to be two men, one woman. Short-haired, beautiful, handsome and proud. We are still trying to change the world, create revolution, in our own ways.

Hell, maybe the three of us are not so different after all.

Jenn and Mel

I've Never Loved
a Person
This Way Before
Jenn Hipps

Jenn hopes to integrate her interest in medicine with her passion for social justice. Her favorite books include [De Saint-Exupery's] *The Little Prince*, [Faulkner's] *As I Lay Dying* and [Foer's] *Extremely Loud and Incredibly Close*. She enjoys childish puns and roasting marshmallows, but not eating them.

His girlfriend, who is, maybe, a wordsmith, calls him a father without children. I think, she says this because of the way Mel is with kids — easy, magical. The gentle cradle of his arms could comfort a sobbing child. His unwavering gaze and calm smile is the much-needed-but-never-requested dose of encouragement from across a crowded room. I don't know if he means to, and maybe that makes it all the more amazing, but he reminds me that I matter. He looks me directly in the eye as I speak, nodding his head, as though swallowing back my words to make them a part of himself. It's the way he knows when I need a reassuring hug. He can make me laugh, or let me cry when he knows it's what I need. It is as though nothing I say or do could possibly make him uncomfortable. Nothing could make him run. He is incredibly steady, strong and permanent. He makes me feel safe.

I try to express this to him, that he is my rock, but irrationally find myself nervous to say those words. Instead, I declare another, related, truth, "I'm excited for you to be a daddy." He thanks me and tells me in response that I'll make a good mother.

Quietly, for perhaps the first time in my life, I allow myself to believe it. I acknowledge (the irony: the fact that I look up to him so often) that there is a chance that he has pegged down what at least part of this love is. Maternal.

I want to make the world better for him.

$\ast \quad \ast \quad \ast \quad \ast \quad \ast$

The first time we met, we didn't meet at all. Looking back, I am surprised and possibly disgusted to realize that I hadn't registered him as a person. I had stepped into an elevator my first week at New York University and was staring off at about knee height, too nervous to look anyone in the eye. I saw a messenger bag dotted with buttons and followed the bag's strap up to the face of its carrier. I looked away immediately. The face was pierced with thick hoops through ears and nose, the hair was gelled back, standing stiffly. The straight line formed by the lips pronounced a distinct lack of a smile; it said, "Beware: hard, unwelcoming and tough." I closed my eyes and inhaled, straightened my shoulders and looked up, "Do you mind if I read your buttons?"

He met my eyes and smiled, "For sure."

I didn't understand all of them. There was one with a person's name and another with the word "SURVIVOR" in teal near a teal ribbon. But the other buttons could have easily been my own. They blared messages of all-encompassing love and "Peace."

We got off of the elevator and walked (in the same direction, though not together) into Queer Union's first meeting of the year. Friends of his waved him over. I found a seat and pulled my bag into my lap, hugging it against my chest. I am no longer sure whether he actually looked over at me with a warm smile and a reassuring nod, or whether, in an attempt to draw a fluid connection in my memory to the person I later got to know, I have assigned these actions to him. Either way, they are truly his.

Two months later, in a reflection period during the Queer Leadership Retreat, someone in our group referred to Mel as "she." I did not remember that the previous day and in every set of introductions since, Mel had asked that we each specify our preferred pronouns and declared, that his were male. I did not recall that he met any questioning glance that came his way with a calm and seemingly confident affirmation. Therefore, when I looked over to smile appreciation for his action as retold by the speaker, I was jolted by the look of pain in his eyes. All at once, I felt the importance and earnest nature of each of Mel's requests. I wanted, in that moment, to correct the person who had misspoken and chastise her for not being careful, for not caring. More than anything, I wanted to be able to comfort the boy sitting a couple of yards away, unsuccessfully trying to shrug off the moment. I promised myself, that I would never mess up his pronouns. While I was not prepared to openly fight for this stranger, I would at least do my best to avoid hurting him unnecessarily.

In another activity, we were asked to identify ourselves as having certain traits and past experiences. Often, Mel and I seemed to be in small or exclusive groups openly identifying ourselves. At other times, I noticed that while

I was not ready to claim a particular experience as my own, Mel was braver. We were the only two who had run away from homes or who had friends who had attempted suicide and were willing to vocalize it. I found myself looking for Mel at each step of the activity — and finding him.

Later that night, outside a cabin in which the rest of the group was painting, Mel and I stood quietly. We looked out into the dark forest, resting against the wooden railing, simultaneously and in parallel, and perhaps together. Without turning to him, I said softly (more surely than I had intended so that my clumsy words sounded more like a statement than the request they really were), "We should be friends."

In the silence, I felt rather than saw his nod.

Shortly after we got back to school, we went for a coffee. Coffee turned into browsing the Strand, pointing out our favorite books (we shared many) and reading passages on the floor. Reading turned into hours of roaming the city, talking and finally sitting on a bench in Union Square Park. I told Mel, amongst a million other things, that I liked to swim because it let me think — the way the rest of the world seemed to fall away, immersed in the rhythm of my strokes and the sound of my own breathing. He told me that he missed swimming, but that he thought he'd decided he would have top surgery. I asked him if he was scared. He told me that he was because it was a major surgery, but that at the same time, he was excited because his body would finally be right, and that binding is temporary and tiresome. If he had the surgery, he'd be able to breathe.

I first understood his statement metaphorically in anticipation of the comfort he would feel in a more appropriate body. I realized that Mel had been speaking literally, that binding breasts down actually restricts one's physical ability to breathe. His words weighed heavily in my mind. I realized that while I understood 'transgender' as a word, I could not internalize the concept. I dressed to cover my body, not to disguise it or attempt to change it. I had felt uncomfortable with my body, but it had always been *my* body. I tried to imagine binding my chest, but was unable to get past a pre-med student's concerns about the strain the practice puts on a person's organs, and the damage it would do over time. Later, it occurred to me that if I did not feel ownership over my body, perhaps I would not be as concerned about the harm done to it.

Suddenly I was questioning everything. I became positively enthralled by the idea of gender, its origin and the impact it has. I attended a lecture on access to healthcare for people who are transgender in hopes of making myself a better, more caring doctor, when the time came. I began to read books on queer theory and on gender and to do endless searches on the internet. I was frustrated by the labels we so quickly thrust upon one another and wondered whether, perhaps, without them, we'd be a bit happier. I stopped looking for a word to describe my own sexuality and began to doubt the ease I had once felt with the gender I'd been raised to embody. I began to think of myself in gender-neutral terms and to dislike the words "girl," "woman" and "daughter," when applied to me. I kept my frustrated questioning to myself, quietly attempting to figure out what any of these labels meant to me, if they meant anything at all.

"*I* realized that while I understood 'transgender' as a word, I could not internalize the concept. I dressed to cover my body, not to disguise it or attempt to change it."

I was hesitant to speak with Mel about it. I had, inadvertently, set rules of conduct for myself in order to not harm this trans man. I never brought up the subject of his body, potential surgeries or hormones, but would discuss the subjects if he brought them up. I began relaying conversations with him to friends, with the ulterior motive of carefully practicing saying 'he,' 'him' and 'his.' In my fear of hurting his feelings, I frequently forgot that Mel was impossibly open and honest about his gender identity, and, more importantly, that he was the single warmest person I knew in New York. When, several months later, I nervously came clean about my practicing thinking of him in male terms, he reassured me that it was okay, and that he appreciated my affirmation of his gender identity. He encouraged me to continue questioning my own identity and our society's social structures and asked me to keep him posted on anything I did, so he could remain respectful of me.

Because Mel is so incredibly patient and compassionate, because he never has a harsh word for anyone, it is difficult to see him upset. It is worse to see him simply take these things in stride, quietly accepting less-than-ideal situations. I hated to see him forced to use a women's locker room to store his coat and bag while volunteering at a food pantry, to hear that a salesperson harassed him about his gender presentation or learning that he was not out at his job teaching elementary school students. When Mel mentioned the latter in passing, I was shocked. Knowing him through school, through the LGBT office, mainly, I know him in a sort of bubble of safety. For me, leaving that bubble and not feeling safe being out as a "sexually deviant person" can feel uncomfortable at times. Being asked whether I have a boyfriend yet or being told I'll make a wonderful mother, as though these are the only possible ways of living, can be uncomfortable. My discomfort is nothing to Mel's. It can't be. Whether I am out or not, I can use the same bathroom, I am referred to using the same pronouns, I can comfortably walk into a store and buy the same things. If, in any setting, Mel is forced to closet himself in order to preserve a sense of safety, all of this changes for him; he is forced to negate his own identity and stay quietly passive.

When I am nervous or scared, when I feel defeated, Mel is always able to comfort me. I do my best to return the favor. I shower him back with the warmth he's shown me. I mirror back the encouraging nods he has taught me.

But I've also learned that as a person who generally feels comfortable in the gender assigned to her at birth, I carry a privilege that Mel doesn't. Mel faces violence and discrimination that I don't. The world is safe for me in a way that it simply is not yet safe for him.

This is where that maternal part of me rears its ugly head; this is the part where I get protective. This is the part where I hold myself responsible for what happens to a person I love. I've learned that because I love someone that the world oppresses because that person is different (for his and my own heart's sake), I must do everything I can to actively combat that oppression. I must work to make this world a better, safer, freer, place for him to be exactly who he is, as he is, wherever he is.

Melissa and Alejandro

Juno and Melissa

My Best Guy Friend Became My Best Girlfriend

Melissa Jeltsen

Melissa is a writer and recent transplant to New York City. Follow her on Twitter at @quasimado, where she tweets about politics and culture.

My friend Juno and I both need to pee. Bad. As the movie credits roll, we shuffle out of the darkened theatre and book it to the restrooms. The men's entrance is on the left, women's on the right. This is the moment when we split and pivot towards our respective labels, like we've done at the countless bars and pit-stops that have peppered our eight-year friendship, but not tonight. For the first time, we go through the same door together.

Until he was 32-years-old, my best friend was a man. She's now a woman. And while she adjusts to this new reality, our relationship is shifting as we search for a new balance.

I met Alejandro by chance when I was 18, living in the student slums of Allston, Massachusetts. He was a laid-back Colombian dude with a thick beard and welcoming smile, and I instantly liked him. Our closeness grew through my early adult years. He cooked for me, helped me through a half a dozen apartment moves and dated my close girlfriend. When I fucked up — jobs, relationships — or felt scared about the future, he'd say, "Don't worry about it! It's just life!"

In 2006, Alejandro moved to New York, built a recording studio and got a job doing sound at a club. But during the summer of 2009, Alejandro came for a visit and was almost unrecognizable. He'd lost 20 pounds and his face was gaunt. Over the next few days, he described to me his recent medical problems: how his hair was falling out, he was having erectile dysfunction, he'd been getting angry for no reason and was severely fatigued.

Genetic testing revealed the cause: Alejandro, then 32, had Klinefelter syndrome. While males have an XY chromosome pattern and females have XX, Alejandro was born with an extra X, meaning he was XXY. He was, as some like to call it, intersex: a condition in which your gender cannot be simply defined as male or female, but is somewhere in the middle.

But what came as even more of a surprise to me was what he said next; the diagnosis confirmed something Alejandro had long felt. He wasn't comfortable as a man. It felt like a charade, fake, like he was acting, he said. He was never truly at ease.

I skipped out on work the next day to try and process what he was telling me. He didn't feel like a man? He had dated a good friend of mine for over two years! He wasn't sure what gender he was? My mind started obsessively running back through all the events of our friendship, trying to see if I could have, should have, recognized that he was unhappy.

"*But* although physically she looked totally different, the defining trait of our friendship, our ability to talk for hours about anything hadn't fundamentally changed."

Six months later, I visited Alejandro at his apartment in the West Village. At a bar, he explained to me that after extensive meetings with doctors and therapists, he had decided to start estrogen therapy. He now identified as a woman; her new name was Juno. And there it was: My guy friend was now my girl friend.

Over the next year, we kept in touch over the phone, and she came to Boston on work. Each visit brought more of a transition. Her face looked softer and more feminine. Her facial hair, thanks to electrolysis, was almost completely gone. Little budding breasts formed.

Juno's visits gave me little, quick, fascinating glimpses into her new life. But I didn't get to spend any extended time with her until November, when I got a job in New York, and she said I could live with her in Queens.

I was moving in with my best friend, but I was also moving in with a stranger. Her closets were stuffed with knee-high boots, skirts and cute shirts. Opening a cabinet door, I found an impressive nail polish collection. But although physically she looked totally different, the defining trait of our friendship, our ability to talk for hours about anything hadn't fundamentally changed. If anything, we had so much more to discuss. Although I knew a fair amount about her childhood growing up in Bogota, I absorbed it again, now through a different lens.

Juno's experience as a woman is so new. Over dinner and wine, we talk about what it means to identify as female. She tells me of the first time she experienced female jealousy, felt the piercing glare from another girl, wracked with envy. She tells me about feeling a loss of personal space as a woman, of having to protect the area around her body in a way she never had to as a man.

It's not always easy. Sometimes, I mess up and say the wrong pronoun, simply out of habit. When we pop over to Duane Reade [a drugstore chain] for snacks, or walk into a party, I'm often flooded with fears that someone will look at her too long, or make her feel uncomfortable. At a bar recently, a man got up and said, *please, ladies, take a seat.* Relief flooded over me. We are ladies, yes.

Small things are cause for concern. Putting a tampon wrapper in the trash, I think, if she sees this will it be painful for her? Is this a symbol of womanhood that she will never get to experience?

I find myself judging new friends by the look in their eyes when I tell them about Juno. I also question myself: Why do I feel the need to tell people the back-story? Am I trying to avoid awkward scenarios?

Our friendship is stronger than it has ever been. A barrier between us, subtle and invisible, slowly disintegrates as we get to know each other on a deeper level.

She tells me about feeling the power of being a woman, how the world can be gentler to you, people smile at you more, treat you kinder. She says physically, she feels more relaxed and engaged with her body. And when she dances, she says, it feels natural and unforced.

For the first time in her life, she feels truly connected to herself. And I too feel connected to her, as a friend, as a sister.

Originally published in "Jezebel," 6/5/2011.

Thea

Wonderful Queers
Thea Leticia Mateu

Thea is a Latina Queer High Femme [gender variant who enjoys extreme expressions of femininity] writer, artist and activist. She has been involved with Queer and Trans communities since the 1990s and has been working for visibility, inclusion and celebration since. She is committed to social justice and to the disruption of binaries and boundaries that limit genuine expressions of self. She currently lives and loves in Southern California.

We drive to the grocery store laughing, singing along to Lords of Acid's song "The Most Wonderful Girl."

"I'm sexy, I'm gorgeous, I'm wonderful, I'm beautiful."

We are enjoying the day and each other. We are beautiful. We have a past as lovers, but now we embrace the future as best friends, the kind of friends who love each other for life. He is a transgender butch. He's a female-bodied boy. Me, a queer high femme. To me, he was always unequivocally he. He was *he* when he danced around in the living room, sporting a feather boa. He was *he* when we walked down the street together. He was *he* when he was watching me do my makeup before a night out, and he dug around my lipstick drawer, put some on and struck a pose. He was *he* when he had to borrow supplies, because his time of the month arrived unannounced. He was *he* when I viewed old pictures of him, in a prom dress looking feminine and beautiful. He was *he* when we ordered a beer at the bar. He was *he* when we were sexual, and I was inside him. He was *he* and that was never an issue for me, never a moment's pause, never a hesitation.

Loving a female-bodied boy who does not believe in the gender binary system [which assumes two, and only two genders], who is transgressive in delicious ways, who is strong in his transgender identity is the easiest thing in the world for me, except when it isn't.

He parks the car, and we set out for the last step in our afternoon of errands: the grocery store. We both love to cook, we both love to eat, both love to share food with each other: getting creative in the kitchen, showing off a bit. Going grocery shopping is comfortable together; we make a good team. I love spending time with my friend. I enjoy his company very much. I love our easy banter, our silliness, our closeness and familiarity. And yet, I hate going straight places with him.

It starts when we step out of the car: the looks, the hostility, the reactions. It starts when we get out of the car; the armoring up, the cold icy heat of anger. We walk together, chatting about this or that, and it starts with the stares and the shift as a family does a double take and moves away from us. He remarks on it, "Already it starts." So interesting to see how people look at us. We are both Latino, brown, beautiful ("sexy, gorgeous, wonderful"). Me, a femme with long dark hair and hips for days. Him, a transgender butch, boyish and solid. And yet confusing.

Walking down the street, people in a car yell out the window, "Are you a boy or a girl?" as if they had a right to ask, as if it were their business, as if it mattered. Even walking down the street with a grrl [alternate spelling for girl, used in the punk rock subculture], minding his own business, smoking a cigarette and talking about life, he is a threat. He doesn't fit the binary. He disrupts the compulsive need of people in passing cars to categorize, boy or girl? He subverts the binary with every breath he takes. He subverts the binary when people see a boy, then do a double take because they scan him to confirm their reading of him, and they see his chest. He subverts the binary when people see a boy and then hear his voice and intonation. "Neither," "Both," "None of the above," "All of the above and then some," none of these are acceptable options. Therefore, he is a threat.

When we enter the grocery store, I ask him to pick up some laundry detergent for me while I get some fruit. He walks over to the display to sniff out the right bottle, and I am vigilant while I fondle produce. I stand guard, ready to jump, ready to pounce, feeling the tension in my body, my posture tall and stiff. I watch people react to him when he says, "excuse me," softly and moves around them. He is soft spoken and kind. He is a loving dad, he is an adoring tio [Spanish for uncle], he is invested in community, compassionate and caring. And people look at him like he's going to attack them, like his non-binary expression is going to somehow contaminate the air around him. I stand guard. Ready to pounce when people shoo their children and keep them away from him. I stand and stare at people who are looking at him with disgust and contempt, hands on my hips, arrogant flame in my feminine gaze, dangerous. And people get nervous when they see the fire, move away, look away, shift. I stand guard. I will protect him and use my femininity as shield and anchor. I stand guard over his right to walk in the world as the boy he is. He doesn't need protecting. He is strong, fierce, courageous and capable. And I see him get tired. I see the pressure build, and I will be his rock.

Loving a transgender boy is the easiest thing in the world, except when it isn't. My anger hurts me. My rage makes me feel powerless and tired. I've experienced hatred and fear directed at me. I've experienced racism, misogyny, homophobia, violence. I've been attacked, threatened, chased and beaten. And the hurt of watching him be threatened is heavy and different. I am essentially powerless to shield him. I can be his ally, his friend, his sister. I can be his advocate, get his back, be his partner and teammate. But I can't stop the gaze that travels to his chest and registers dissonance. I can't stop the questions, can't stop the pronoun wars, can't stop the entitlement to question his gender, his body, his sexuality, his Self. I am powerless to do anything but rage, stand witness, work to educate, listen to his frustration and kiss the tears of anger and hurt.

I've been on the phone with him when a drunken asshole harassed him, insisted he was a girl and put his hands on his body. I wanted to jump through the phone and kill him. I've been out with him and physically put myself in between him and a man who was being threatening. I've used my body to distract attention from him. And it hurts. It hurts because I want to protect him. I want him to be safe and comfortable walking through the world. I want him to be able to walk down the street without being in triple jeopardy: brown, queer and recognizably female. And sometimes my anger boils up, wells up inside me until I can taste it. My peaceful, loving self wanting to hurt people, because I see their gazes cut through him. I see the cumulative effect of every comment, every stare, every flinch, every attack.

"I want him to be able to walk down the street without being in triple jeopardy: brown, queer and recognizably female."

I have boiled inwardly when I see him flinch when we are asked, "What can I get you ladies?" at the gay bar. I bite back rage when people contest his identity when he takes the time and trouble to explain. I let it go when a friend persists using *she*. I step up when the stares become hostile, prepared to do whatever it takes to keep him safe, using my femininity as a shield. I scan the crowd for reactions, carefully gauge the responses looking to see what direction trouble might come from. On guard, on point, ready to defend him and his right to be exactly what he is, and my right to love him that way.

My anger hurts me because I have to keep it away from him. He is my support. He is the person who sees me and loves me, who has had my mocos [Spanish for mucus] all over his beater [a type of sleeveless shirt] stained with mascara as I sob. He is the person I turn to when life is beating me up, and he sees me and loves me and understands. And I keep my anger from him as much as I can. It hurts me because I don't want to burden him with my exhaustion, with my frustration, with my pain. I stand silent guard. He knows. But I can't add to his burden by letting him see how much it hurts me when he is a target. I won't add to his pain.

My anger hurts me because of my own gender identity. I am a queer femme. To most of the world, I am invisible, indistinguishable from any other beautiful woman, read as straight, read as normative, invisible. I am challenged in some queer spaces, my membership contested, my high heels making me suspect. I am forever struggling to be seen. Invisibility hurts me. Being silenced hurts me, and yet it protects me. For me, a lover of cognitive dissonance, a fan of complexity and paradoxes, a fluid soul who can easily reconcile the irreconcilable, this one contradiction is agonizing. I am only seen as queer when I am in the company of someone like him. As much as it hurts to see him be a target, I long for the power that being SEEN provides.

I went through a period in my life when I could not be a femme anymore. I could not be invisible anymore. It had worn me down to the point where I simply had to be recognized, I needed to be seen. I cut off my hair. It had once reached below my waist, and I kept the long braid when I went from that to buzzing the nape of my neck. I threw out all my girly underwear. I replaced everything. No more thongs, as I switched to boxers exclusively. No more sexy bras. I wore constricting sports bras. I couldn't bear to throw out my makeup but I put it away, not to see the light of day in a long time. I bought my clothes in the men's section and affected masculine toughness instead of my sassy feminine fierceness. I wore combat boots, because I was armored up. And I relished every angry "dyke!" directed at me. I would bask in the hostility, finally I could take it myself instead of watching the people I loved be attacked, instead of looking invisible to the world, instead of looking like the people doing the attacking, I could now be read as angry. I wore my anger on my sleeve. I put it on display for the world to see. It freed me in so many ways. And yet, it was a betrayal. It was a betrayal of my own gender identity as a femme. It was an act, a suit of armor that I wore out in the world and that hid the person I really am. I had become complicit in my own invisibility, and I could not sustain that.

Out of that gender experiment emerged new confidence, strength and understanding of my own gender expression. Out of the experiment came new ways of seeing myself in the gendered world. I learned to resist. I learned to stand firm in my stilettos. I learned to fight back when the world insisted that the butch on my arm would only define my being a femme. I learned to build allies for myself as well.

I share with him my anger and frustration as a femme. He understands the dissonance. He understands that my pain at my invisibility still knows his pain as a target. He gets angry with, and for me, and seeks out ways to support me without oppressing me, without participating in my invisibility. We are gender warriors, we are on the same team and we are working toward the same vision. We both subvert and pervert the binary in the ways that make sense to us, and we are angry together. We each bear witness to the other one's pain.

After being out in the world, after the anger, the pain, the armor of daily interactions we can sit together and take a deep breath. Home. Safe space. We can share space where we can just be, where his right to be exactly who he is, a "sexy, gorgeous, beautiful, wonderful" transgender boy, is protected. Where my right to be a "sexy, gorgeous, beautiful, wonderful" femme is sacred. We know our partnership can protect us from the daily assault, and we can be at rest and recharge, ready to face the world and build hope.

Lorelei

Best Friends, No Question
Lorelei Rutledge

Lorelei has a passion for learning, exploring new opportunities and using big words. In her free time, she enjoys reading, connecting with friends and spiritual exploration. Professionally, Lorelei is a librarian at a research university with an interest in information literacy.

Dear Friend,

I remember the first time I met you. I had convinced my parents to drive me from my small town home up to our state university to do a campus orientation. I spent the whole ride terrified that they would somehow figure out that this orientation was for GLBT students, although they never did figure it out. I remember walking into the GLBT resource center and seeing you arrive, the first masculine woman who openly identified as somewhere on the GLBT spectrum that I had ever met. I disguised it well, but I remember several furtive glances while you spoke, watching you carefully adjust your belt and smooth your tie. I felt like we were part of the same tribe.

When I came back in the fall to start school, things had changed. You went by a new name, and testosterone had already started to deepen your voice and add a tiny bit of coarseness to your features. I saw you at social events, and I still watched and waited, looking to you, in some way, for information about how to navigate being queer, being other. I remember brushing my fingers through my long hair after seeing you one night, holding it close to my head and wondering how it would feel to have such short hair. I wondered what I would look like wearing your clothes, adjusting my belt and smoothing my tie.

When you started to date my roommate, I got to know you a little bit more. I watched how the T [testosterone] changed you and also watched you struggle with your temporary decision to stop taking it. Hearing you talk about the gender spectrum brought all that I had learned in classes, all that I had experienced, to light. Although I would have denied any gender confusion or difference at this point, your words still penetrated me on a deep level.

When you left town to take a job far away, I remember feeling like my heart was breaking. I had a community, but life was not the same. I remember trying to listen so carefully when we talked, trying to read between the lines as you told me the stories of your life, how you were harassed. You tried for a light tone when you told me about how the postwoman wouldn't sell you stamps or when the people you worked with ignored you because of your gender identity, but I could tell it had an impact. Every time you came back to visit, you seemed a little bit more tired, a touch more frustrated. I felt like the proud warrior I had once known had been replaced.

I don't know if we ever talked about your decision to transition. I never blamed you, because I knew that I would never really know what you had survived to get where you were, but it still hurt. Seeing you pass, seeing our relationship change as you became more interested in hanging out with "the boys" was hard. I remember my roommate, now your fiancée, talking nonchalantly about how you were "for all intents and purposes, a straight couple," and it made me want to scream. I felt like all of the struggles we had shared, the stories, the deep kinship bond was erased. Now, you and she passed in the street, went to conservative churches and blended into landscapes where I never have and never will belong.

"*Most* of all, though, I want you to know that I wrote this letter to tell you one key thing; I love you."

Even now, I lack words to articulate much of this initial rage, perhaps in part because I am ashamed, and in part because thinking about the past still twinges that old pain that I have buried in some small part of my heart. I do remember, however, looking at you, and my roommate, and feeling, in some way, utterly powerless. I felt such rage that someone who once seemed like me, who had breasts like mine, a body like mine, could take a medicine, have a surgery, and in some way be able to blend into a world where I always seem to stand out.

When you decided to get legally married, I remember being both happy and grief stricken. Where I felt once so close, now I felt this legal and social divide that I could not define. I felt like you had become, once again, what I could never be, and that feeling was agony. I realized, watching you get married, that your wedding was just a wedding, your love was just amazing love, while my wedding will be a queer wedding, my love will be homosexual love, always marked and always standing out.

I remember later, when you helped me shop for clothes for my new job. I pulled and twisted in each outfit; watching the way each one seemed to accentuate my curves, cling uncomfortably to my extra flesh. I found one pink shirt that seemed to look okay. You were so sweet then, so gentle, telling me that I looked good, that pink was fine, that you wear pink. I still remember, though, doubting your opinion, thinking that of course, you could wear pink; who would judge you. "Men wear pink all the time," I thought "but on people like me it is just confusing."

I also remember, though, how many times you soothed my hurts over the years. When I came to you weeping because a trans friend about to become a lover told me that "he wished body parts didn't matter," but that, despite his appreciation for my masculinity, he couldn't love someone without a penis. I remember how you promised me that it wasn't about me, how you used your words to build a cocoon around me, reminding me of what a beautiful and strong woman I was.

When my mother died and life seemed so difficult, I remember how you came to be with me, a calm and comforting presence. I remember how you nursed me through the break-ups, the family troubles and the other hard times, and these stories are so much more important to me than the stories of my fears about your transition. You have always been the same amazing person, regardless of your gender presentation.

Most of all, I appreciate how you have given me a space in our friendship to be unapologetically myself, and I hope I have done the same. You have seen the roadmap of scars on my heart, mourned them with me and celebrated the joys as well.

I will freely admit that I am terrified to have you read this letter, and almost as terrified to have an audience read it. Perhaps they will think that I am transphobic, that I am not really a good friend or that I need to get over my own internal hang-ups. In my defense, however, I will say that I have never stopped loving you, and I recognize that much of my anguish is not about your transition in specific, but about my own sense of being ill-at-ease in a heteronormative, gender-policing world.

Most of all, though, I want you to know that I wrote this letter to tell you one key thing; I love you.

Your friend,
Lorelei

"Even sadder still, some of these same people are pushed aside or condemned by churches who ignore Christ's call for welcome and inclusion for *all* of God's children."

—Bishop Bennett D.D. Burke,
   ally of the transgender community

Allies

Allies of the transgender community come from many places. They are family members, friends, teachers, clergy and helping professionals just to name a few. Through personal interactions, study and prayerful consideration, they find the courage to stand with and stand up for, those in the transgender community. On a daily basis, they use their privilege as non-transgender individuals to educate those around them about transgender people. They recognize the problems of a transphobic society, and the wounds that many transgender people have endured. There is no one way to be an ally, as this section demonstrates. For some, being an ally means actively engaging in organizations and speaking out in public ways. For others, being an ally is a less public endeavor. These stories too remind us that the SOFFA categories are not so orderly, but rather only a convenient way to talk about a shared experience, or relationship, with a transgender person.

In this section, we hear from clergy who promote the recognition of transgender persons in their respective faiths (Burke, Hassler, Monroe, Nicewander). A counselor who paved the way for others in her community to meet the needs of the transgender population shares her story (Tiv-Amanda), as a performer speaks of his self-discovery and evolving development of an ally to the transgender community (Toscano). The voices of a professor (Grant), students (Irby, Yamamoto), and political activists (Hodges, Perez-Darby) situate the realities of transgender folk in all of our lives. Still, the messages received from these very different perspectives are remarkably similar: advocate for the transgender community by listening to your transgender loved ones. Be willing to learn from what they are willing to share. Know that you will make mistakes even with the best intentions and never forget to celebrate difference.

FAQ

Q. I was a tomboy growing up. Why didn't I turn out to be transgender?

A. Girls have more latitude in their gender norms growing up. Being a tomboy is considered good, particularly if the girl is athletic. Being a feminine boy, however, is not ok! There are many variations of gender: people who like to dress and perform as the other sex (think drag queens and kings), people who work in non-traditional gendered occupations (male nurses, female construction workers), people who enjoy transgressing gender boundaries (women who smoke cigars, men who like to knit) and lots more. But playing with gender boundaries or even pretending to be the other gender, which all of us have done from time-to-time (think Halloween), is *not* being transgender. *Here is the important distinction:* you may be transgender if you perceive yourself to be the other gender. If you do not identify with either gender, you may be genderqueer. If you identify with the gender you were assigned at birth, you are "normal," or cisgender (check the glossary at the end of the book for definitions of words you don't know).

Q. What pronoun should I use to refer to a trans person?

A. It is best to ask the trans person themselves. Some trans people don't mind being called the gender they were born while they are transitioning (for instance, my daughter is transgender, she dresses like a man and is taking male hormones). Some trans persons want to be referred to as the gender they perceive themselves to be even while they are transitioning (my son is now my daughter, please call her by her new name, Debbie). Other trans people prefer a gender-neutral pronoun, like ze (refer to the glossary, for a complete list). Just ask, it might open up a good conversation.

Q. So how do you have sex?

A. Has anyone ever asked you this question? Remember this isn't usually asked of non-transgender people, and like all sexual activity, it is very private and individual. But trans persons do have sex and may be attracted to and have sex with trans people or not, it varies. If you really want to know how a particular person has sex, make sure you have a very special relationship with them, as more than likely they will be offended by your asking. In an intimate relationship, this is a perfectly acceptable question, but probably not anywhere else. A good guide to remember: Would you ask your mother this question?

Q. What is all this GLBT stuff? Why are trans people lumped together with gay people?

A. Gays, Lesbians, Bisexuals, and Transgender (GLBT) people came together to prevent being stigmatized and discriminated against. In fact, it was trans people, really drag queens, who began the movement by standing up for their rights in the Stonewall riots in New York City in 1969 (this is a fascinating story; there are lots of good books and videos if you want to know more). So GLBT is a political movement of marginalized people, because of their sexual orientation *or* their gender identity. It works to the benefit of trans people because there are larger numbers to effect change, but it also is a problem because people tend to confuse sexual identity (the GLB part) with gender identity (the T part). Sometimes Q will be added to GLBT meaning queer, and sometimes I, meaning intersex.

Q. Why should I support transgender equality?

A. All people, including trans people, deserve the same rights. GLBT rights are not special rights, they are civil rights already afforded to most other people. However, discrimination based on gender identity is still legal in many states: your trans friend may be fired, your trans child may be unable to get married and your trans significant other may be sexually or physically abused. Young trans people, particularly, face potential abuse in schools across the country. Trans people need the support of all of us: for instance, contribute to trans organizations or volunteer at PFLAG. Once you get started, you will find out there are lots of things you can do.

Julia

Teaching Gender and Transgender

Julia Grant

Interviewed by Cameron T. Whitley

Julia is Professor of Social Relations and Policy at Michigan State University and Associate Dean of James Madison College of Public Affairs. She has enjoyed teaching and writing about childhood, gender, disability, sexuality and masculinity throughout her scholarly career. This summer she will lead a study abroad program on "Sexual Orientation, Gender Identity, and Sexual Politics in the Netherlands,"(which includes a visit to a gender clinic), about which she is very excited. She and her partner and two children live in East Lansing, Michigan.

What does being an ally to the transgender community mean to you?

Being an ally means first that I consider the claims for justice of the transgender community as central to any conversations about social justice. I see my role as challenging misconceptions about people who are transgender in multiple settings; from discussions with my family to classroom conversations. Having relationships with people who are transgender that are deep and meaningful has also enhanced my appreciation for the unique challenges such individuals face as well as the particular insights they bring to our understanding of the role of gender in our society. More importantly, though, is appreciating what we share as human beings. I sat along a canal-side café in Amsterdam with a woman who had recently transitioned, and we shared a very special moment when we confided that we both felt that we were "late bloomers," — she because of the confidence and self fulfillment she had felt because of her transition; me, because of the confidence and sense of hopefulness I had recently identified in myself at a later stage of life. We both felt empowered and blessed by a newfound sense of possibility.

How have you constructed a classroom that is open to various identities and experiences?

In my classes, especially my class on "Sexual Politics" (about 30 students), I immediately lay the groundwork for exploring the multiple gender and sexual identities that students bring to bear on course materials. Although these classes are largely made up of heterosexual cisgender students, starting with an open climate, where I talk as a matter of fact about being a lesbian, who has both a partner and children, seems to empower students to bring to bear their own personal experiences to class materials. Immediately, I create an open environment that is inclusive of diverse perspectives and experiences. Because of this dynamic, this class has become a major venue for self-disclosure about various sexual and gender identities that have provided some of students' most profound learning experiences.

Have transgender students come out in any of your classes?

Yes, when a transgender student, whom many of the students had known from previous classes came out, students were moved and transformed both by the student's story and by the experience of finding out that someone that they respected, admired and considered to be cisgendered, had a unique history. A number of the females in the class confessed that they were sexually attracted to this person, which challenged their conceptions of masculinity and heteronormativity. Just this week (the second week of classes), a student admitted that his partner was a transgender female. In all cases of self-disclosure, transgender individuals and their partners have been positively responded to, and I know that students are appreciative of the courage involved in sharing these experiences. When transgender students sense that their peers have learned to appreciate the complexity of gender expressions, they are more likely to open up. At the end of the class, many students acknowledge that these moments of self-disclosure were among their most positive memories of class.

Are there assignments that you give to help students understand the difference between gender identity and sexual orientation?

Yes, an assignment that I do right at the beginning of this class seems to further students' understanding the multiple meanings of gender and sexuality in different people's lives. I have students work in groups on a "language use study" that explores the meaning of different words and phrases in both heteronormative culture and in various subcultures. This brings the class up to speed on various ways of talking about sex and gender that are unfamiliar to them. For instance, students investigated the numerous meanings of the term "tranny" both from a historical and contemporary usage context (even noting that the phrase "hot tranny mess" was first used on Project Runway!).

What would you recommend to other teachers trying to create an open classroom for all individuals and identities to flourish?

I suggest opening up dialogue in the classroom from the very beginning, by reminding students that it is legitimate, and useful, to speak about sex and gender from the inside out and not just from a theoretical perspective. Designing activities. whether academic or experiential, that help students to become familiar with the discourses and experiences of different sexual and gender communities also opens up a space for dialogue.

Bennett

Why Weren't You (Your Name Goes Here)?

The Most Reverend Bennett D. D. Burke

Bishop Bennett is Bishop of the Liberal Catholic Diocese of Arizona. He has been involved with Tucson's transgender community since 2005. Bennett's partner, Wendy Pawlak, is completing her Ph.D. dissertation in transgender representations in film at the University of Arizona. Learn more about the Liberal Catholic Church at www.azlcc.org

Light from dozens of candles flickered in the darkness of a November night in Catalina Park, during Tucson's annual Transgender Day of Remembrance. But neither the darkness of the night nor the darkness of the violence and hate crimes inflicted upon those whose memories we had gathered to honor, could overcome that light. On that day in 2005, I had not yet fully embarked on a ministry to Southern Arizona's transgender community. Earlier that year, I had moved to Tucson from Casa Grande, where I had spent the last nine years ministering to another marginalized community — low-income Hispanics who were often treated like second-class citizens by the local Roman Catholic parish. Baptism was often denied to babies whose parents were not married, or not married through the Church, or who had not made significant financial contributions to the parish, and for many other reasons.

I came to Tucson when my full-time employer assigned me to a management position here (Liberal Catholic clergy are self-supporting and do not receive compensation from the church). This move also offered an opportunity to establish a Liberal Catholic mission in "the Old Pueblo," as Tucson is often called. It was in that spirit that I began to attend a number of community events, to learn more about my new hometown and to find out about marginalized people and communities here. Sadly, no matter where we go, there are people pushed aside by society, or actively oppressed or even hated and attacked and sometimes killed, for being "different." Even sadder still, some of these same people are even pushed aside or condemned by churches who ignore Christ's call for welcome and inclusion for *all* of God's children.

Through my attendance at Transgender Day of Remembrance and other events, I began to see that Tucson in general offered a more welcoming environment for the LGBT community than I had seen in other places I'd lived. In addition to city ordinances preventing discrimination in employment for those identifying as LGBT, Tucson's Mayor Robert E. Walkup had actually proclaimed "Transgender Awareness Week" as an official event on the city's calendar. But where were the churches and clergy at transgender events? Yes, I met some wonderful lay leaders of some of Tucson's very welcoming and inclusive churches. Yes, I met a number of people in the LGBT community who had found churches where they felt comfortable, comforted and loved. And yes, I occasionally met local pastors — very busy people doing wonderful work — who helped make their churches open to everyone, including those identifying as transgender.

During the next year, I attended a number of events at Wingspan, Southern Arizona's LGBT support and advocacy center. Through Wingspan, I became involved in a successful effort in the fall of 2006 to defeat Arizona's "Proposition 107," an anti-gay-marriage amendment (to date the only successful defeat of such legislation in any state in America), which to their great credit involved a number of Tucson's visible and influential religious leaders.

Yet it was still rare to see members of Christian clergy at trans-specific events and activities. So in November 2006, I attended my first monthly general meeting of the Southern Arizona Gender Alliance (SAGA) and my second Transgender Day of Remembrance event, as part of what would become one of my Tucson ministries for the newly-founded Our Lady of Peace and Hope Liberal Catholic Mission.

Now, I have to admit to lots of double takes, awkward stares and discomfort with attire and presentation in the beginning of my relationship with Tucson's transgender community. No, I don't mean *my* reactions to trans folk — I mean the looks I got when people walked into a meeting to see a priest sitting there, in black suit and white collar!

I didn't take it personally. I know how badly churches — and leaders of so many congregations — have treated people in the LGBT community. And how badly many churches *still* treat them. And I know how human it is to make assumptions about people based on how they're dressed. For example, just as so many people assume that someone born male, but who now presents as female, must be some kind of deviant or worse, people assume priests show up in places like this to condemn or convert or otherwise devalue them.

The funny looks lasted through a few meetings, during which I tried hard to learn to use respectful terminology and forms of address for everyone present. I learned that people "identify" as belonging to a certain gender, regardless of whether or not that matches the one they were physically and externally born into. I learned that people of courage and determination eventually wish to "present" themselves in that gender, with the appropriate attire and speech and movement and mannerism, and sometimes even medical and surgical intervention. And I learned that all everyone wants is to be accepted for whom they really are, without having their character and intentions judged solely on their appearance.

By my third SAGA meeting, though everyone was polite and respectful to me, I was still getting lots of funny looks, then came time for introductions. When it was my turn, I said, "Hi. My name is Bennett. I'm bishop of the Arizona diocese of the Liberal Catholic Church International. I get the feeling some of you are a bit puzzled, or even a bit put off by my presence or maybe it's just the way I'm dressed. Allow me to explain. *I identify as a priest. This is the way priests dress.* I hope you won't make assumptions about me based *only* on the way I dress. I'll try hard to do the same for you."

A few eyes widened. A few jaws dropped slightly. A few eyebrows arched in surprise, and I think, in realization. Then everyone laughed. That's the deal I always look for now, with everyone I meet. I'll try hard not to make assumptions about others based on the way they identify or present (though I'm sure I'll fail at this from time-to-time, as humans tend to do). I'll try instead to get to know the person inside, and I hope others will look past how I dress and present, to get to know me from the inside out.

I think that's a fair deal and an honest one. The Liberal Catholic Church doesn't exclude, or condemn, or seek to change those who are "different," when that difference is a matter of sexual or affectional orientation, or gender or gender identity — or for that matter, race, color, national origin, ancestry, marital status, economic status, age, disability, theological viewpoint, familial status or issues of individual conscience. Our church welcomes to its altars all who sincerely and reverently desire the sacraments, regardless of whatever reason those same sacraments have been denied by other churches.

Actually, the welcome I've received in the transgender community has been wonderful and very affirming to me as a person, just as I've tried to be affirming — personally and professionally as a member of Christian clergy — to everyone I meet. In April 2008, for example, I had the opportunity to attend the annual conference of the International Foundation for Gender Education when it was held here in Tucson. I also had the honor of co-presenting at the conference, with my friend Erin Russ, a discussion called "Did the Bible Really Say That?" which focused on its timeless and eternal messages of inclusion and welcoming, rather than the contextual and time-limited cultural messages of exclusion and discrimination. I can't begin to describe how wonderful it was to help the Church be present with the transgender community at this first-of-its-kind Tucson event, though sadly once more, I believe I was the only ordained member of Christian clergy to attend. Again and again, people went out of their way to thank me for attending or to share a personal story, or even to ask for counsel and spiritual advice. But there were two sides to this coin. The joy and surprise so often expressed to me about my attendance also indicates how unusual it is for those in the transgender community to find religious communities or religious leaders to whom they can turn for the same kind of spiritual comfort they — like any other person — should be able to much more easily find.

"The Liberal Catholic Church doesn't exclude, or condemn, or seek to change those who are 'different.' ... Our church welcomes to its altars all who sincerely and reverently desire the sacraments."

So does that mean that Our Lady of Peace and Hope is rockin' the house with transgender members or members from the wider LGBT community? Sadly, it does not...at least not yet.

Again, I don't take this personally. We're new here in Tucson. I know that millions of people from all walks of life, not just in the LGBT community, have rejected or ignored Christianity. Many people think the Church lacks relevance in their lives or feel that they have been actually and actively harmed by Christians. In the LGBT community and among transgender people, these problems are even more acute. As one extreme example, which is by no means an isolated one, someone I met in my ministry was once beaten unconscious by a Christian deacon in his church, when as a teen he revealed he was gay.

So many people in the LGBT community have been treated so badly, they're scared to take the risk of walking through the doors of a church, even in the small and family-style congregations of a Liberal Catholic Church.

They're understandably afraid to trust, to take a chance on faith, only to find that "welcome" really means "you're welcome until we get a chance to change you." So many in the LGBT community have been insulted by Christian preaching, which often denies their humanity or condemns them as sinners simply for being who God made them.

We have our own unique challenges in the Liberal Catholic Church, too. Because we're a small denomination, lacking in financial resources, we often begin our missions around kitchen tables, or in rented rooms (May I take a moment to point out here that the Christian church *began* in a rented room, rented for a small gathering we now call "The Last Supper.") Because we're a small denomination, it takes us years to get to what we've put together in our first Arizona parish, St. Michael and All Angels Liberal Catholic Cathedral in Casa Grande, Arizona, about midway between Phoenix and Tucson. There in that small rural town, we now have a 200-member congregation, in our own 3,500 square foot facility, with all of the trappings (priests, deacons, altar servers, music, child care, Sunday School and so on), while in our new local mission, we're still struggling to fill a small room for Mass on Sunday mornings. Unfortunately, many people still think of "church" primarily as a fancy building, with lots of programs and choices of services and events. Many people choose churches based on those outward "identities," rather than basing their choice on the "soul" of a congregation or denomination, including how those churches view the inclusion of lesbians, gays, bisexuals and transgender people. In this regard, let's consider for a moment something called "queer theology." While I don't have time to do it proper justice in the space of this essay, "queer theology" basically posits a very different view of LGBT "inclusion" in the Christian faith.

Here's one way to explain it. Today, a number of so-called "mainstream" Christian denominations are debating the issue of LGBT "inclusion" in their congregations. On one end of the spectrum, we have Christian churches, which condemn all the component identities included in "LGBT" as hopeless sinners. On the other end, we have churches which encourage the LGBT to come out within their congregations or which actively reach out to the LGBT community (or at least to the LG, if not quite so actively to the B and T). Some denominations are in the middle somewhere, and some face the prospect of splitting their church in two based on differing interpretations of Biblical teaching on same-sex relationships or gender identities. Often, the clear intent of Christ's message is ignored or even contradicted by the all-too-human leaders of Christian denominations, the "popes and councils" derided by Martin Luther, whose interests often seem to be more about earthly power and control than loving and welcoming strangers. But queer theology takes a different and much more radical approach.

Remember what Christ said in Scripture beginning in Matthew 25:34? That as we did to those marginalized by society in his day — the hungry, the thirsty, the stranger, the poor, the sick, the prisoner — we actually did it to Christ himself? That if we shunned them, we shunned Christ? That if we hated, punished or even neglected them, we were hating, punishing or neglecting Christ, too? That's what Christ actually said and also how he lived. As Christians, we call his teaching — but more importantly the flesh-and-blood reality and example of Jesus Christ — the Word of God.

Remember also what Christ said when he was criticized for the company he kept, those same marginalized people and others, who were shunned by religious leaders in Christ's day as "unclean?" Christ told us that those were the very people for which he had come. Christ condemned the religious leaders and exalted those on the margins. Christ made those considered by mainstream society to be "the least" of God's children the very *core* of Christian faith and of his ministry. That, too, is the Word of God.

In this way, theologians speak of Christ's "preferential option" for the poor and oppressed. Queer theologians, among them the Liberal Catholic Church's own Bishop Elizabeth Stuart, speak of the same preferential option for *everyone* who is marginalized and oppressed, especially for those in the LGBT community who function today as a direct equivalent of those Christ saw as marginalized in his day.

Therefore, it is *necessary, but not sufficient* to merely "welcome" those who identify as LGBT into our congregations. Instead, the Church must renew its focus on Christ's "preferential option" for the marginalized and oppressed, find those who are among the marginalized and oppressed right here and now — certainly that will include lesbians, gays, bisexuals and transgender people — and make them not just "welcome" in Christian faith, but actually reach out to them as a new "core" of Christian faith.

Those who identify as transgender must insist, I think, on finding this value made explicit in any Christian church which is deserving of their participation: "I was a stranger and you welcomed me." For Christ says today as he did 2,000 years ago, "Truly I tell you, just as you did it to one of the least of these who are members of my family, you did it to me." Again, this is the Word of God as revealed to us in Scripture, and it stands in triumphant and glorious contrast to those who quote the Bible out of context to humiliate, embarrass and condemn.

But finding welcoming churches continues to be a challenge. Hence, the latest phase of my ministry, a discussion and support group we're calling "Come Again? Recovering from Spiritual Malpractice and Abuse." The idea for this actually came from a discussion at a SAGA meeting in early 2008, centered around the negative and harmful messages directed against the

LGBT community by so many who identify as Christians.

This group was created for those who still find that Christianity calls to them, but who seek to understand and overcome the ways in which some Christians have used techniques and messages of what I call "spiritual malpractice and abuse." We're using a process similar to the "transtheoretical model of change (TTM)," which deals with a person's success or failure in achieving a proposed *behavior change*, such as developing different habits (like returning to a faith community). The model attempts to explain how changes can be made successfully — or why they fail.

Based on more than 15 years of research, TTM posits that individuals move through a series of five stages (precontemplation, contemplation, preparation, action, maintenance) to make significant behavioral changes. Similarly, people who seek reintegration into a church or faith community, or simply wish to rediscover Christ's message of love and welcome, can benefit from *talking and thinking* about faith — that is, precontemplation, contemplation and preparation — before seriously considering taking that scary step — the action part — of walking through a church door. I'm also excited about some one-on-one work with transgender friends, especially those who are in early stages of transition. This work involves helping them to have safe and productive coming-out conversations with their families or friends, particularly where faith issues may be involved in family dynamics. A few of us are also beginning to discuss the creation of spiritually-based coming out or transition "blessing ceremonies," to mark these important rites of passage, much as Christians have traditionally celebrated other rites of passage like baptism, communion, confirmation, marriage, ordination and the end of earthly life.

But enough about theology and our church. There's something else that's at least as important about my work in the transgender community. At least it is for me. And that's how the example of so many of my new friends, fighting against tremendous societal, financial, emotional, familial and medical odds, have found the courage to be themselves, whatever the cost. Ultimately, that quest doesn't belong only to the transgender — it belongs to all of us who seek to live authentically, to be truly ourselves, to be the best "me's" we can be, while reaching out in love to our neighbors and to God. But my transgender friends, and all those in the LGBT community throughout Tucson and the world, who struggle to make themselves over into their own true image — well, they inspire me every day to try to do the same.

We are all pulled to live according to the expectations of others. In my case, that might be the expectations that go with my "day job" of corporate executive. Or my family obligations. Or the expectations my congregations have of me as their pastor and bishop. The challenge I have, that each of us has, can be met by learning the lesson my transgender friends have to teach.

That lesson, so difficult to apply, yet so simple to state, is this: we must truly be ourselves, regardless of how many obstacles stand in our way.

A popular legend from the Hebrew tradition comes to mind. A Rabbi named Zusya died and now stood before God's throne. As he waited for God to appear, he anxiously and ashamedly began to reexamine his own life — how little he felt he had done, how poorly he felt he would fare when compared to the lives and accomplishments of others. He was certain that God was going to ask him, "Why weren't you Moses? Why weren't you Solomon or David?" But when God appeared, the rabbi was stunned and amazed. God simply asked him, "Why weren't you Zusya?"

All of us who seek to be who we really are face an uphill climb. We face disappointment, frustration and opposition. In my case, while most people in our two congregations have welcomed our LGBT members, we *have* had a few who have resigned — pointedly citing our outreach to the LGBT community. We continue to struggle financially, while we work to establish our new mission in Tucson. I still get hate mail from time-to-time, from people who identify as Christians, but who cling to what I call "Old Testament Christianity," seeing a wrathful and vengeful God who sends plagues and locusts and frogs, rather than the all-merciful and loving Christ who tells us our creator pours life-giving rain on us all. These challenges, of course, pale compared to the challenges faced by those in gender transition. So we must take strength from each other. We must help each other in love and support and community.

For those in transition who also identify as Christians, we must remember that there is only one requirement for the "identity" known as "Christian," and that's baptism. Regardless of the neglect of so many faith communities or their condemnation or even hatred, we must stand here together and proclaim our faith in God and in each other. We must insist that Christian churches that are worthy of preaching in Christ's name must welcome the stranger and love everyone. We must choose churches wisely, or counsel and advise those churches to which we currently belong, letting our own lights shine to better illuminate the path for all people of faith.

For those of us who identify as Christians, we must stand secure in that faith, in belief in ourselves, in pursuit of our true identities, in the process of our transitions, despite attacks on those identities, on our Christianity and even on our essential humanity. Consider the example of Martin Luther in 1521.

When attacked at the Diet of Worms for what were considered at that time his unorthodox Christian views and his adherence to the dictates of his own conscience — in fact, his very rebellion against the Christian and societal norms of his day — Luther refused to recant, retreat or resign from the

Church. He knew that the Church belongs to all Christians by virtue of nothing other than baptism, and that we must stand firm in our faith and in our Church, despite those who accuse us of not being "real Christians," or "good-enough Christians."

May we stand humbly yet confidently in our current congregations, or failing that, find new and more welcoming congregations, where we too can voice the words spoken by Martin Luther to his accusers; where we can say to our fellow Christians and to those who question our true identities and our right as members of the LGBT community and their allies to proclaim the Good News of Christ; where we can be the light shining in the darkness, which no darkness can overcome; where we can proclaim our faith as Christians and simultaneously and proudly *be* who we really *are*; where God will never have to ask us, "Why weren't you who I made you to be?" and where we can say what Martin Luther said — and say it again and again until we actually believe it ourselves:

> "*Unless I am convinced by the testimony of Scripture or by clear reason (for I do not trust either in the pope or in councils alone, since it is well known that they have often erred and contradicted themselves), I am bound by the Scriptures I have quoted and my conscience is captive to the Word of God. I cannot and will not retract anything, since it is neither safe nor right to go against conscience. Here I stand. I can do no other. God help me. Amen.*"

"Fall" by Hilary Brenneman © 2012

In the Image
of God
Rev. Emily C. Hassler

Emily is an ordained United Church of Christ pastor who began her ministry in the Presbyterian Church upon graduating from Austin Presbyterian Theological Seminary with a Master's Degree in Divinity in 1991. In 2000 she transferred her clergy credentials to the UCC upon winning her six-year court battle in the Presbyterian Church Courts. Because Emily came out after she was ordained, she retained her clergy credentials as a minister in good standing, despite living as an out lesbian in a committed relationship with her partner of 18 years. In 1997, she co-founded a Denver organization called Rainbow Alley, a drop-in center providing a safe place, case management and health education for the GLBTIQ (gay, lesbian, bisexual, transgender, intersex, queer) youth of Denver and the surrounding areas. She served Washington Park United Church of Christ as their senior pastor for eight years where she gave this sermon. She currently works at Arapahoe House in their adolescent in-patient treatment center.

$\star \quad \star \quad \star \quad \star \quad \star$

In many ways I've probably been writing this particular piece my whole life. I know I've been writing it since I was a little girl growing up in Wyoming. When I was 13 years old (c. 1970), the northern Wyoming culture finally decided to allow little girls to wear pants during the winters. Sub-zero temperatures were common, and it was not uncommon for folks to freeze to death. It's curious to me even now why it was more important to maintain a certain gender image than to keep little girls warm during the horrendously cold winters in Wyoming.

But there's really no other boundary issue that raises more discomfort in the general population than the issue of gender roles. You'll remember the backlash of the women's movement in the 60's.

I'd like to think that I am a truly evolved child of the 60's, having broken through a gender barrier or two of my own. I don't know why I cared at all about what Michael Jackson did except that he refused to fit into any of comfortable categories I've constructed for myself around gender and race.

Feminist theologians like Virginia Ramey Mollenkott [*Omnigender*] suggest that: "Any person who deviates from [the standards of heterosexuality and patriarchy] is a gender transgressor, outside the pale of genuine humanity, undeserving of full human consideration … [This] binary gender construct is assumed to be …the order of creation, the will of God, unchangeable and beyond question" (p. 1)!

Well, isn't it? I mean, men are men, and women are women, right? One thing in this ever-changing world upon which we should be able to hang our hats is that God made us male and female. It's right there in Genesis 1:27: "God created humans in the image of God, in the image of God was humanity created, male and female God created them." God did not create Michael Jackson that way; Michael did that all by himself with the help of his plastic surgeon and hairdresser.

Except, you know, there *are* two creation stories. Some of you have heard of the famous exegesis of the Genesis texts by Phyllis Trible [*God and the Rhetoric of Sexuality*] in which she suggests that the *Adamah* in Genesis 2:7-8 is more properly interpreted as 'earthling.' A being with an *undifferentiated* gender, neither male nor female; it is not until divine surgery is performed in vs. 27-28 that two other genders are created. What's truly disturbing about this accurate translation is that it indicates that God actually created three genders: adamah, male and female (p.141).

"When we put on the robes of Jesus, some of us may be cross-dressing and/or dressing for the cross. I believe only the later truly matters to God."

Those of you who know about intersexed people also know that as many as 1 out of 100 people are born with biological indications of both genders. The archaic language used to describe these folks was *hermaphrodite*, a word now considered by many to be inaccurate because it implies a full set of both genders present in one human being. This is not the case. Intersex people are rather an ambiguous biology somewhere between the two accepted genders, shades of *Adamah*. What does that mean to our socially accepted binary [or gender binary assumes that there are two and only two genders] gender roles? If God created us male and female, who are these people? Are they perhaps the *Adamah*? Why is it so important for us to conform to a set of idealized norms instead of honoring the vast and delicious diversity of what has been created?

OK, it's true. We have a number of biological indicators that a binary world is part of creation's plan. Most of us have two eyes, ears, arms, legs, etc. But what if these binary constructions are simply here to teach humans the first steps towards seeing them for what they may actually be, two ends of a continuum? What if binary constructions are our Creator's best riddle? What if intersex people are posed to help a world understand that nothing under the sun is outside of our Creator's plan.

It's like a pop quiz from God, you've got your basic left and your basic right, so what's all this in-between? Christians have tended to suggest throughout the ages that whatever doesn't fit into the boxes we've constructed must be of Satan. But that leaves vast amounts of creation in the hands of the fallen. It's your basic fall-redemption theology. I believe something else.

As Mollenkott suggests "Our society has such a powerful cultural desire to [make all categories binary], that to threaten any one *boundary* is to threaten them all" (p. 74). If that boundary actually equals the *status quo*, oh we better watch out. And there's one thing that has become abundantly clear to me in my brief years of study of the life of Jesus; this man from Nazareth had a particular aversion to the social constructions of the *status quo*. Which is why one of the supreme lessons of my faith is to take great care in looking for God outside of what my culture says is holy, perfect and acceptable. Jesus was considered neither holy, perfect nor acceptable by the culture of his day. I believe it was only when his story became part of the status quo that his *perfection* was achieved. Ironically it was Jesus' self-appointed ad man, the Apostle Paul who did the most to disassemble the false binary social constructs of his day, when he penned one of the greatest marketing statements of all time. You've heard it before:

> *But all of you are the children of God, through faith, in Christ Jesus, since every one of you that has been baptized has been clothed in the Robe of Christ. There can be neither Jew nor Greek, there can be neither slave nor free, there can be neither male nor female, for you are all one in Christ Jesus.*

This is one of the hallmarks of our faith. It is why we chose to be an open and affirming congregation. For in doing so, we have agreed to serve as a bellwether for a culture that demands binary conformity on nearly all fronts. Instead, we have proclaimed that creation exists on a continuum, be it attraction or gender identity. Nor do we need to judge which part of the continuum is more holy, for it is all God's, all of it: male, female, intersexual, homosexual, heterosexual, bisexual, Michael Jackson. God is much more interested in the ways which we love each other rather than the ways in which we define, exclude and devalue each other based on political or cultural notions of gender and power.

Even if we decided to purge from our cultural Christian theology of gender the disturbing ambiguities of the *Adamah* in the Genesis 2 account, we are still left with the Genesis 1 account, which tells us 'In the image of God was humanity created, male and female God made them.' If male and female are the truest image of the one God, then you tell me…which person is closest to the image of God? The one who has lived as only one gender or the one who has lived as both genders? When we put on the robes of Jesus, some of us may be cross-dressing and/or dressing for the cross, I believe only the later truly matters to God. Amen.

"Church" by Jackie Frances © 2012

Jean, her son Ben, his partner Wayne and
her daughter Beth

Evolution of an Ally
Jean Hodges

Jean was a founding member of PFLAG Boulder in 1993 and was its president from 1996 to 2010. She is currently the National PFLAG Vice-President and chair of the Regional Directors Council. Her passion is to make schools safe and inclusive of all LGBTQ students. Jean is a former high school teacher and theatre director. She and her husband have three adult children, one of whom is gay, and three grandchildren.

My first experience of interacting with trans folks was at a PFLAG meeting some 15 years ago. We invited several representatives from the Gender Identity Center in Lakewood, Colorado to present a program to our Boulder PFLAG Chapter. Some half-dozen M2F people arrived, shared in our support circle, and then presented in front of our larger circle, with all our members. I sat next to a self-identified cross-dresser named Jane. When she came to our group, she was decked out in makeup, wig and female attire. Jane explained to us that she identified as male and presented as such on a daily basis. Where she works, on a ranch, she was known as Joe and dressed as a man. For fun and recreation as her female persona, Joe preferred female attire and being referred to as Jane with appropriate pronouns. I was puzzled by this double identity, as she told us about dating men as well as being a father to adult children, and so I asked a stupid question: "So do you consider yourself gay or straight?" (S)He smiled at me and with a twinkle in his eye asked, "What do you think?" My brain was doing cartwheels as my cognitive gender box exploded. Blushing, I mumbled with some embarrassment, "Maybe, it doesn't matter."

There's nothing that has taught me more about gender variance than to know some people in transition. PFLAG and my work with the Boulder Valley Safe Schools Coalition (BVSSC) led me to learn what it means to be transgender in profound ways. When Serenity quit high school in 1998 because of harassment as a lesbian, I was motivated to work to change school climate by starting the BVSSC so that no one would ever quit school just for being who they were. I also kept in touch with Serenity and witnessed her transition to He over the next several years. We talked fairly often. I asked him questions such as the pronouns he preferred. I was getting my head around the idea of the fluidity of gender. I saw the confusion and dissatisfaction when she identified as a lesbian and then become a settled and confident young man finally "at home" with his evolution as a transsexual man. He took me to visit my first Sex Shop on Dupont Circle when we were in Washington, D.C. together as consultants to National PFLAG's development of Safe Schools materials. Once again, my mind whirled in wonderment at the novel ways that people expressed their sexual energy.

"*I* am proud to be part of a national organization that recognizes the importance of working for Trans Equality."

My third mentor who expanded my understanding of gender variance was the whole Bond Family (names have been changed). The parents came to PFLAG Boulder when they began to understand that their six-year-old girl was really meant to be a boy. As they studied more about what it meant to have a transgender child, they stretched our understanding about children who know early on that they were born in the wrong body and feel as though they must transition to live happy and healthy lives. I became a surrogate grandmother to the two Bond children since their own grandmother was not available nor understanding and accepting. It has been a privilege to share in their journey over the past 10 years. I am in awe of the parents' passion and love that led them to make many presentations to parents, faculty and schoolmates to make their son's school a place where he would feel respected and accepted. No grandmother could feel prouder than I do of their success in educating an entire K-8 school on transgender issues and school acceptance. I also know that as in all parenting, the challenges are never done. They are now supporting their child in his adolescence into the uncharted territory of hormone therapy and future decisions about surgery. I stand by to listen and offer emotional support and lots of love to their family.

My fourth vicarious learning experience was through a PFLAG family whose college-age lesbian daughter declared her intention to transition to male. Her mother and father have two great children, both of whom had come out at different times when they were in high school. As the parents were part of PFLAG for several years, I witnessed their struggle to adjust their thinking about having two gay kids. Now there was a new layer to incorporate in their love and acceptance of their children. I think it only took a matter of months for them to shift their reticence about gender transition to total acceptance. The mother told me recently that she can hardly remember that there was much struggle because her new son is so happy, so at peace with himself. Even I cannot remember with any clear image the perky high school lesbian that I first met because his strong male presence is so right, so complete at age 25.

For at least the past seven years our PFLAG Board has chosen to make transgender education a priority because of all areas of LGBTQ experiences, gender variance is the least understood by both LBG's and straight PFLAG families and allies. We have offered support for families and individuals as cited above, *education* through programming a minimum of one PFLAG meeting a year dedicated to increasing our knowledge of a complex subject. In addition, we received a grant to bring Mara Kiesling, Executive Director of the National Center for Transgender Equality, to Boulder to do trainings for teachers in our schools as well as offering a PFLAG program. Advocacy, the third leg of the PFLAG mission, is an ongoing challenge. When I lobbied legislators in Washington, D.C. for trans inclusion in the Employment Non-Discrimination Act, I realized the misconceptions of people in power. This awareness led to my becoming Executive Director to create a film, *Faces and Facets of Transgender Experience* [www.pflagboulder.org] to break down stereotypes. This film recently won an award at the National PFLAG Convention for its impact on education, support, and advocacy on behalf of gender variant persons. I am proud to be part of a national organization that recognizes the importance of working for Trans Equality.

Megan and Allison

Are You a Boy or a Girl?
Megan Irby

Megan is a 29-year-old female-bodied, gender androgynous queer who currently lives in Portland, Oregon with her beautiful femme partner. Megan has an undergraduate degree from the University of Colorado, Boulder in Psychology and Sociology. She is currently attending Lewis and Clark College for her Masters in Counseling, focusing on Community Counseling with children. Her goal is to be a mental health therapist specializing in working with queer, trans and sexual minority youth. She also has many years of experience educating the public about issues of intimate partner violence and sexual assault as well as working directly with survivors.

✴   ✴   ✴   ✴   ✴

"Are you a boy or a girl?" was a comment I became familiar with as it was often echoed as I walked past groups of heckling boys and petty girls during my school-age years. "Why do you dress like a boy?" or "Do you like being a 'tomboy'?" they would ask at recess and in the hallways. I hated my body back then. I hated the way I didn't fit into how girls were supposed to dress and play. I hated the way I would never 'pass' on the boys' side of the schoolyard. I now have grown to love this existence of being in the middle, living in the gray and confusing the hell out of strangers. I would have never come to this point without first being a friend and ally and deconstructing the social construct we call 'gender.'

I think most of us can agree, the childhood years can be rough. Life only gets rougher as adolescent hormones kick in and subsequent changes shape our bodies and how we view these physical vessels of blood and bones. Our self-perceptions are distorted in light of what others think, whom we loathe while simultaneously seeking their approval. It wasn't until college that I realized I could be what I wanted to be: in the middle of the gender spectrum or genderqueer (even though I wasn't aware of this term quite yet). When I first starting working at the Gay, Lesbian, Bisexual, Transgender Resource Center (GLBTRC) on the Boulder [CO] campus, my eyes mirrored that of a child going into the toy store for the first time. I finally found my world, and the people I had always hoped existed, to validate my reality and mere presence. I knew there had to be people who not only understood my experience with being out of sorts with gender, but people who could model images of what it means to be living with confidence and not conforming to the gender binary [assumes that there are two and only two genders].

"I now have grown to love this existence of being in the middle, living in the gray and confusing the hell out of strangers. I would have never come to this point without first being a friend and ally and deconstructing the social construct we call 'gender.'"

Over the last six years, I have met and formed many friendships with trans-identified folks who represented all parts of the beautiful spectrum called transgender. I have considered myself a SOFFA ever since I heard the term from my good friends and co-workers at the GLBTRC. I knew there were elements of being transgender I could identify with and at the same time other aspects that were not related to my personal experience. My biological sex is female, and I have always "felt in my body" as much as one can in this material world focused on "one ideal body." Although I've had times, like I mentioned earlier, where I hated my body, it was just the usual stuff (I'm too skinny and boney, my boobs are too small, my butt is flat, no one will ever find me attractive, etc). When I talked to folks who despised the body they were born in because their biological sex and gender identity didn't match, there was a level of discomfort beyond what I had experienced. I quickly realized this community could use as many allies as possible, and I became dedicated to being an ally, much in the same way I expect my heterosexual friends to be to the queer community.

I realized I still saw transgender in specific terms and conditions, though, and only if you met these requirements could you identify as transgender. I noticed I wasn't alone in this feeling when I heard many within the trans community discuss the exclusionary boundaries many of them were held to, such as the pressure to pursue surgery. It was as if you had to change your body physically to be included in the community, similar to how bisexuals are told they need to choose a side. It is odd to me how people, who are excluded by mainstream society everyday, could be so exclusionary themselves. I had this underlying feeling of being a fraud if I considered myself trans since I had no desire to change my physical genitals. For a while I saw myself as the A(lly) and F(riend) in the term SOFFA, as I am not a transgender person.

With no job in place, no apartment lease signed and no friends to help guide me once I got there, I moved to Portland, Oregon, in the summer of 2004 after graduation. With all my worldly possessions packed in my dad's truck, and my cat as my only partner in crime, I started what would be a journey of self-exploration. The first couple years were a struggle in terms of forming a friendship circle in the midst of trying to stay afloat financially. Six months after moving, I cut my hair short, voluntarily and intentionally, for the first time. The closest I had ever come to a "boy's" haircut was in the 3rd grade when I fell asleep with gum in my hair, and my mom refused to spend the time to get it out. The biggest differences between 3rd grade and cutting my hair at 23 were the elements of choice and what it meant to my identity. In 3rd grade, the 'do' was another way to be pointed out as different and weird by my classmates. At the age of 23, I cut my hair to make sure the plethora of lesbians in Portland saw me as part of their community. What I didn't come to realize until much later, was the act of cutting my hair was actually me taking my first step towards transitioning into my gender identity.

The first year of sporting the short hair, I still wore tight shirts and continued to play the role of "feminine." I was careful to only shop in the female side of department stores and looked enviously at the men trying on clothes I really wanted to wear. I would end up buying clothes that made me feel more like a drag queen with no skills. I feared I would be found out as a gender imposter by binary living folk at any moment. The short hair was a saving grace and was the only thing I liked about my physical self, but I still felt out of place in the world. It's an odd reality; feeling proud of my breasts and clit[orus] when I look at myself in the mirror or feel my body alongside another female, yet the way in which society recognizes females doesn't include me.

When I embraced the androgynous presentation, I realized I didn't have to choose a box. I came to expand the definition of transgender and not get bogged down by exclusionary thinking of whether my androgyny qualified as trans. I find many people are afraid of the gray and non-compartmentalized identities because it somehow threatens where they stand. Reminds me of the basics of object-relations theory: "If there is not a clear definition of what you are, then how can I possibly identify myself as opposite?" I sometimes forget there are people who accept the illusion of social constructs and never stop to question the validity of demographic labels and consider they may not even fit into those manufactured identities.

I proudly identify as a queer, genderqueer, female-bodied, androgynous-presenting, woman-loving trans ally. When deciding what to focus on in this piece, I wanted to balance and paint the picture of my dual roles; being trans and being a SOFFA. It wasn't until I met my current partner, Alison, when I felt confident enough to live and present as the gender non-conformist I truly am. My relationship with her has been the catalyst for me to arrive at a place where I can live confidently within the gray. Now, I can shop in the men's department and come home with clothes I actually want to wear. Actually, Alison found most of my current wardrobe because she is a Goodwill star and finds the best clothes for me. I love being dressed by my femme.

The vehicle that led me to this transition came way before my partner though. It was the presence of the trans community in my life and other activists who made me realize the issues unique to them. I remember hearing bathroom horror stories of friends being mistaken as male by female patrons and having uncomfortable encounters at best. Now, bathroom discomfort and being called 'sir' is a daily reality for me, and I understand on a personal level how the binary restricts space for us constantly.

I also have come to love this androgynous existence because I finally feel at home. I almost feel privileged at times when I can be "read" as male and female in one day. Plus being a sociologist at heart, I get daily information about how being male or female will change the way in which people interact with you. It's a researcher's dream to know what it feels like to be mistaken as a gay boy in a bar, a Portland dyke, a straight male and a 12-year old boy all in one day. I have been able to take these interactions with a grain of salt and a sense of grace since I am aware of how strongly people are ingrained with gender roles. Being a trans ally and friend, I am able to empower myself to present how I want to in the world: androgynous, genderqueer, gender-f**k, whatever term you want to use. For me, the nature of being a SOFFA and trans-identified are intertwined and cannot be isolated from one another. I credit my friendship and allyship with the transgender community for my pride around identifying as trans and the confidence I now have to be who I want to be, regardless of how much I stray away from the socially constructed binary between male and female.

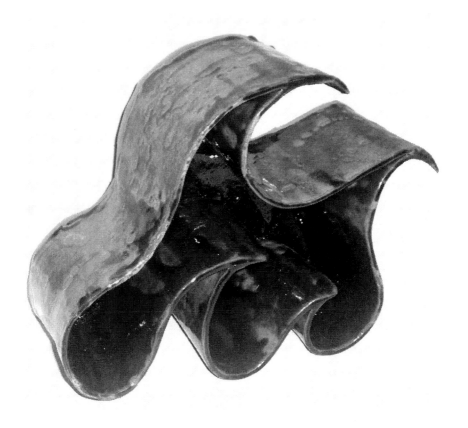

"Waves" by Hilary Brenneman © 2012

Irene

Transgender, Victimized and Black

Rev. Irene Monroe

Irene is an ordained minister, a Huffington Post blogger and a syndicated queer religion columnist. Her columns appear in 43 cities across the country and in the United Kingdom. She was chosen in October 2009 by MSNBC as "10 Black women you should know." Irene has been profiled in *O, The Oprah Magazine*, and in the Gay Pride Episode of "In the Life," where the segment on her was nominated for an educational Emmy. She has received the Harvard University Certificate of Distinction in Teaching several times. Irene is in the film, *For the Bible Tells Me So*, an exploration of the intersection between religion and homosexuality in the United States and how the Religious Right has used its interpretation of the Bible to stigmatize the gay community. She sits on the advisory boards of several national LGBTQ organizations. website: www.irenemonroe.com

∗ ∗ ∗ ∗ ∗

It's not easy for any person of African descent to be LGBTQ in our black communities, but our transgender brothers and sisters might feel the most discrimination.

The National Black Justice Coalition (NBJC), in collaboration with the National Gay and Lesbian Task Force and the National Center for Transgender Equality (NCTE) released a groundbreaking study in September [2011] called *Injustice at Every Turn: A Look at Black Respondents in the National Transgender Discrimination Study*, exposing both the structural and individual racism transgender people of color confront. The study is a supplement to the national study *Injustice at Every Turn: A Report of the National Transgender Discrimination Survey* [Available at www.thetaskforce.org/ reportsandresearch/ntds].

Because misinformation about transgender people in our country is rampant and egregiously offensive, its impact is deleterious. Transphobia in black communities has left these members of our community especially vulnerable. The statistics are stark:

Black transgender people had an extremely high unemployment rate at 26 percent, two times the rate of the overall transgender sample and four times the rate of the general population.

"*H*alf of Black respondents who attended school expressing a transgender identity or gender non-conformity reported facing harassment."

A startling 41 percent of Black respondents said they had experienced homelessness at some point in their lives, more than five times the rate of the general U.S. population.

Black transgender people lived in extreme poverty with 34 percent reporting a household income of less than $10,000 per year. This is more than twice the rate for transgender people of all races (15 percent), four times the general Black population rate (9 percent), and eight times the general U.S. population rate (4 percent).

Black transgender people were affected by HIV in devastating numbers. More than one-fifth of respondents were living with HIV (20.23 percent), compared to a rate of 2.64 percent for transgender respondents of all races, 2.4 percent for the general Black population, and 0.60 percent of the general U.S. population.

Half of Black respondents who attended school expressing a transgender identity or gender non-conformity reported facing harassment. Nearly half (49 percent) of Black respondents reported having attempted suicide.

On a positive note, many Black transgender people who were out to their families reported that their families were as strong as before they came out. Black respondents reported this experience at a higher rate than the overall sample of transgender respondents.

Adding insult to injury is the lack of recognition our trans brothers and sisters receive for their contributions to our community. If any recognition is doled out, it is usually posthumously.

For example, the annual Transgender Day of Remembrance (TDOR) is an international event memorializing transgender people murdered because of their gender identities or gender expressions. The purpose of TDOR is to raise public awareness of hate crimes against transgender people and to honor their lives that might otherwise be forgotten. This event is held every November and honors Rita Hester, a 34-year-old African-American trans individual who was murdered in her home just outside of Boston on Nov. 28, 1998. The crime kicked off the "Remembering Our Dead" web project.

Another example, in June 2006 the Ali Forney Center (AFC) in NYC, the nation's largest LGBTQ youth homeless services center, aggressively launched an advertising campaign asking the simple question: "Would you stop loving your child if you found out they were gay or lesbian?" Carl Siciliano, Executive Director of the Ali Forney Center, stated, "Our goal was to address the rising rate of LGBT youth homelessness, particularly in communities of color."

Ali Forney, for whom the center is named, was an African American transgender individual known as Luscious and was also a throwaway. And like many throwaways, Forney earned his living as a prostitute. Once stabilized with a roof over his head, Forney spent his remaining years dedicating his time helping his peers. On a cold wintry December night in 1997 at 4 a.m., Forney was murdered by a still-unidentified assailant.

Black transphobia, in this present-day and in its present form, many opine, has a lot to do with the social alienation from the dominant white LGBTQ community and the cultural and religious isolation from the African American community...

The study *"Injustice at Every Turn: A Look at Black Respondents in the National Transgender Discrimination Survey"* gives us just a small window into the everyday lived reality of my transgender brothers and sisters.

Originally published in "The Huffington Post, Huff Post Black Voices," 2/30/2012.

Kari

All God's Children
Rev. Kari Nicewander

Kari has served as the pastor at Edgewood United Church, United Church of Christ since 2007. She was ordained into the Christian ministry in 2003 after completing her Masters of Divinity at Harvard Divinity School. She has served in pastorates in Massachusetts and in Michigan. Kari is very involved in advocacy and education around issues including HIV/AIDS, religion and LGBT concerns, international development and the intersection of faith and social justice. In addition to her pastorate, she serves as the Outreach Coordinator for Lola Children's Fund, serving HIV-affected children in Ethiopia; the Chair for the Executive and Advisory Boards of Church World Service, Michigan Region; and a regular volunteer for the Lansing Area AIDS Network.

⋆　⋆　⋆　⋆　⋆

I distinctly remember that phone call from three years ago. I was in my office, at Edgewood United Church, United Church of Christ, where I serve as a local church pastor. The voice on the other end came from a representative of our national body, a woman calling from the Office of LGBT Concerns.

"There is a member of the UCC who is moving to East Lansing soon, and he requested that I call you, in order to make sure that he would be welcome in your church."

It was an easy question for me to answer. Of course he would be welcome. After all, we are an Open and Affirming Church. We have been welcoming LGBT folks at Edgewood for decades and engaging in advocacy, outreach and education on issues of LGBT inclusion since 1998. We said it every Sunday morning, as a matter of fact: "No matter who you are, or where you are on life's journey, you are welcome here."

So, I responded with ease and affirmed that our church was a safe, welcoming space for all people. The woman was not so easily pacified. "Well," she replied, "I went to your website, and although it says you are Open and

Affirming, it says nothing about transgender individuals. And the person I am speaking about is transgender."

Again, the answer was easy. Yes, we are welcoming of transgender people. Of course we are. Open and Affirming means we welcome LGBT folks. Doesn't it say that?

My answer was still not satisfactory. "It says in your Open and Affirming statement that you welcome people regardless of sexual orientation. It doesn't say anything about gender identity."

I tried again to argue, but the realization slowly began to dawn on me and a question crept into my consciousness. Were we really inclusive of transgender people? Did we really pay attention to the "T" in LGBT?

And so began a process of education, conversation and reflection within our church on transgender issues. In the three years following this phone conversation, I have learned a great deal, and the church has learned a great deal, and we have been greatly blessed in this process of creating and maintaining a safe space for transgender people at Edgewood church.

In March of 2009, shortly after this phone call challenged my assumptions about our congregation, we hosted a showing of the film, *Call Me Malcolm*, about a transgender minister, who is now ordained as a pastor within the United Church of Christ. This film offers reflections on what it means to be Christian and to be transgender, and the conversation afterwards affirmed the lack of education about transgender issues within our congregation. In fact, after the showing of this film, there was a great demand for more education, and more conversation, on transgender issues.

We scheduled a panel discussion as a follow-up that fall and began to discuss a language change in our Open and Affirming Covenant. It was generally agreed upon that we needed to include transgender and gender identity within our statement of welcome, but that there needed to be greater education leading up to this change. And so, in the fall of 2009, we hosted a panel discussion with two transgender people and one family member. The room was packed full of people from our congregation, and students from Michigan State University came as well. As the conversation progressed, there was laughter, beautiful stories and honest questions, and the atmosphere was one of interest, learning and solidarity. Soon after this panel discussion, we knew the church was ready for a change in language.

Our Open and Affirming Statement, which we passed in 1998, did not explicitly include transgender people, or include gender identity, within its statement of welcome and affirmation. At our annual meeting, in February of 2010, we presented this change to the congregation, in writing, to create an Open and Affirming Covenant Statement that reads as follows:

The Call: Guided by the love of Jesus Christ, Edgewood United Church seeks to be a community of healing, hope, and hospitality. We celebrate the diversity that God created and seek to reflect that diversity in our community of faith. In the Edgewood United Church Covenant Statement on Justice and Peace, we covenant "to conduct our common life in ways that reflect God's inclusiveness of people of all nationalities, races, ages, abilities, genders, gender identities, and sexual orientations." We believe we are called as disciples of Jesus Christ "to discover God's message by standing with the poor, the victims of injustice, and those on the margin of society."

In standing with those who have been marginalized because of sexual orientation or gender identity, we feel the need to speak and act with enhanced boldness as a congregation and to be more explicit in our inclusion of lesbian, gay, bisexual, and transgender people into the common life of our church. The Christian church has often judged and excluded lesbian, gay, bisexual, and transgender persons from the community of faith or has been complicit by its silence. These actions have served to justify, if not encourage, discrimination and violence against lesbian, gay, bisexual, and transgender people. It is time for Christians to declare that such practices are incompatible with the gospel of Jesus Christ.

"In standing with those who have been marginalized because of sexual orientation or gender identity, we feel the need to speak and act with enhanced boldness as a congregation and to be more explicit in our inclusion of lesbian, gay, bisexual, and transgender people into the common life of our church."

The Covenant: Therefore, in response to the call of the 1985 General Synod of the United Church of Christ, we declare ourselves an Open and Affirming congregation and we covenant anew:

To affirm that people of all nationalities, races, ages, abilities, genders, gender identities, marital statuses, and sexual orientations are embraced within the family of God and the fellowship of Edgewood United Church.

To honor, support and celebrate the partnerships and families of lesbian, gay, bisexual, and transgender people.

To encourage all persons to share their talents and energy in the worship, ministry, mission, educational programs, and leadership of Edgewood United Church.

Not to discriminate on the basis of race, gender, age, disability, sexual orientation, gender identity, nationality or marital status when hiring church staff and contracting for goods and services.

To condemn acts of homophobic violence, to confront the continuing injustice of institutional discrimination, and to advocate equal protection under the law for lesbian, gay, bisexual, and transgender people.

To empower the Church Council to establish a Task Force to work with the congregation and its boards and committees to implement the covenant statement in the life and ministry of Edgewood United Church.

On February 7, 2010, this new covenant was adopted by a unanimous vote, which maintained the language of the 1998 covenant, while explicitly speaking of transgender people and gender identity. However, we knew that changing the language certainly wasn't enough. In our discussions leading up to this language change, the congregation began to realize that while we were very comfortable advocating on issues affecting lesbian, gay and bisexual people, we lacked knowledge of transgender issues. And so, we continued to explore what kind of work we were called to do in order to live out our covenant on transgender issues.

Our Open and Affirming Task Force decided to create a survey to explore knowledge about, and understanding of, transgender issues. We spent a few months creating, distributing and compiling survey results, and they affirmed our theory that while the church was very well educated on issues affecting the lesbian, gay, and bisexual community, they felt a lack of education on transgender issues. In addition, there was concern within the congregation that we were not doing enough to minister to transgender people.

As the fall of 2010 approached, we decided to educate the congregation about Transgender Day of Remembrance, and we agreed to co-host a vigil with the transgender student group at Michigan State University. In preparation for this day, we spread fliers among the congregation, letting them know about the event, and about why we needed to honor Transgender Day of Remembrance. I was able to speak at the vigil, as did one of our other members. The event was moving, and heart-wrenching, as names were read, brutal deaths recalled, and the horror of discrimination and hatred revealed over and over again. It was a stark reminder that there is much work to be done to combat transphobia and that the church must be involved in addressing this violence and oppression.

By the beginning of 2011, we began to discuss a transgender connections group, and our desire to support transgender people within our community, by creating a safe space for conversation, fellowship and mutual support. The congregation connected with TransMichigan, and other churches in the area, to spread the word that we were in the process of forming this group.

At the Michigan Pride rally, which we have participated in for over 10 years, we spread the word about the formation of a transgender connections group. Over the summer, we continued to advertise, connect and make plans. By the fall, we were ready to begin. We now have a monthly meeting here at Edgewood, which is open to people in the community, for connection and conversation among people who are transgender.

We continued our annual observance of the Transgender Day of Remembrance this fall, as well, and recognize the need to continue in our education, welcome and advocacy for transgender people. The church itself has been blessed to welcome transgender members, and we are overjoyed to see the ways in which we are growing, learning and connecting. It is a blessing to be a part of a congregation that truly seeks to welcome, love and affirm all of God's children.

As a minister, I am often asked to speak about transgender issues and asked questions about how I reconcile my faith with my affirmation of transgender people. My response to this question is always the same. I don't know how I could reconcile my faith with not affirming transgender people. God created us, as we are, and God loves us, as we are. And so if I do not value God's creation, I am insulting God. Transgender people are God's creation, and if I do not value them, I am insulting God.

I will close with the words I spoke at the Transgender Day of Remembrance Vigil, in November of 2010:

I stand here as an ordained Christian minister, well aware of the violence that has been done in the name of Christ against transgender people. And on this day, where we remember those who have died because of this violence, because of the hatred that is sadly spewed from pulpits, I begin by sadly acknowledging the culpability of the Christian church in oppression, ostracism and silence in the face of suffering and violence.

Joelle Ruby Ryan writes, "I recognize that many conservative Christians believe the binary gender system [assumes that there are two and only two genders] to be God-ordained and biblically endorsed. I cannot believe, however, that any of them would endorse murder or suicide as justifiable means for protecting, enforcing or advancing that system. And yet those who speak for conservative Christians in America are largely silent on the matter of these deaths.

To those who are prone to these kinds of violent acts that silence implies that violence is indeed justified. To the young straight man who has discovered that a gay classmate has a crush on him, the church's silence says, 'It's okay to rough him up a little.' To a 12-year-old boy who has known all his short life that he needs to be a girl, the church's silence says, 'We'll all be better off if you'd just put the gun in your mouth and pull the trigger.' To the parents of a teenage girl who refuses to stop seeing her girlfriend, the church's silence says, 'Of course you're justified in kicking her out of the house and onto the street.' When the voice of moral authority refuses to speak, hatred and injustice hear all the permission they need to hear."

Truly, it is time to speak. On this day, when we hear about suicides, murders and hate crimes against people because of their gender identity, when we think of lives cut short through hateful, heinous violence, we know it is time to speak. We need to say, "No. Hatred and violence do not have permission to act in my name, or in the name of the God that I serve."

But not only this, I believe it needs to be taken a step further. As a Christian, I believe that we not only need to condemn the violence, we need to condemn any sort of theology that values one gender identity or one sexual orientation over another. We need to move far away from the notion of "tolerance" and towards the firm statement of affirmation. We do not tolerate one another; we tolerate headaches and traffic jams, we are not called to "tolerate" groups of human beings. No, we celebrate and affirm and honor one another. We celebrate and affirm and honor each human being as an image of God.

And so, I stand here as a Christian minister to say, "We celebrate and honor people of all nationalities, races, sexual orientations, gender identities, types of families, marital statuses, ages and abilities. Indeed, we are grateful for the diversity that God has created."

On this day, I pray for a celebration and an affirmation of every one of God's children. I am deeply grieved by the pain, suffering and death that has come as a result of the church's silence and complicity in violence against transgender people. But I stand here in hope, in hope for change, in hope for healing, in hope that we can truly create a world where all people are valued, honored and cherished as the sacred, beautiful, beloved human beings that they are. Thank you for being here and standing in that hope.

Shannon

"Hey, I Thought You Were Gay:"

On Supporting Our Loved Ones Without Giving Up Ourselves

Shannon Perez-Darby

Shannon lives a fabulously boring life reading, gardening, working with LGBT youth and supporting fat girl runners (herself included) in Seattle, Washington. For questions, comments or to find out just how fabulous she is, contact her at perezdarby@gmail.com

✶   ✶   ✶   ✶   ✶

He reaches down and grabs my hand and for a moment my heart skips a beat. I look around and wonder who is watching. It takes me a moment or two to realize that no one here is reading us as queer. Here, in this grocery store, we are a newly dating straight couple flirting in the aisles. I'm relieved and dumbfounded all at once.

I didn't really start dating until college, which was a result of not knowing how to express my queerness in my relatively small high school as well as generally being on the coy side when it comes to dating. When I finally figured out how to ask people on dates, I was fully engaged in my queer communities. I've mostly dated people who percieve me as queer. My own queer visibility has changed over time and is largely based on where I am, how long my hair is, what I'm wearing and who I'm with. All of that is to say that I've had plenty of practice in all sorts of spaces being seen as queer with queer lovers.

A number of years ago I started dating a wonderful guy. He is by no means the first trans person in my life, but he is the first trans guy I've dated who always passes as male. Our relationship is special in so many ways, not in the least because he's the first person I've really seen myself building a life with. What surprised me most when we first started dating was how easy it was. I'd spent so much time with previous lovers fighting battles, both big and small. Fighting about visibility, fighting about who we were out to and why, fighting about how others saw us both as individuals and as a couple. With this new sweetie there was none of that: we didn't fight about our identities, we didn't fight about visibility, we didn't fight about being out or not. The most surprising part was how weird it felt not to have to fight these daily battles, not the big fights, but the small ones so many of us are fighting to try and be seen as who we want to be. I didn't have to justify my femininity or queerness to him, we just went on dates and got to know each other. We talked about our childhoods and shared interests, and we laughed a lot. It wasn't until that day in the grocery store, when I even thought about how others saw us.

My sweetie and I have each had different versions of the same conversation. My version starts when I mention something about having a boyfriend. I see that confused look starting to form, the question on the tip of their tongues, "but I thought you were gay?" Now there are endless responses to this exclamation, and I usually pick and choose my responses based on how well I know the person and where we are at the moment. Often I respond, "Ya, I am queer and so is my boyfriend." Ninety percent of the time, that's the end of the conversation. I don't offer any more information and often people don't ask for it. The way I see it, it's not my job to "out" my sweetie as trans, the "we're both queer" response is, as far as I'm concerned, answering the question they've asked. What they are really saying is, "I'm reading you as a dyke (or you've told me you're queer), and now you're telling me you have a boyfriend and usually girls with boyfriends are straight so now I'm very confused." This interaction happens to me most often with people who identify as gay or lesbian. It used to break my heart when I would see that slight look of betrayal on their faces, like when they read me as a dyke I was on their team and now they clearly see that I've been fooling them this entire time and now don't know what to think.

That day in the grocery store was so stunning because it was so clear to me that others were not seeing me as I saw myself. As someone who is mixed-raced, I have a lot of practice being seen as different than I see myself. I am intimately familiar with what it is like to interpret the words and looks of others to try and make sense of the "me" they think they are seeing at any particular moment. What changed in that moment, holding the hand of my new date, was that this was something we were seen or not seen as together.

Relationships don't just happen to us, we choose them. The romance myth wants us to believe that it's magic, that the actions we take in relation to romance and desire are something that we have no control over. I have desires I don't act on, and desires I love to act on. I have desires that have faded away, and new desires I never saw coming. For me, there is no real or core desire, but an entire sea of desires that I wade through, which shift and change depending on my time and place.

I've been thinking a lot about whom I date, how I date and how this relates to the communities we create together. I've been with mostly trans guys for the last several years in part because as a queer girl doing intentional femininity that's who is available for me to date in my communities. Relationships exist in the context of other relationships. I'm not making these choices in a bubble. I make them based on my identities, community, who surrounds me, what my dating pool looks like and what society says I can and cannot do. There are patterns and maps in my sea of choices.

I'm femme and my femme identity is about a constructed, intentional queer femininity. For me it's about doing femininity wrong. It's about missteps. It's about constantly engaging with sexism. It's about deciding how I want to use my voice, and how I want to live and carving out the space to do that. It's about being feminine and visibly queer. My femme identity is inextricably and specifically linked to my identities as fat, mixed and Latina. My identity as femme is connected with all of my identities. As a fat woman, I do femininity wrong, my fat body means I will never do femininity like society wants me to. My Latina mother taught me a version of femininity that is definitely wrong. It's loud, bossy, wordy, brazen and super sassy. It's not taking any shit, and it's definitely frowned upon in so many of the spaces my mom and I spend so much time in.

In building community and allyship with other queers, I've seen so many wonderful and beautiful moments of love and support. I've also seen a lot of sad and difficult moments, moments where we stumble, where we are not our most fabulous selves, moments where we're fighting each other for resources and cutting one another down. I've seen a scarcity mentality that keeps us believing that there is only enough time, space, visibility, love and resources for some of us.

It's a set-up for everyone that socially acceptable masculinity relies on misogyny to maintain itself. If you're the wrong kind of guy then you're punished, you're called a fag or you're denied access to the boys' club. That's a big deal for most guys, particularly if you're told you'll never be a "real man," because you were born a girl. We think of men as people with cocks and only certain kinds of junk qualify as the right kind of cock (i.e. trans guys cocks aren't thought of as "real"). So what do you do if you're trying to construct a masculine identity for yourself, especially one that you're told you will never do right? Misogyny is a pretty quick and easy pass into the boys' club. Talking shit about women with other masculine folks helps to keep you in the boys' club, objectifying women helps, defining femininity as weak, stupid and less than helps. Cutting down other guys who are doing masculinity wrong also really helps. A great way to stay on the inside is to point out who is on the outside.

I get the shitty set-up that the trans guys in my life have, and I know how easy it is to access misogyny and I get why people do it. I think we can do better. When I'm thinking about how to support the trans guys and masculine genderqueer folks in my life what I really want to do is support them in creating alternative forms of masculinity. That means supporting folks when they chose not to create a masculine identity by cutting down femininity and doing what I can to reward intentional masculinities by acknowledging how awesome and hard that is. Part of supporting folks is also calling out when the guys in my life are complicit in misogyny. It means not standing by when anyone hates on women and femmes. It means not privileging masculinity. Sexism hurts everyone, and while sexism disproportionately affects women, men are not free from the harms of sexism. Sexism, like other forms of oppression, hurts privileged folks as well as marginalized folks because oppression stops everyone from being their most fabulous and full selves.

"When I'm thinking about how to support the trans guys and masculine genderqueer folks in my life what I really want to do is support them in creating alternative forms of masculinity."

It's important for me to call out transphobia and fight against gendered violence in all its forms. It's important to talk about health care and health insurance and the many ways that trans folks negotiate those systems. It's important to look at the rates of incarceration for trans folks, the way trans people's lives are criminalized for trying to live and survive the conditions of oppression. It's important to talk about all gender-segregated spaces and the policing of those spaces that means that every gender non-conforming person in my life (including me) from genderqueer folks, trans folks, boys who wear make-up and girls with short hair, have been policed in some way.

Everyone should care about this. I think it's important to have non-trans allies who are using their privileges to leverage space and to sit with other non-trans folks and have long tough conversations and to do this in a way that centers trans folks. That means having trans folks in decision-making places, checking in, asking when folks want to use their own voices and when they'd like you to step up. This is not a science. You will mess up. I mess this up all the time. The idea is to be engaged in the process and to understand that oppression is real, and in order to maintain itself it works really hard at convincing you that it doesn't really exist. Please see trans folks; know they exist, but also don't out trans folks, don't use trans folks as examples to prove whatever point about gender you're trying to make. Don't ask trans folks questions about their medical histories just like you wouldn't ask upon meeting me if I've had any surgeries lately. Check in about pronouns, allow space for movement but also for bottom lines. Listen to what people have to say. Be intentional. Being an ally isn't a goal we get to check off of our to-do lists, it's a process, much more about intention and engagement than perfection.

I want to be supporting the queer folks doing masculinity in my life but not disproportionately so and not at the expense of myself. Transitioning can be a pretty self-centered time, and rightfully so. It makes sense to focus a lot of energy on yourself when you're renegotiating social scripts and having shifting relationships with your body. I think people should have that time and space and we should honor that for folks. What I see happening with so many trans folks is that transitioning takes up their whole lives, it's all transition all the time. As transitioning takes up more space in people's lives, everything else takes up less space. Sometimes it feels it's like all we can talk about. I want people to have those spaces; I think it's really important to have peer groups and spaces to talk about things that are hard. I want to talk about people's experiences of their gender identities and expressions, just not all the time.

I've seen too many partners of trans folks who make themselves less in order to make the space for their partners to transition. I think people do this for so many reasons, either because they want to, we're told that's what good, supportive allies and partners do or because that's what we (queer and trans communities) expect them to do. I can think of so many times where I've seen the queers in my life fighting each other to be seen, competing and cutting each other down. Making ourselves less, so someone else can be more will never be the answer.

I don't know what the answer is. I come from queer and trans communities where there are many trans folks with as many different ways of expressing their genders as there are people to express them. In my early twenties, I dated someone who came out as trans shortly after we started dating. At the time, there were no lack of people in my life who were both trans and/or partners of trans folks. At the same time, I felt isolated and unsure where and how to talk about the stuff that came up for me. People looked to me for answers, as someone to give them cues about his name and pronoun preferences. That's not something I could offer them, not because I didn't know, but because it was in flux. For a long time there weren't pronouns and identities that were set in stone. There was fluidity and different spaces had different name and pronoun combinations. People wanted simple answers I couldn't give them. This is the set-up for partners of trans folks, that we expect them to offer us the answers, the clues to the identities of their partners with the hope of knowing how to proceed less awkwardly when it's our own uncomfortableness and gender shit that's really in the way. As someone who's committed to supporting trans folks, I think it is important to hold the space for other people's uneasiness. What I'm not willing to do is play into the game that says it's you or me; there is only enough space, time, energy and resources for one of us to get what we need.

I thought that being a trans ally meant supporting my partner no matter what. I had an overly simplified understanding of ally that was translated into "support at any cost." In trying to be a good ally I put too much of myself on the shelf. What I didn't understand at the time was that there was enough time, love and community support for both of us. I didn't understand that I wasn't supporting him by putting his needs above mine. The trick to allyship is balance; it's understanding systems of oppression and how they affect our everyday lives without setting up hierarchies of oppression. Allyship is about getting out of our heads and our highly developed politics and actually being with and seeing each other.

I'm not willing to let that scarcity mentality win anymore. Being a smart, sexy, feminist, queer femme is not an inherent contradiction with creating intentional (queer) masculinities that don't rely on sexism and misogyny. Everyone deserves to feel seen, and everyone deserves to feel supported. It's not an either/or. If we keep fighting amongst ourselves then we're not looking at and fighting sexism, homophobia, the prison industrial complex, transphobia, poverty, capitalism and all of the interconnected oppressions that affect our lives every day.

I'm happy to say that I'm battling less and less these days. I've simply had more time to sit with these questions and decide who I want to be in relation to them. In my life I don't feel like a spectacle, I see myself and my relationship reflected by those around me. My boyfriend is a feminist, and as I try to be a good ally to him, so too is he an amazing ally to me. When guys pull misogynist, sexist bullshit, he continually steps up and interrupts it. I can speak up for myself when that makes sense for me, but also I'm continually impressed with how he is there to speak up and call stuff out.

Because of this, sometimes he does masculinity wrong. One of the things that is most impressive in how my sweetie creates an intentional masculinity for himself is how firmly he sits in that identity. Being trans takes up a proportional amount of time and space in his life. I want him to have all of the space he needs to work out what visibility looks like for him, and I want him to talk about his trans identity as he needs to just as I want to talk with him about his work, friends, dog and anything else important in his life. He passes as male and passing is a tool that allows him to speak up, yet I've seen him time and time again refuse to engage in so many of the behaviors we think "real men" should do and still his masculinity is intact. That's pretty radical if you ask me.

I firmly believe that we can do this, as queer folks, as trans folks: as partners, friends, family and allies of trans folks. We can support each other and create the spaces to really see each other and get to be our whole selves. I am not doing this perfectly. We need more voices, more spaces to share and really be able to see each other. We need to have each other's backs and stop setting each other up for failure. I believe that we can support each other and hold our multiple identities together, not stacked in that hierarchy of oppression that messes us up every time, but woven together to honor how beautiful and complex we all are.

Soltahr

Community and Ceremony
Soltahr Tiv-Amanda

Soltahr holds a Master's degree in Transpersonal Counseling Psychology from Naropa University in Boulder, Colorado. She is currently in private therapeutic practice. She has published an article in the *Journal of Counseling and Development*, entitled "Compassionate Curiosity." She is one of the featured healers in a book released in 2001 by Carol Kronwitter entitled: *Women of Grace: Women Healers and Healing Practices* from D&S Publications. Currently Soltahr is preparing for the release of her own book entitled: *She of Many Colors*, chronicling her journey on the Goddess path.

For three years, I had the honor of facilitating a transgender support group in Boulder, Colorado. I "inherited" the group from Kim and kari (she always signed her name in small letters — I'm simply honoring that choice) who'd been running it successfully until then. When Kim asked me to take it on, I was actually sort of stunned, as a therapist I had been teaching multicultural graduate classes at Naropa for a few years and always made sure to include LGBTQ people into my course syllabi. However, I had no direct experience with the transgender population. I reluctantly agreed, only because I felt that I could learn something as well as be able to help a population I did not have much previous contact with.

It was easy for me to take over the group, as it was already up and running, and they had received a grant from Boulder's Community Foundation. Space for the group was given freely by the Safehouse Progressive Alliance for Non-Violence. We met each Monday evening.

The group members came from all walks of life, from a 16-year-old high school student to a retiree. Being representative of the larger population, folks came from all possible career areas you could imagine. We had a lawyer, a computer programmer, a self-employed craftsperson and many others. Because the group was an open group, each week was a different configuration, and drop-ins were always welcome. The array of situations that each individual brought gave the group wonderful color and spontaneous discussion.

To my surprise, the next three years that followed were some of the most amazing learning years of my life. Through self-education and open discussion, I learned all about the transition process that trans folks go through as they begin to live as the gender they wish to be. I also became familiar with and ultimately saddened and angered by the many maladies that trans folks face in the larger culture. Being a woman of color, I found it easy to relate to their struggles and felt glad that I was able to lend the support they needed. The group became a safe haven that they could come to, in attire they preferred, bringing their multitude of differences and stories from their lives.

As a therapist, during that time, my private practice also began to be filled with folks from the trans community. In this more intimate and confidential setting, I got to see the tears, the heartaches, as well as the joy they experienced as they moved closer to their true selves. I was continually astounded at the tenacity that folks displayed in moving toward their goals, as well as the courage beyond anything I've ever seen, to find money with which to attain surgeries that would complete the picture of who they knew themselves to be. I felt called to this population, honored that I could share in their journeys. Many spoke openly of the fact that, at the time, few therapists in the region were comfortable seeing transgender clients, and that only a couple of doctors would prescribe hormones.

One evening, we were graced by the presence of kari Edwards, the former group leader, writer and trans activist, who has since left this life. She said something that was for me a turning point in my understanding of this population. She was speaking about a memorial service she'd attended for a person who was trans who'd been killed because of this, in San Francisco. She said, "I was standing there at the candlelight vigil, and when I looked around me, I realized that there were hundreds of genders on display." This statement helped me to understand not only the complexity of this amazing group of folks, but gave me a deeper understanding of human beings in general. She brought light to the idea that we as humans indeed have a vast range of gender expressions, and what freedom there was in that idea!

Native Americans have always spoken of trans folks and the LGBT population as "Two Spirits" — they were seen as being very magical, in that they could see into what they saw as the polar opposite expressions of male and female — hence making them very special in their tribes — they were seen as the Shamans [spiritual leaders]. As Shamans, they have the capability to look into the realm of spirit to bring healing to their people.

It would be my understanding from my work with the trans population that this idea of magical beings has a great deal of truth to it. We as humans, in order to grow and develop, must ultimately embark on some sort of personal spiritual journey. When I ponder the notion of the "transition" that trans folks go into as they seek and eventually come to their truer self, I am struck at how similar this is to the Shamans' journey. There is a particular journey in Shamanism called "dismemberment," where one goes into shaman trance and visions one's physical dismemberment, all of the physical body is literally envisioned to be taken apart, piece-by-piece, by one's "power animal(s)" and other helpers. After the body is stripped down, there is a time of releasing disease, and anything that the body no longer needs. Then, the same helpers reassemble the body lovingly, leaving out what is no longer needed. Hence when the person re-enters life, they enter whole and healed.

"*I* was standing there at the candlelight vigil, and when I looked around me, I realized that there were hundreds of genders on display. This statement helped me to understand not only the complexity of this amazing group of folks, but gave me a deeper understanding of human beings in general."

I have actually often thought it important, given my spiritual orientation to see that trans folks are able to take part in various sorts of ceremonies along the journey to their "reassembled" selves if they choose that route. Ceremonies meant to acknowledge and honor the change that has taken place, as well as to honor and grieve what was lost. Then, to create a place of healing and renewal meant to help them to re-enter into life, strong and ready to be the new being that they have become.

Many trans folks make the transition with a minimal amount of help; yet, it is my belief that community support is crucial. Many, sadly, lose their mates, families and friends through the process. No one should have to go through this alone, and indeed, should have a number of support people to stand with them and to make sure that they always feel loved, accepted and cared for.

$$\star \quad \star \quad \star \quad \star \quad \star$$

I also had the pleasure for a few weeks, to facilitate a SOFFA group sponsored by the Boulder PFLAG group. Again, this was yet another amazing and wonderful experience as part of my connection with the trans community. There were parents, mates, other family members and friends present for this intensive group. I was so moved by the open hearts of these folks who so wanted to understand and get help with how to best support their trans loved one. There were so many tears shed, and in the safety of this grouping, anger, fear and deep sadness. Again, like the "dismemberment" journey, the person comes back changed and hence totally unlike whom they used to be. For the SOFFA's, this acceptance was often so very difficult for them — like most humans, they wanted things to remain the same, for their loved one to just be who they assumed they always were. I cannot, and will not say that all of these folks came to a place of total acceptance, yet, the fact that they were willing to show up, to explore options, to share feelings and stories spoke to their commitment to grow with their trans loved one.

I have to add here that for me personally, the journey alongside the folks in my group, in my practice and in the SOFFA group also changed me forever. I learned to go to deeper levels of compassion than I even knew to be possible. I came to understand and accept trans folks in ways I could not have predicted when I started the journey with them the night of the first group I facilitated. Sadly, along the way the journey has not always been easy for me. One of my trans clients committed suicide and a number of others have wrestled with similar feelings. Sometimes these moments make me question my work. What I do know is that working with a population that has a high rejection and suicide rate can be very difficult, but also very rewarding. From my interactions, I am confident that my work has helped many trans folk, but the loss of one life is still painful. Ultimately, I know that this was a choice made by an individual who was experiencing deep pain and loss. They had lost the love of a close family member, been rejected by someone they so desperately wanted in their life. Isn't that what we all want acceptance and love?

My last experience was wrapped up last evening (January 15, 2012) as I helped to facilitate the memorial service for a spiritual community member who had died of cancer on December 16th, 2011. I was struck at the amazing diversity of this Two Spirit community member, as friends and family spoke of her life. It was my honor to have been with her as she transitioned yet again out of this life. We created a ritual that honored her life, and it was such a powerful way to allow her friends, family and community to honor her life.

In conclusion, it is my honor to have worked with, and to continue to work with, the trans community. I have learned so much and grown so much as a therapist and group facilitator through the interactions we have had. It is my sincere contention that community and ceremony will come to serve trans folks as well as those of us who work with them, as we move forward into an evolving time in our world.

Peterson

Confessions of an Unlikely Ally
Peterson Toscano

Peterson is a theatrical performance activist using comedy and storytelling to address social justice concerns. He writes and performs plays that explore LGBTQ issues, sexism, racism, violence and gender. Peterson lives in Central Pennsylvania with his partner, Glen Retief.

★　★　★　★　★

I remember my first encounter with a trans person. I desperately desired to be the perfect Christian husband, to the extent that I spent 17 years and over $30,000 on three continents trying to de-gay myself. Yet at age 26 living in New York City, I struggled daily with temptation and an ever-growing gravitational pull towards anything queer. Still I insisted to myself, and to anyone who would listen, that God was turning me into a fully functioning heterosexual. To keep myself on the straight and narrow path, I steered clear of gay men, but my biggest temptation that year proved to be Rebecca. Six-feet three-inches tall with mini skirts that showcased legs that any Rockette would envy, Rebecca was an open and vocal M2F transgender person.

The alternative school where I taught had hired Rebecca to oversee all of our computers and the network. In my mind, and out loud to my students, I immediately denounced her as unacceptable and woefully misguided. According to my Evangelical [a Protestant Christian who believes that the Bible is literally true] mindset, I asserted that a man was a man — period — *God doesn't make mistakes.* Yet no matter how much I judged Rebecca as a deluded sinner, I found reasons every day to hover near her workspace before I guiltily dashed back to my classroom. I eventually spoke with her, first to ask for paperclips, then computer advice and ultimately her story.

I fell hard for Rebecca, not sexually, she presented far too successfully as female to stir my gay desires. I lusted instead after her authenticity and her audacious freedom. She represented a liberated queer, something that lured me and repelled me at the same time. I liked Rebecca, her geeky humor, her willingness to launch into the Time Warp dance as a Friday afternoon celebration ritual and her charm. I also hated Rebecca because she stood as a threat powerful enough to bust me out of my straight jacket.

Throughout that summer with our relaxed schedule, I began to feel comfortable around Rebecca, and every day went out of my way to chat with her, yet I worried that my resolve to be straight was beginning to erode. In July during my lunch breaks, I started to peruse men's fitness magazines on the nearby newsstands. By August I began to buy gay porn during my lunch hour, then in a fit of frustrated repentance, I threw it away before leaving work only to repeat the cycle again the next day. I asserted to myself that it was wrong to be gay no matter how much I wanted it and began to look for influences in my life that might be undermining my resolve to destroy the gay in me. By the time autumn came, I ramped up my involvement in church and started to pull back from visits with Rebecca. Ultimately I informed her that she was going to hell. She told me to go f**k myself.

At age 34, after many bizarre failed attempts to de-gay myself, I finally came to my senses and subsequently came out as gay. I then saw my rejection of all things queer begin to fade. The more at peace I felt with myself, the more I opened up to others around me. My self-acceptance created the necessary conditions to turn me into an ally of fellow queer folks, particularly transgender people, but this gradual transformation required essential specific steps.

I eventually left the Evangelical Church and four years after I had come out, I attended a lesbian, gay, bisexual and transgender gathering, Queer Quakers, the Religious Society of Friends. Although I had been to other LGBTQ events, this one was the first queer gathering I attended that actually included active participation of and leadership from transgender people. Up until then I had seen the T in LGBT as simply an accessory, a token gesture without any real representation. This three-day event included a variety of trans men, trans women and genderqueer folks with plenty of time for us all to hang out together. We chatted, shared meals, attended workshops, slept in bunk beds 10 to a room, sat in silent worship and then joined in spirited discussions.

This proved the first and perhaps most essential step in my journey to becoming a trans ally, the power of friendship and simply spending extended time with transgender people. In that gathering I heard stories I had never heard before: about transition, horrendous medical care, self-discovery, loss and great gain. I also heard familiar stories about identity, coming out, the challenges of romance and the complicated roles that non-LGBT families play in queer lives. I left that weekend with personal knowledge of some transgender people from varying backgrounds and identities. Assumptions and misconceptions challenged, I saw these trans folks in a new light, and then over the next few years met up with them again and again at gatherings, in their local Quaker meetings and in their homes.

The next step, like the first, was not intentional and did not feel like a step at all. Passion has its own choreography and offers its own deep lessons. I met a man: sweet, smart, secure and oh so sexy. Ivan with his sinewy body and facial scruff oozed my ideals of masculine sensuality. We spent time sharing our stories, my struggles to accept my gay side and his struggles in a world that insisted that he must be female because he was female-bodied. Ivan overcame cruel church oppression that declared he was a deformed human and a threat to others and came out the other end a self-made man still in physical transition. We talked and talked and then simply held each other. I felt the weight of Ivan's body on mine as we intertwined limbs. We kissed, and then with our hands and our kisses we explored each other's bodies, speaking through the physical journey, revealing to each other our f**ked-up body image issues. I told him how I never liked my body, that to me it always seemed too short, too fat and too flabby, that the reflection I stared at in the bathroom never mirrored the one I saw inside me. He told me he understood completely. On a twin-size bed in the bright morning sun, we exposed our bodies to each other, stripping away the covers, the clothing and the jokes we told to mask our fear and shame. We then made love, embracing the person in the body as we delighted in each other's touch, all the more precious because of the hell we knew the other had endured. It was the most satisfying sex I had ever experienced. Thoughtfully and intentionally, we gave each other pleasure without rushing, knowing we explored unchartered territory, and that at any moment either one of us could do or say something to spook the other.

Because of geography and other relationship commitments, we never became partners, but we have remained close, regularly checking in with each other. When I think of Ivan, I smile and feel joy inside. I have a connection with him that I believe will hold for the rest of my life, a tender sense of belonging and responsibility. He is not just another person in the world or even simply a friend: we are now kin. I carry part of Ivan with me, and I imagine he carries a part of me with him. It sounds trite and disrespectful to me to state that loving Ivan helped make me a better trans ally. Yet I recognize that my connection with him has had a web-like effect in connecting me to so many other trans people. My love for him has multiplied.

In addition to the sex we shared, Ivan and I spent many hours talking and listening to each other. I learned from Ivan about some trans men's experiences. Listening has proved vital to the process of becoming an ally. Regardless of the group or individual a perspective ally approaches; we often come with ignorance and misinformation. We need re-education. The greatest tool we possess and the greatest gift we offer is the ability and willingness to listen.

My intimacy with Ivan and the growing friendships with other trans folks stirred in me a desire to know more. As we would say in my Quaker circles, I felt a leading. Informally I began researching transgender lives. I sat, listened, asked questions and soaked in their stories. Based on suggestions from various trans people and allies, I read books and watched films highlighting transgender experiences.

"The most painful and humbling part of being an ally comes when I make mistakes. No matter how much I care about transgender people and how informed I become, I will at times get it wrong."

About this same time, I began doing formal research into gender variance in the Bible, a topic that captured my attention and stoked my imagination. I discovered that the most important people in the most important Bible stories transgress and transcend gender. Fusing the stories I absorbed from the trans people I met with these Biblical narratives, I created a one-person play called *Transfigurations — Transgressing Gender in the Bible*. In it I play multiple characters and multiple genders, highlighting the diversity of gender expression and identity. To my great surprise, trans and non-trans atheists and believers have responded well to the presentation, perhaps because it has little to do with religion and much more to do with authentic human experiences of discovering and asserting the self often in spite of great pressure to conform to society's demands.

As I began to perform my play, I met trans people throughout North America, Europe and Africa. We found each other through the internet, mutual friends, and as we presented jointly at conferences then spent hours talking about issues that moved us. Out of these conversations, working partnerships and projects have formed. For instance, I met Mila and Jayna Palvin through their popular *Trans-Ponder Podcast*. They affirmed to me and their audience the importance of my *Transfigurations* performance work. Skilled artists, they have begun the process of transforming my play into a graphic novel so that it can reach as many people as possible. Mila, Jayna and I have spent hours together chatting online and on the phone, hanging out in their home sharing our favorite snacks, partying at conferences, goofing around with audio recordings and developing creative ways to communicate. Through the mutual trust we have built, we have also joined forces to take on injustices towards trans people we have witnessed perpetuated by cisgender gay men. The executive director of an international LGBT organization in Philadelphia, in response to the violent murder of a gender non-conforming, gay-identified man, decided to hold a vigil the same night as the Transgender Day of Remembrance. Jayna, Mila and I connected with others horrified by this thoughtlessness, and through blogs, podcasts and direct contact with leaders, highlighted the offensive and unjust act while we deepened the public discourse. As a result, we have formed a team that seeks to use art, humor, the internet and partnerships with still others to address oppression within our communities while helping people in the process of becoming active and engaged allies.

The most painful and humbling part of being an ally comes when I make mistakes. No matter how much I care about transgender people and how informed I become, I will at times get it wrong. With more and more opportunities to speak with other cisgender folks through my stage work, lectures and in the media, I have asked Mila, Jayna, Chris Paige, Michael Eric Brown, Allyson Robinson, Ethan St. Pierre, Autumn Sandeen, Diane Lombardi and other trans people who know my work, to call me out when I unwittingly say or do something that is inaccurate, unhelpful or offensive. I trust their honesty and helpful critique. Still it hurts when I learn I messed up. I feel aggrieved, defensive and embarrassed. It smarts to see that my good intentions alone are not good enough to ensure I will do good. It especially pains me when I see that my intentions are not always pure. Confronted with my limitations and missteps as an ally, I have needed to cultivate a graceful resilience as I tell myself, "Of course you will screw up some times." I remind myself that I need to listen more, learn more and stay in partnership with my fellow activists. In the midst of listening though, I cannot be guided solely by others and their opinions. I also need to listen to my own inner voice. Then after considering multiple views, I can make informed choices.

$\star$ $\star$ $\star$ $\star$ $\star$

Earlier in my life I tried to be the perfect Christian husband. I embarked on what I believed to be a righteous mission to annihilate anything queer in me and in the world around me. Thank goodness I failed miserably. My pursuit for perfection harmed others, exhausted me and wasted a lot of time; I do not want to repeat that madness again. Today I have a new mission — this time to understand transgender lives and experiences, to work with trans folks and allies for equal rights and access and to foster greater understanding in other non-trans folks. Important work indeed, but for me it does not feel like a chore. I see that my role as an ally arises out of friendship, partnership and love. Also, being an ally has its own rewards. The people I have met and their stories have enriched my life. I also hold onto a special hope that one day through my travels I will run into my former co-worker, Rebecca, and get the chance to sing out, "Let's do the Time Warp again."

"Portrait #30" by Autumn Yamamoto © 2012

Autumn

The Problem of Being Earnest
Autumn Yamamoto

Autumn was born in Los Angeles, California. Among other things, she is a self-described Blackanese (Black and Japanese) nerd, poet and spoken-word artist. Currently, Autumn is a dual masters degree student of Clinical Social Work and Human Sexuality Education at Widener University in Chester, Pennsylvania. An academic nomad at heart and avid people collector, she has lived in many places across the world and befriended people from all walks of life. She often contemplates the complexities of donning various identities in a society that both loves and loathes being true to oneself.

☆　☆　☆　☆　☆

If I have learned anything from being true to myself and being friends with someone who is transgender is that identity is a funny and complicated thing, particularly in America. Many people in America would like to think that America is a very individualistic society, but I think at times we are far less accepting of individualism than is thought. It is a weird juxtaposition of being so individualistic yet also suffering from groupthink. Many would like to define what is "normal" and what are deviations from that norm. Yet people like to take it upon themselves, as a collective at times, to define what normal is. What it looks like, who is in and who is out, who is considered real and who is not. Unfortunately, to me, this just leads to all sorts of misunderstandings and arrogance. Misunderstanding of what it means to be real, to be normal, to be true to oneself. And arrogance as to thinking one knows how to conceptualize it.

From a young age one grows up with the notion of normality and honesty. "Be yourself." "Be true to yourself." "Keep it real." "To each their own." All of these slogans and clichéd phrases remind us to just be honest with ourselves and honest with others. There is wisdom in those words of simply being earnest. But there is folly that follows since people are left to their own devices and those devices are clouded by one's own personal experiences, biases and prejudgments.

And therein lays the problem of being earnest.

If there is one thing I have thought about for a long time, it is the capacity one might have of fluidity of identity. The question of who am I is a central life theme. To some degree we all want to be accepted. My friend and I want to be embraced as people who are worthy of love and acceptance. We all want to be loved and accepted for who we are by someone or at the very least by our own selves. As individualistic as one would like to believe one is, we inevitably gravitate to being part of something more than ourselves. I have experienced this very same conundrum that attempting to self-identify presents. I have felt a part of something yet apart from that same something.

Here are some of my identities. I am: Black, Japanese, mixer, daughter, sister, friend, lover, a Libran, Pagan (not Wiccan), goth-lite, nerd, sex geek, goofball, woman, cisgender, heterosexual and ally. I enjoy a bit of identity fluidity as much as I can be restricted by these identities. There is a multitude of privileges and oppressions that comes along with trying to be earnest with my identities and myself. I used to joke in sardonic fashion that being Black, Japanese, Pagan and female opens me up to being lynched, interned, burned or raped. Harshly put I know. Nevertheless some truth to it, since society's tree bears strange fruits.

$$\star \quad \star \quad \star \quad \star \quad \star$$

Part of the privilege of my identities is that I do not often get questioned whether or not I am and always have been a woman. Most people assume correctly that I am a heterosexual woman. I get to try on various hats without being too bogged down by intrusive and sometimes ultimately offensive questioning as to just who I am. Moreover, even with the large potential for assumptions, most of these assumptions appear benign in nature. I do not often worry if harm will come to me if I seemingly fit into someone's assumption about me, especially if it matches. For instance, if someone assumes I am a heterosexually-identified woman, and I do not present in any other fashion to negate this assumption, I am largely left alone to my own devices. Yet, if I were not to present or match up to someone's assumption of my person, then I could be rendered vulnerable to personal attack. My friend who is a transboi (also known as a trans boy or man) is not allowed this same privilege all the time. If his personhood does not match up to someone's expectation he is vulnerable to personal attack. This has sometimes worried me and made me pray to the gods and goddesses for his and his family's safety.

As a collective, many of us are ignorant. Now, this does not have to be pejorative in nature. Honestly, with ignorance comes not bliss but the opportunity to learn. To grow. Ignorance simply means to be uneducated or unaware of something. So within this context it means we can learn from each other if we are willing. Unfortunately it is this willingness to learn from each other that makes being earnest with ourselves and others difficult. Piaget, a Swiss psychologist known for his theories on the cognitive development of children, spoke about a sort of cognitive dissonance experienced when something we know to be true (more like hold to be true and normal) is confronted and challenged by something that does not fit into a neat little box. And face it, I and others, like things to make sense, to fit into a neat little box. Even though some people strive to not conform to categorization, the trap has already been set, because sometimes in one's attempt to not conform one conforms. Seems nonsensical I know. But think of it. If a person belonging to a nonconformist identity branches from that said apparent non-identity they risk being ostracized, ridiculed or at the very least, questioned by potential peers.

It is at those moments that identities become tricky. From personal experiences and vicariously, I know how muddy the waters get when identity is not allowed any flexibility. Being someone who is racially ambiguous, people try even harder to fit me in a nice little bento box of identities, and if unsuccessful, I am just written off. I am both Black and Japanese and my acceptance in these communities varies with time, individuals or groups and how I present to others. I am both a part of these communities, yet set apart from these communities that are so integral to me. I sometimes wonder if that is how my friend or other people who are trans feel. Feeling a part of the gender they identify as and yet not a part of it, because of the potential non-acceptance from the community when deviating from what is expected.

I think that is why I simply accepted whichever identity my friend, who happens to be a transgender male, adopted at various transitions in our lives. Wanting to be accepted as whoever I was at any given time with little to no guff about it, I felt like it was just elementary logic to treat others the same way. To give a little more background, I met my friend more than 15 years ago when I first moved to Colorado from Los Angeles, California. When we met he was biologically female with long blond hair, a bit mischievous, and best friends with another crazy/sexy/cool gal. Those two were who helped me have a life in high school.

Eventually, my friend began using terms such as *gender dysphoria* to describe what he was feeling about being male, although born female. As odd to others as it may seem, I did not question him in what this all means as he explained it. I just knew that he was still my friend and what is the de/construction of gender identity to do with that fact? So another transition began as one of my best gal pals became one of my best homebois (also known as homeboys). However, even though I was not concerned about what I would think, say or do with regards to our friendship, I often was concerned about what others might think, say or do when he was earnest with them about who he was.

I recall the time he spent in the Virgin Islands doing work with risk-reduction of Sexually Transmitted Diseases and Infections (STD/Is) and HIV/AIDS transmission in the islands. I am open to embrace his or anyone's identity(ies), not everyone is like that, and this sometimes becomes more apparent in communities of color. Or perhaps, it becomes more apparent to me, because of my own personal biases of being part of the communities and knowing what it feels like to be different than the collective. That is where some of those feelings of oppression can intermingle with the privileges one is granted, given any identity one carries.

Within various communities of color, historically and presently, many of us are not allowed the same privilege and unfettered access to adopt a myriad of identities that we choose but instead are sometimes imposed on us. I have learned in classes teaching future social workers and counselors that one should speak of their own experience and not speak for others. Although that can be the ideal and is often wise, it is not always possible or supportive. Many people of color and marginalized "others" sometimes share a sense of responsibility and kindred spirit with each other that has helped us through trials and tribulations. Thus, although many people of color may often identify in the singular there is an undercurrent of the shared experiences and feelings being Black, Asian, Latino, Indigenous brings. Black/Yellow/Brown/Red pride speaks to this thread that binds us as individuals.

"*People* are sometimes not willing to accept someone without condition, because to do so means that at some time one will have to turn inward and accept themselves without condition."

Unfortunately as this thread binds us to make us stronger, it has sometimes invoked a feeling of "us" against "them," with the "them" being thought of being equated with Whiteness. For instance, being anything that might go against what some think of what it means to be Black just makes you White or an Oreo: Black on the outside but White on the inside. I have dealt with this for most of my life and will continue to deal with this tug of war of what my and others' identities mean to myself and others. I have often been called out as sort of a traitor to my people as I befriend people considered to be brainwashed by White society and culture or being friends with ole Whitey in the first place. Identifying as gay, queer, lesbian, homosexual, transgender, gender variant, genderqueer, etc. is sometimes equal to burning up one's "Colored" card, committing cultural genocide and joining the ranks of and becoming White.

To be honest, this fear and suspicion is not entirely unfounded. People of color have often suffered at the hands of a culture and society that did not entirely understand or accept them and wanted to ultimately wipe out their culture through indoctrination and subjugation. So I get it. Blame it on my quintessential Libran qualities that like to play both Angel and Devil's advocate, but I understand the fears and contempt of some communities of color. Does not excuse the prejudice or hatred of people no matter one's cultural or ethnic identity, but I get it. People are sometimes not willing to accept someone without condition, because to do so means that at some time one will have to turn inward and accept themselves without condition. This ultimately could mean taking an in-depth look at our own negative qualities, prejudices, biases, judgments, flaws. In turn, being introspective wields the potential for learning to forgive, love and gain increased knowledge of ourselves and others, breeding self-acceptance. But self-acceptance proves even more elusive than acceptance by others oftentimes. In those thoughts I am reminded of Kurt Vonnegut Jr.'s *Mother Night* in which the main character concludes that sometimes people hate so much that they want their god/religion to hate as much as they do.

It has sometimes proven extremely difficult and emotionally disruptive to follow my own lofty ideals. Being friends and an ally to people within the transgender community and queer community has meant to sometimes be perceived as being Eurocentric or not *really* being Black/Asian. Consequently being friends and an ally has afforded me an opportunity to plant the seed of acceptance in others. I have had many heated conversations and encounters with others who were not entirely accepting of variant peoples — whether variant in gender, sexual orientation, religion and more — with open arms. Upon respectfully challenging a person's concept of what is acceptable and unacceptable, normal and abnormal, change or expansion of someone's "truth" is possible. Sometimes people being confronted with this cognitive dissonance and resistance experience an opening up to the beginnings of trying to understand and embrace another perspective and identity. This does not mean one will start going to pride fests of any kind or even fully accept variant identities, but sometimes one cannot help but question what they already knew when encountering the unknown and being introduced to the once feared and dreaded mysterious. At times it is much harder to hate or be intolerant of someone with whom you find yourself up close and personal and not among the masses.

Creating opportunities to break down a bit of what someone knows by constructing and incorporating new knowledge. Essentially, infusing the person with a desire to know and learn. Which is why I continue to make an effort to speak patiently and with positive regard for someone who is only speaking from their truth whether I agree with it or not. I believe promoting this disequilibrated state in a people of color from a place of respect, love and acceptance would help bridge the gaps these communities and sexually and gender variant communities exist in. I was afforded the privilege of wanting to accept people like my friend and others as they and I come, because of my own desire and experience of acceptance of me and my kin.

Ultimately, we all seek in conscious and unconscious manners to be loved and accepted. Someday hopefully, person-by-person, and community-by-community the problem of being earnest will not be such a problem. People like me; my friend and other people who supposedly deviate from what some consider the norm can be accepted as just a person. Language becomes more inclusive and less constrictive to recognize and sit in comfort with the idiosyncrasies, oxymorons, paradoxes and contradictions life and its inhabitants may involve.

"Portrait #4" by Autumn Yamamoto © 2012

"*I* started telling family close to me: my mother, father, brother, a few cousins, my pastor and one person at school. I received so much support, but some disheartening issues too. I believe it is just as much about transitioning for family and friends as it is for someone who is transgender."

—Elijah Henry Burton, husband, father, and F2M

TRANSGENDER PEOPLE

Transgender Persons

As Billie Jean King noted, "Everyone has people in their lives who are gay, lesbian or transgender or bisexual. They may not want to admit it, but I guarantee they know somebody." We all have been touched or will be touched by the transition of a transgender person. Perhaps this person is a child, parent, sibling, significant other or friend, or maybe this person is on TV or in our local newspaper. Our journeys as humans are infinitely different and yet quite similar. We are all looking for acceptance and love, from those whom we have chosen to share our lives with. Because we have focused on Trans-Kin, not transgender people, in this book, this is the smallest section. There are many resources where the curious can learn more about the trans experience (Transgender Recommendations in the Book List in the appendix, for instance). Still we think it is important for Trans-Kin to hear a sample of experiences from transgender people about their experiences with SOFFAs.

Our collection of voices begins with a personal perspective from a Two Spirit Indigenous American (Little Bear) who discusses identity, performance and spirituality in relation to one's community. From a transgender perspective, one of the authors (Beemyn) suggests how to be an ally. The rest of the section deals more concretely with relationships between trans people and their significant others, parents, siblings, friends and allies. Some common themes mentioned in this section include: how SOFFAs transition as their trans loved ones transition (Burton), how the transition of a loved one ripples through SOFFA relationships in both challenging and beautiful ways (Alyson), our desire to be loved regardless of our transgender status (Hayward, Palermo) and the importance of community (Diamond). These themes extend beyond our relationships with transgender individuals into our understandings of ourselves and our own personal and psychological needs. In all of these themes, we see a desire to be recognized, respected and loved, a shared desire among transgender and non-transgender people alike.

"Untitled" by Jonas Jaeger © 2012

FAQ

Q. Will my family and friends be as supportive as the people who wrote in this book?

A. We don't know, but we certainly hope so. Every family, every friend is different. What we do know is that the more comfortable you are with your gender identity, the more comfortable other people in your life will be. Seek professional help if you need to, encourage your family and friends to seek help if they need to, but most importantly give it some time. You probably have known you were "different" all your life, and if you are transitioning, it will probably take several years. So don't expect the people in your life to change any more quickly than you have. Have patience, as often the first response is seldom the last.

Q. How do I know if I am transgender?

A. This is a difficult question to answer. The best thing you can do is to seek resources, try a support group or talk with a professional or friend. Ultimately, be gentle with yourself and take the necessary time to explore your own identity. You do not need to figure it out instantly.

Q. Somewhere I heard that there are trans people in other cultures. Is this true?

A. Absolutely. There have been people who transgress and transcend gender in every society and in every historical time. In our early history and in many places still today, trans people are shamans or considered holy members of their communities. In India, for example, hijras are usually physiologically male, but with feminine attributes. Culturally, they are often considered to be a third sex. Check out the reading list for books that will give you more information.

Cody

Two Spirited
Cody Little Bear
Interviewed by Cameron T. Whitley

Cody is a 32-year-old scholar and spiritual explorer. Cody is Mexican-American and Hopi Indian and identifies as Two Spirit (as both gender identity and sexual orientation). Cody has spent countless hours working with underserved populations including GLBT youth, the gender variant community and people of color. Cody is also a seasoned drag performer and has performed in over 250 shows during the last 14 years.

How would you describe your gender journey?

It has been both exciting and fabulous, while at the same time completely turbulent and heart breaking. My path to true authenticity is an incredible ever-evolving adventure that has been filled with both the best and most difficult times in my life...and it has been worth every moment.

How do you identify now?

At this point in my journey, I have really pulled away from labels for the most part. I see myself as a spiritual being that is having a human experience, and my human experience requires me to have some sort of gender identity. The only label I really identify with these days is "Two Spirit." This identity reflects my gender as a spiritual path and is part of my culture and heritage. Aside from all of this, I also identify as a drag performer. I use the term "performer" instead of "king" or "queen." To me, drag simply means, "performing gender," and my drag is all over the gender spectrum.

Can you talk more about your drag performance? Specifically, how long have you being performing? Has your family seen you perform? If so, how do they feel about your identity as a drag performer?

I performed in my first drag show during my senior year of high school in 1998 and haven't stopped since. My family is very supportive of my connection to the drag community and has seen both my friends and I on the stage on numerous occasions. Although issues related to gender identity sometimes make my parents uncomfortable, they are always very supportive of my drag identity. One of the most legendary drag queens in Denver is my mother's cousin, so the drag world is very accepted in my family. I think it is seen as entertainment more than anything else, which makes it safe on many levels.

How has your family been supportive of your Two Spirit identity?

They have been supportive, but not always in a direct way. My mom and I have been able to talk about my identity and she supports me as being Two-Spirit. In regards to my dad and extended family, we simply don't talk about it. They know that I am different, but it isn't something that is talked about. They take me as I am, but we don't have a lot of big discussions about it. I think a lot of this stems from the stoicism within our culture. Overall, I have been given the impression that to live as Two Spirit is fine, but to medically transition would mean sacrificing something about myself that was sacred and that would not be okay.

How does your Two Spirit identity fit with your culture/ heritage/race, etc.?

I think the most difficult thing for me is that I don't particularly fit in a binary black and white world (or Western society). My gender is both female and male. I am a person of color, but my skin is pale white. Sometimes I don't feel like I fit anywhere. I wrote a poem about this that was published in my school's literary journal last year (Cody's poem, entitled *It*, follows).

Have you found that your gender identity has changed throughout your life?

My identity has changed a great deal in my life. When I was a teenager my gender was simply fluid and I didn't think too much about it. As I grew into an adult I felt extremely pressured to conform to society's ideas of gender, to be either male or female. This eventually led me to have a strong transgender identity and to consider transitioning to be male. Although this initially seemed like a good fit, I began to feel a bit lost in this identity too. To medically transition meant denying a part of myself that was spiritually sacred and having the gift of living a life of both male and female experience. These days my gender and sexuality are completely fluid. It took a really long time for me to understand and accept this.

Where have you found support for your identity?

I have found support, but ironically not in the places I would have ever thought it would be from. My greatest support has come from my friends who are "camp drag" queens. Most of them are gay "bears" and identify on the butch/masculine side of the gay spectrum. When they perform drag, they do so by putting glitter in their beards and facial hair — and letting their chest and body hair show. This type of drag performance often counters what 'traditional' drag is. I have even heard some people say that this type of drag is transphobic, but I don't see it that way at all. It is another way of expressing gender, of expressing gender in a drag performance. They are simply performing gender and embracing it in their own way. I have not met many other Two Spirit people, and even when I do, I don't necessary feel as if I belong. My skin is light, and some assume that because of this fact I do not have the validity to refer to myself as Two Spirit, what they fail to see in my skin color is my heritage. My drag family is really the only place where I ever feel like I belong.

Have you found support in the transgender community? If not, why?

The short answer is no, although at another point in my journey I might have answered a bit differently. When I first started spending time in the transgender community, it felt like being "home" and being free to be myself. The more time I spent in the community, the support I had once had began to feel like pressure. According to others, I wasn't presenting masculine enough. I wasn't "really trans" because I wasn't on hormones and had never had any surgeries. My effeminate mannerisms made many of the straight F2Ms in community uncomfortable — and I was ridiculed for identifying as "mostly gay" and dating gay men. At one point, a well-known transgender woman in my community encouraged me to moderate a speaker's panel series we were presenting instead of speaking on it. She said that "my identity as Two Spirit/transgender was too confusing for people," and that it took away legitimacy for "real trans people." I can't tell you how painful this was coming from 'my' own community.

I helped start a transgender program at my local GLBT community center and devoted countless hours, time and money for over a year to help get the program started. I was bullied out of the program that I helped create. Largely this was the result of me not 'medically' transitioning. Other transgender people stigmatized my journey, as someone who does not identify distinctly as male or female. Eventually, I left the community, because I could no longer take the bullying and pressure to medically transition. In doing so I was left with little to no community resources. Even when my former partner, a transgender woman in our community, committed suicide last May, I was essentially blacklisted and left to deal with the loss on my own. Trying to fit in the heteronormative boxes of gender and identity were always difficult, but finding a home in the trans community was even more difficult. It will never stop being part of who I am. I can't help that. I just wish I wasn't the bastard child.

Can you talk about how your family has reacted to your journey?

I am extremely close to my family, and they mean everything to me. In my traditionally stoic Mexican-American family, we don't talk about feelings or emotions much until they get to a point that they boiling over. (Incidentally, this way of living is what made me want to go into the field of psychology and counseling.) My only sibling, my older brother, is 12 years older than me. He came out as gay at 18, and this was an extremely difficult time for my family (what I remember of it). Although I was a complete tomboy and never encouraged to be "girly" (my mom was a tomboy, too), there was a lot of pressure to be the "normal kid." During my teen years I came out as "gay," although for me it was 85 percent gender identity and 15 percent liking female-bodied people. This would all get figured out later in my life. These days my parents are both extremely supportive of my brother and myself. My parents aren't bothered by my gender presentation, but I know they wouldn't be thrilled if I chose to medically transition. To do so would go against what makes me special — being "Two Spirit." Ironically, I also have some major health issues, which makes medical transitioning impossible.

You have a long history with being involved in GLBT community outreach, development and action. What would you like to see from the community? What could the GLBT community do better in terms of supporting transgender/gender

variant/gender creative persons and their significant others, family members, friends and allies?

This is a question I have asked myself many times, and honestly the answer is quite simple. Love one another. Do not judge. Embrace all people and know that we are all unique and special beings. Don't segregate or create a hierarchy of gender. Honestly, I think gay, lesbian and bisexual people are making great strides in embracing the transgender community. I think it is often the trans community that wants to discard those who do not fit within binary constraints. We are all beautiful and fabulous.

It
Cody Little Bear

White skin, Brown heart

Female body, Boy soul

Childlike smile, Jaded quintessence

Lover, Fighter

Gay, Straight, Everything-in-Betweener

Spiritual, Non-Believer

Fiercely unique, Painfully ordinary

Passionately Apathetic.

Two Spirits, One Body

Sacred, yet Meaningless

Fitting everywhere, Belonging nowhere

Everything, Nothing

Never existing in black, white or Technicolor

Only gray.

Never home, Always visiting

Concrete Contradiction.

It.

"Hilary" by Hilary Brenneman © 2012

"Jayne" by Kai Tierney © 2012

Growing Into Your SOFFAs
Jayne Alyson

Jayne is a full-time artist and sometimes writer. She has been taking her best shot at happily-ever-after since early 2004.

I don't always have the greatest memory. I don't remember names or faces very well. Sometimes, I forget sequences of events, what state/city/country I was in when something happened, or who was there.

I don't remember exactly where I was when I made the call but I remember staring at the phone being terrified. I mean, really terrified, knowing I was about to change my relationship with my mother forever. I remember the emotions like a picture. Even thinking about it eight years later, I can remember — I can feel — the pounding pulse and shallow breaths as I held that shitty, Nokia phone in my hand.

I like to think of myself as independent. I was raised to make my own decisions and to do things for myself. I had done all the planning and preparation for my transition, by and large, by myself. And until I came out to my mother, my transition hadn't really affected anyone else.

I mean, I had come out to friends and some of the people around me. They were important to me, but I had just moved; started from scratch. I could have found new friends. New mothers are harder to find.

After a few deep breaths and some hand trembling, I managed to call my mom. It's not exactly the first bit of news you want to start a conversation with, but if you wait too long you'll never get it out. If you get too deep into a normal conversation, you can become paralyzed by nostalgia for something you haven't even lost yet.

So, I blurted it out.

Silence.

It's hard news to take. I get that. I really do. I had had 23 years to come to terms with my gender identity. I had been researching it in books and later on the internet for most of my life, desperately trying to understand who I was and why I felt the way I did, and still, I could barely come to terms with the fact that I was transsexual. How was my mom supposed to take that all in, in just a few moments?

As much as I was terrified of having this conversation for me, I was also sad for my mom.

"*I*t's hard news to take. I get that. I really do. I had had 23 years to come to terms with my gender identity. I had been researching it in books and later on the internet for most of my life, desperately trying to understand who I was and why I felt the way I did, and still, I could barely come to terms with the fact that I was transsexual. How was my mom supposed to take that all in, in just a few moments?"

There was no screaming, no rejection. My mom reassured me that she loved me, she was thoughtful and considerate in the way she answered me, but there was a heaviness to her voice. I could almost hear her concept of self and family changing. Suddenly, she didn't live in a world where people grew up, got married. Suddenly, those people, included her.

Maybe I shouldn't have felt bad. Maybe I should have felt entitled to shake my mom out of the 1950s vision of a nuclear family she had been raised with — but, I did feel bad.

Being trans has never been a political identity for me. I'm not making a statement by transitioning, I'm just living. It's something that's always been a part of me, and I think somehow, it always will be. I'll never know anything different, but my mom, the people around me, the people I had grown up with, they had worlds, with world views. I never asked for this — for my life to be so complicated. Somehow, it seems like my very existence is transgressive. Just being has impacts, involves ramifications and negotiations. And now, after a few minutes on the phone, my mom's life had that too, and I felt bad.

Transition is one of the most intimate and personal decisions a person can make. You're changing your gender, it's kind of a big thing. It's kind of your big thing.

It's life changing.

It's your gender, it's your life, it's your decision alone — but no matter how you do it, other people are involved. There are ripples. Our transitions can affect the lives of those around us and their reactions, or even the fear of their reactions, can affect our transitions. Our lives.

Sometimes, our loved ones, in their grief, will accuse us of suddenly springing this news on them. Of not thinking of them and how our transitions, our identities, will affect their lives. They don't know how much time we've spent thinking, obsessing, about them and how they'll handle it. How much effect our imagined versions of them and their reactions have already had on our lives.

I tried to tell my mom once, when I was twelve. I tried to start a conversation. It didn't work. I went back into the closet for a decade. She doesn't remember.

The most bright-burning, courageous-terrifying, scarring moment of my 12-year-old self's life, was just a thing that kids say. She feels terrible now, but how was she supposed to know that a half-started, fear-stuttered sentence and an offhand, cutting remark, would change the course of my life for a decade?

When I finally did decide to transition, I ran.

I ran from everything and everyone I knew. I ran because I'm willful, and I wanted to do things my own way, and I ran because I was scared. I was scared I would lose everything I had known and loved. So instead of risking the loss, I ran. I was also worried that if I didn't leave the things I was afraid to lose, I would never figure out who I was.

The day after I graduated from college I packed all my worldly belongings into a tiny car and drove 1600 miles away from where I grew up.

From family.

Friends.

Everyone.

Everything.

Some people think of me as a strong person; some would go so far as to say leader, but the truth is, I'm a people pleaser. I am desperate for love, affection, approval. I cast myself as a strong person in hopes of garnering admiration — admiration, is close to affection. Sometimes, it works; rarely, is it healthy.

I knew this about myself.

I knew if I transitioned close to home, I would never figure out who I was. I would play to others. That, or I would have to constantly fight to be taken seriously. All my actions would either be playing to or fighting against expectations.

I would never be able to just be.

1600 miles, it turns out, is a really long way. I ended up in the middle of the country, in an unfamiliar city and a completely foreign environment, with one dubious contact, no friends, no job and no social network to speak of.

I might suffer from a low self-image with people pleasing tendencies, I might have a desperate need for love and affection, but I can take care of myself.

I know artists have a reputation for being flaky and unable to make practical decisions or to take care of themselves, but in the space of a few weeks: I found a terrible job, a terrible apartment, I started making contacts in the artistic community and picking up piecemeal freelancing work where I could find it.

<Insert montage of being poor as f**k, deciding between gas and groceries, dragging a mattress from the alley so I would have something to sleep on and the occasional cross-dressing>

I started establishing myself without telling anyone what I was planning. Everyone assumed I was a boy. I was starting to make friends — friends I wanted to like me. Transition is a huge step, there are irreversible ramifications, both physical and social (you really can't un-tell people you're a transsexual). I hesitated out of fear and uncertainty. I was in danger of finding myself in exactly the same position I was in when I left my home. Trapping myself in the expectations I had created.

But, there was a difference this time.

The difference was that with these new friends, I was a significantly different person than I was to the people from my hometown. I was presenting as a much more feminine person — and weirdly, people still liked me. When I did decide to transition, no one was surprised. It helped that I had moved to a very accepting town, and most of my friends were artists.

Still, I was terrified of rejection.

Right here, I'm going to take a moment to say: I am privileged.

I am lucky.

Things could have gone much worse.

I've seen it.

My mom didn't throw me a parade, but she didn't throw anything at me either. Even if it was very uncomfortable for many years, I have always been welcome in my parents' home. Not a single one of my friends has ever said anything cruel or rejecting to me. At least, nothing has ever gotten back to me, and honestly, I don't care if people have terrible thoughts they keep to themselves. It's my life, and I don't need to hear about their bullshit.

I'm not saying that the road has been perfectly smooth. I can't say I've never experienced prejudice or that people haven't said or done horrible things to me because of my history, but my social transition has gone so well that sometimes it feels unreal, and I feel spoiled for having difficulty dealing with the relatively minor annoyances it has brought me.

I didn't know that before I came out. Before I told people, I had to assume that everyone I knew could disappear from my life. That I would never be able to go home again. It seems silly now, but you don't know until after.

Weirdly, I found myself in almost the same situation years later when I moved across the country again. This time, from the other side of transition.

I had stayed in the city where I started my transition for three years (give or take some random roaming here and there). My friends got used to me. I got used to me. It's one thing to dream about waking up as a girl for most of your life; it's another thing to actually wake up as a girl. It takes some getting used to, for you and for those around you.

After a while, I settled in. I started to get a grasp on my identity and my friends were starting to get used to me — some of them started to forget that they had ever known me any other way. I was getting used to the idea that people weren't able to guess my past if they didn't already know.

It was comfortable. I was comfortable, but I wanted more. From myself and from my art. So, I packed up my little car again and moved across the country again, to study my art full-time. No one looked at me twice on the street or in the store, but I had never lived in a place where no one knew.

I didn't mean to do art school in stealth — it's just that once I got there, no one asked and I didn't feel like telling them. In a way, my time there was awesome. Without the burden of *being trans* to all my friends, I learned a lot about simply *being*. I was making friends as myself and in that environment, I was able to figure out who *myself* was. However, close friendships, were tricky. I had only been a girl for a couple of years at that point, and there was so much in my life I couldn't talk about.

I had no stories. I had no history. You'd be surprised how often people talk about things that happened more than three years previous, and how much a change of gender changes the meaning and significance of even the simplest childhood story.

Even though the situation was completely different, the question was the same: *would my friends still be my friends if they knew?*

Eventually, as a kind of pressure release, I told some of my closest friends. Some of those relationships eventually faltered for reasons that friendships normally falter, but some of the people I told are still among my closest friends, and I feel closer for having told them. My stories make more sense. I don't have to cover my tracks.

I can breathe a little.

However, I still haven't told most of the people I went to school with about my past. I consider them friends, but there's no reason for them to know. I'm comfortable with that.

With time, I've grown more comfortable with myself. I started transition when I was 23 years old, fresh out of college, at a time when most people are beginning to form their adult identities. I've changed and so have the people around me.

For the first few years coming home to visit was difficult and awkward. Before I left home, I had spent my entire life in the same city, in the same house, surrounded by the same people. My parents still live in that house and are still friends with many of the same people they were friends with when I was a small child.

The name and pronouns were difficult for people. They were trying, but every slip was a little knife in my heart. Conversation topics were difficult to come by: I was poor, I was trying to make it as an artist, and I was a transsexual. Their kids were graduating from college, looking for normal jobs and having normal relationships. There was a lack of understanding in our conversations; some resentment from my side and maybe a little pity from their side.

However, things don't always go *normally,* even for *normal* people.

As some of my parents' friends' children have struggled to make their way in a difficult economy, as they themselves have had difficulties — divorces, unemployment, unexpected health problems — it's kind of opened a door for them to understand, that sometimes life is complicated and more difficult than you'd want it to be.

In the past eight years, I've gradually moved from dragging mattresses from alleys, trying to coast into work on the last sip of gas and trying to get the very last scrapings out of a jar of peanut butter so I wouldn't have to go to sleep hungry, to supporting myself with my art, being able to feed myself, pay my bills and afford small luxuries. I've traveled the world, learned a second language and started to build a small reputation for myself in my field.

Now, when I come home to visit, I stop by the local bar that serves as a kind of community meeting place for my parents and their friends. People are excited to see me. Conversations are normal and easy. My parents' friends, some of whom have known me since I was eight years old, call me over to find out where I've been and what I'm up to. They're even proud of me.

That feels good. It feels like living.

Dealing with people from my past can still be frustrating at times, try as they might, they just don't see me the same way other people do. There's baggage there. There's a certain coloring to our interactions, that's absent from relationships I've formed after transition. Still, for me, being able to interact with people I knew before transition allows me to see my entire life as a whole. Not partitioned into bright-sunny, post-transition happiness and dark-gloomy, pre-transition sadness. It's taken a lot of work to get here, from them and from me, but my parents and their friends are starting to see that being transsexual isn't the end of the world, and that maybe for some people, it's only the beginning.

The Staff of the Stonewall Center, Genny is in the back, far right.

How to Be an Ally to Transgender People

Genny Beemyn

The director of the Stonewall Center at the University of Massachusetts-Amherst, Genny has published and spoken extensively on the experiences and needs of transgender people, particularly the lives of gender nonconforming students. Ze [Genny prefers gender-neutral pronouns) has written or edited seven books/journal issues, including special issues of the *Journal of LGBT Youth* on "Trans Youth" and the *Journal of Homosexuality* on "LGBTQ Campus Experiences." Genny's most recent work, written with Sue Rankin, is *The Lives of Transgender People*, which was published by Columbia University Press in 2011.

* Validate people's gender expression. It is important to refer to transgender people by the pronoun appropriate to their gender identity. In other words, if someone identifies as female, then refer to the person as "she;" if someone identifies as male, refer to the person as "he." If you are not sure, ask them. Never use the word "it" when referring to someone who is transgender. To do so is incredibly insulting and disrespectful. Some transgender people prefer to use gender-neutral pronouns: "hir" instead of "her" and "his," and "sie" or "ze" instead of "she" and "he."

* Use non-gendered language to avoid making gender assumptions. Refer to people by name, instead of calling them "sir/ma'am" or "Mr./Ms."

* Challenge your own conceptions about gender-appropriate roles and behaviors. Do not expect people to conform to society's beliefs about "women" and "men."

* Do not assume that someone who is transgender is lesbian, gay or bisexual, or that a person will seek to transition to become heterosexual.

- Use the word "cross-dresser" instead of "transvestite," as the latter term is often considered pejorative, because of the word's clinical and pathological history.

- Never ask transgender people about how they have sex or what their genitals look like. This is inappropriate in every situation.

- Do not share the gender identity of individuals without their permission. Do not assume that everyone knows. The decision to tell others about one's gender should be left to the individual.

- When you learn about someone's transgender identity, do not assume that it is a fad or trend. While public discussions about transgenderism and transsexuality are a relatively recent phenomenon, most transgender people have felt themselves to be gender different from early childhood and have often struggled to be accepted by others. It is important to trust that someone's decision to identify as transgender is not made lightly or without due consideration.

- Educate yourself and others about the experiences of transgender people. Introduce trainings, readings and other resources to your colleagues to continue educational efforts to deconstruct social norms around gender, sex and sexual orientation.

- Work to change policies in areas such as housing, employment and health care that discriminate against transgender people and seek to include "gender identity/expression" in school, company, city and state non-discrimination policies.

Some material adapted from the Southern Arizona Gender Alliance: www.tgnetarizona.org

"Challenge your own conceptions about gender-appropriate roles and behaviors. Do not expect people to conform to society's beliefs about 'women' and 'men.' "

Elijah and Lucy

TRANSGENDER PEOPLE

From Oma
to Daddy
Elijah Henry Burton

Eli lives in suburbia with his partner, Jessica, and their two-year-old, Lucy, who runs the show. They also have two cats and a dog. Eli stays busy serving at his church, singing in the choir, playing handbells, taking care of honey-do lists and helping facilitate a transgender group. Eli celebrated his one-year T-versary [the anniversary of taking testosterone] in March 2012 and hopes to have top surgery checked off his list the same year. Eli's family plans include marrying Jessica, adopting a few kids and adding a few more animals.

Starting the journey of transition is a difficult task for anyone to undertake, however. starting it at 30-years-old creates a whole new layer. I had been struggling internally for a few years about being transgender and I considered many different reasons for my feelings. I worked up the courage to tell my partner Jessica after about a year of research and internal debates. She encouraged me to keep researching, keep talking and most importantly to reach out to others.

About that time, I met my biggest support and ally. On June 15, 2009 my partner gave birth to our daughter, Lucille (Lucy). A beautiful blue-eyed, curly-haired little bundle. I was so proud to be a parent, something I had for years longed for, but something felt off. The term "mom" didn't fit me. I couldn't figure out how to refer to myself in my daughter's life. We played with a lot of ideas, but eventually gave into referring to me as Oma (short for Other Mother.)

Well as any parent knows, the baby days go by too quickly and before we knew it, our little one was walking and talking. It was a seemingly ordinary day, when I learned one of the biggest lessons of life. Children should run the world. They see things for what they are, no fluff. Lucy, who had only ever heard me referred to as "Oma" by us and other family and friends, called me "Daddy," and she's never stopped. That was the push, the bump I needed. I knew I was on the right path, and that it was time to further my journey.

I began much more actively transitioning. I starting telling family close to me: my mother, father, brother, a few cousins, my pastor and one person at school. I received so much support, but some disheartening issues too. I believe it is just as much about transitioning for family and friends as it is for someone who is transgender. No matter how much you look, feel or act like your chosen gender, even you still need a brain adjustment period. (I'm sure I'm not the only one who still whips their head around when I hear "Heather.") There are habits and traditions ingrained so deep in you, and it can take awhile to retrain your brain. I know I spent a long time making this decision; I try not to expect instant changes in others.

I've made a lot of friends and acquaintances in my life, I have a pretty large extended family, and I've never been a very shy person. So when I started my journey, I had to give some consideration as to who I would tell, who I'd just let discover it and who, if anyone, I would just let slide out of my circle of life. Along the way, I've learned just as much about the people that surround me as I have learned about myself.

Jessica and I have been together 10 years. We have moved a lot, struggled financially, dealt with school, families, being ostracized by people for being a lesbian couple and even harassed for having a child because I'm transitioning. However, Jessica never wavered in her support of me. Sometimes, I worried she was bottling things in. I urged her repeatedly to seek out a support group for herself or to see a therapist. She showed no signs of struggling with this transition; she helped me to "try on" different names, switched pronouns when I expressed interest, encouraged me to let my facial hair grow out and helped to educate others about my journey. I had heard so many stories of partners who weren't ready or left after someone transitioned; I was becoming paranoid.

I stopped doubting her the day I broke down in tears. Dysphoria had been building in me for a few weeks. My therapist at the time kept "forgetting" to write my T letter she had promised (two months late). One of my doctors wanted to put me on a female hormone pill, I had been called "Ma'am" countless number of times, my binder was cutting into me, I had fought with my mother on the phone and I was just ready to quit transitioning. Jessica hugged me, let me cry for a while and said,

> I love you as a person, not a gender. I didn't choose to love "Heather" because she was a woman, and I won't stop loving Elijah because he's a man. The person I fell in love with can never leave this body. So I will follow this body through whatever journey it wants to take.

She always knows just what to say to motivate and lift me up. I think she gets her way with words from her dad.

My father-in-law, Bob, was head of the class when it came to acceptance of my journey. The conversation with my in-laws was pretty relaxed. I explained a simplified version of what transgender meant for me, and what I planned to do. My father-in-law explained how they had just had a speaker at church talking about being transgender and being accepting as a congregation. And by the end of his story, I was completely male to him. He has never slipped up on pronouns or name and has given me nothing but support since.

The most negative experience for me was with someone I thought I could count on in my support system. I really struggled with how to tell this person, and what I wanted them to understand. I ended up writing them a letter, and I had to wait a few weeks to hear back. I was expecting a discussion to ensue with this person. They are the type that would carry on a conversation with me forever. Instead, I was treated to a letter of selfishness. What were they suppose to tell other people? How was this fair to them? And stating that I definitely shouldn't expect him to switch everything so quickly. It's taken over a year, and he is finally starting to make an effort.

"*I* know I spent a long time making this decision; I try not to expect instant changes in others."

I have had plenty of other supporters who have given me positive experiences in coming out though. A few cousins, friends from years back and friends more recent, a former supervisor, a recent co-worker, my pastors, grandparents, my church family and my parents even came around. So many people seemed to see the happiness this decision gave me, and many saw that it wasn't really different than how I had been living my life. My positive supports far outweigh my negative experiences. Unfortunately, there are still some that just don't try to be accepting. I have struggled with those who slip into an old name and gender when it's easier for them, but they are fine with my transition most of the time. I remind them that at this point, their lack of trying only makes them look bad. If we're out in public and they holler "Heather" to me, strangers aren't going to judge me. They'll wonder if my family/friend is losing their marbles, calling this big hairy man a woman's name.

No matter what though, I know I wouldn't have made it this far into my transition without amazing support. People like Jessica, Lucy, Ryan, Jackson, Liam, Cameron, Bob, Kari, Amanda, Ranelle, Bill and my Mom have all given me strength, words of wisdom and even a swift kick when I needed it. Having strong people by my side is just as important to my transition as making that first decision to change.

"Heleconia" by Hilary Brenneman © 2012

Morty

Raised by Community
Morty Diamond

Morty is a Jewish transsexual writer, artist and filmmaker currently living and working in Los Angeles, California. Morty has edited two anthologies showcasing the trans experience from the perspective of transgender writers: *From the Inside Out* (Manic D Press) and *Trans/Love* (Manic D Press), published August 2011. Morty is currently working on publishing a literary and arts magazine focused on the transgender and transsexual community, titled: *Bodies Of Work Magazine*.

Just four months shy of my 21st birthday, I shoved all of my belongings into three suitcases and declared that I was through with Los Angeles. I had what most teen queers had at the time: an intense need to be in the city everyone hailed as the Queer Mecca: San Francisco. With about $300 dollars in the bank and a hand-me-down white Nissan Sentra, I drove up the I-5 freeway until I hit the Bay Bridge, thinking to myself, *You're here! Now where are you gonna sleep?*

Struggling to get on my feet, I immediately set out to find the like-minded, young queers who shared my love of Manic Panic hair dye and goth puck music. I was a drummer, albeit without a drum set, in love with The Pixies, Siouxsie and the Banshees, The Smiths. When I walked past the most punk rock video rental store I'd ever seen, Leather Tongue, I knew I might find my people. Beside the VHS tapes, Leather Tongue had a huge wall plastered with flyers. People offering and looking for housing, bandmates, jobs, whatever, this wall was Craigslist before the internet existed. On that enormous wall of flyers, stapled upon flyers, I found a bright purple piece of paper with serial killer style magazine letters cut out one-by-one. This ad looking for a drummer changed my life overnight.

I called the number and the next day, met Rhani Lee, a hot femme with a blue-black bob, skintight blue jeans, a short brown, tattered leather jacket and a T-Rex shirt. Rhani Lee and I connected immediately. Both of us were young musicians and artists just recently moved from Los Angeles. We both had natural facial hair. We were both into zine [online magazine] culture. She was going to the local art college and playing bass in a band called Leper Sex Killer On The Loose.

She invited me to see her band play at the Purple Onion in North Beach. When I got to the venue, for the first time in my life, I saw a slew of gender bending queer and trans people pogoing and moshing to the Leper Sex punk rock rhythms. Later on in the evening, a big crew of us went out for burritos at Cancun, and Rhani Lee introduced me as the new queer on the block.

It was in this community that I would grow into the transsexual I am today. Turning 21, I was just coming to understand my gender identity. As a fraternal twin, I was always the boy; while my sister asked for Bongos, I wanted Wranglers. As a teen, hidden beneath the goth makeup and baggy black band tees, was a boyish girl who didn't know what transsexual was. As a dyke, the queer community felt as wrapped up in gender as the straight one did. I always felt too feminine to be a butch and too masculine to be a soft butch. I didn't watch enough football to be a sporty lesbian. I wasn't crunchy enough to be granola. Plus, I didn't know the code. There seemed to be an unspoken butch code I sensed from other butches and their femme dates. I felt like an outsider no matter what community I was in. Rhani's friends didn't seem like the LA gays that I knew. Rhani's friends were freaks, and they were proud. I was happy to finally find my freaky queer community.

> "*I*t was this community who raised me, this community who saved me and this community that I now work to make healthier."

San Francisco was filled with out trans women who saw something in me that I didn't know was there. On a rainy night of drinking 40's [40 oz. of malt liquor beer] with Darla, one of my trans female friends, I was gently led to think about gender in a new way. Darla took me aside and asked, "Well, have you thought about what it would be like to be a man?" Her words seared a hole right through me. After meeting trans folks, and seeing for the first time changing genders was possible, of course I had thought about it, but I never acknowledged these ideas as real. Every time I thought, "Well, maybe I am a guy," I would enter this dark space in my mind. It felt like I was about to step into the most terror-inducing dream imaginable. At the time I was prone to anxiety attacks and tried to stay far away from life altering questions like "Are you trans?" and "What if you're trans?" as much as possible. Still, Darla, with her wide brown eyes, half-covered by her inky black hair pressed her hand into mine and asked again, "Honey, if you could change into a man, do you think you would? Because you just don't seem happy....as a girl."

Conversations like these, mostly with young trans women just beginning their transition process, helped me come to see my gender as something malleable, something I could change. These fearless, beautiful trans women helped me become courageous enough to jostle myself out of a mild depression and see myself for what I truly could be.

My parents were not there to hold my hand during my transition. I felt I had let them down for being the bad child: dying my hair green at 13, ditching school, drinking in the back of the gym. Yet, once I skimmed by high school and got my diploma, they washed their hands of me and cut me loose. No college, no "make something of myself," just a hundred dollar bill as a graduation present, and I was out the door. Though I had come from a solidly, middle-class background, I had no support and struggled to pay rent and eat.

I felt I fit right in because of all the queers and trans people I was surrounded with. This mirrored my story of a parent-less life. Together, we made this team of young trans misfits, and we stuck together. If someone needed a place to sleep there was always a floor. If someone needed a meal, we would pitch in our food stamps. Rhani Lee and I would start the Cud Club, a once-a-month dance club, for our little trans community. The Cud Club would end up, through word of mouth, to become a meeting place for young trans folks to meet and live the dream of a few hours of total abandon from the harsh lives we lived.

It was this community who raised me, this community who saved me and this community that I now work to make healthier.

Eva

It's Natural
Eva Hayward

Eva has taught at the University of New Mexico, Uppsala University in Sweden and Duke University. Her scholarship focuses on the intersections of gender and the environment. She also writes for the *Independent Weekly*, her work is archived here: http://www.indyweek.com/indyweek/Article Archives?category=2497995

A love affair broke out between a transsexual woman — male to female — and a transgender man — female to male.

I have lived as a woman for years, and he had recently transitioned from female to male. I define as transsexual — someone who feels an essential need to modify her body — and he is transgender — not necessarily wanting sex reassignment. I always desired men, and he always women. While sex and gender identity do not define one's sexuality, we moved across cultural categories of gay and lesbian, man and woman. Neither of us was looking for a transgender lover, but we found each other and became a different kind of heterosexual couple.

Although relationships can be complicated, love is often quite simple. In many ways, our relationship is no more or less convoluted than any other: Do you desire me as much as I desire you? Has this relationship changed me, or not? And in other ways the coupling feels novel.

Transgenderism and transsexualism are expressions of life-loving invention. Simply, transgender people, like all people, are part of life's exuberance, the planet's investment in change and potential. Even a casual reading of Charles Darwin reminds that organisms flourish because of their ability to transform or adjust, not because of their capacities for strength or intelligence. And a more careful reading of Darwin invites us to see how nonreproductive members of a species are not detriments but advantages. So, might it be true that variation in sex, sexuality and gender is indeed "natural?"

What makes this male-to-female and female-to-male couple fresh is that bodies shift across seemingly inherent cultural codes. Rather than suggesting the apocalypse of society (although I confess that on some Monday mornings I long for nothing else), this couple expresses elasticity in identities that most Americans assume are true and enduring. Bodies are potentials rather than absolutes. The interest in Chaz Bono, Thomas Beattie ("the pregnant man"), *America's Next Top Model* candidate and trans woman Isis King and author Jennifer Finney Boylan demonstrates this as a cultural truth. If you need more proof, watch the Oprah Winfrey Network for a few hours.

"*I*t's common to read about why people transition gender ... but the question is often irrelevant. How do any of us know how we became gendered? Or why we desire a particular gender or sex?"

Trans people define themselves in numerous ways. There is probably no single term that adequately conveys this diversity. Self-identifying language in the trans community is rapidly changing. What worked a couple of years ago — for example, "tranny" — is suddenly wrong or misrepresenting. "Tranny" is now viewed as offensive, a slur. These changing definitions are not arbitrary, but indicate a people finding their voice in a larger context.

It's common to read about why people transition gender — it seems some researcher is always searching for some biological code or psychological event that triggered it — but the question is often irrelevant. How do any of us know how we became gendered? Or why we desire a particular gender or sex? Perhaps too much misguided time and money is spent on defining a genetic code or a traumatic experience that will account for all the ways transgender people become transgender.

The real question is why we pose these questions. Are they meant to secure better health care or to foster social justice for a politically disenfranchised population? Or are their purposes less altruistic? Behaviorist psychologist John Money studied why transsexuals feel an innate need to change their sex and concluded that such feelings are indicators of mental illness. Consequently, the American Psychiatric Association listed "Gender Identity Disorder" in the 1994 revision of the diagnostic manual, which has since impacted the lives of transsexual and transgender people.

Usually transgender people are written about. Their stories are interpreted by sometimes-sympathetic writers, but more often than not by insensitive journalists, interviewers, academics or health care providers. This isn't to dismiss our political allies; they are crucial for solidarity projects and cultural change. But even allies should give voice back to a community that has for too long been named, defined and pathologized.

Even the inclusion of "T" in LGBTQ (Lesbian, Gay, Bisexual, Transgender, Queer) pays only lip service, and lesbian and gay organizations ignore issues that are unique to trans people. The Employment Non-Discrimination Act (ENDA) introduced in Congress would prohibit discrimination against employees on the basis of their sexual orientation. In 2007, The Human Rights Campaign Fund, one of the largest lobbyists for the lesbian and gay community, refused to extend ENDA's protections to include gender identity: transgender and transsexual.

A lot of education is needed even in local news reporting. Sam Peterson, a local artist and activist who organized ChestFest at The ArtsCenter in Carrboro, described an encounter with a local person who *"looked like* a man." The interviewer told Sam that he didn't *look like* a man to him. The irony of course is that all men try to look like men, but without the assumption that they are not actually men.

In general, news stories constantly refer to trans people using the wrong pronouns — "A man dressed in women's clothing was found murdered," read a Baltimore news article, or "*She* tricked this other woman into thinking *she* was a man," a British publication reported. But it is not just disrespectful misrecognition that is the problem, but the way trans people are either criminalized or represented as deserving victims of violence.

Far from resembling the character Buffalo Bill in *The Silence of the Lambs* or Norman Bates in *Psycho,* transgender women as a group risk being assaulted and killed at a much higher rate because of who they are. The Transgender Law Center conservatively estimates that one in every 900 homicides in the U.S. is an anti-transgender, hate-based crime.

As for claims of deceit, there is nothing about having sex with someone that requires disclosure about one's trans status. Don't we all risk some self-discovery when we are intimate with another person? Is the anxiety of non-transgender people that they will be tricked, actually a fear that sleeping with a transgender person could affect their own identity?

By living their lives, trans people invite everyone to question his or her assumptions. The invitation is a reminder to us all that change is what we are.

We don't sustain ourselves because we are intact or perfect, but because we embody the reach and possibility of our experiences. Our sense of self is created out of ingenuity and necessity. We should not only want to live and love according to variation, but we must.

Originally published in "The Independent Weekly," www.IndyWeek.com, 6/1/11 as Transgenderism and Transsexualism are expressions of life-loving invention.

Must We Be Extraordinary to Be Ordinary?

Eva Hayward

Clacking away at my laptop, chunky Dior glasses sliding to the end of my nose and lips pursed in concentration, with a lifted finger I momentarily held off the doctor while I crafted a last sentence.

Surely a well-rendered sentence matters as much as a steady heart rate. I was writing my February opinion column for the *Indy* on love, desire and the Roman holiday Lupercalia, while receiving blood transfusions in a Cincinnati hospital bed. Landing there was my own bloody valentine — ironic comeuppance for downplaying the holiday's savagery.

My gesture was not simply a power play, Ph.D. versus M.D., but an insistence on being respected. Because without exception, every doctor who came into my room was fascinated to distraction to learn that I am transsexual. One doctor asked me if I were born female or male, and when I told him, he seemed perplexed and asked if I had had sex reassignment surgery, and then asked about cosmetic surgeries and then still seemed confused. But the most troubling issue was that I had wound up in the hospital for reasons unrelated to my sex. I needed care for pain and blood loss, but with an IV in my arm and secured hospital floors, he had me positioned to satisfy his curiosity.

Over the last two years, I have been in three hospitals: University of New Mexico Hospital, Duke University Hospital and University of Cincinnati Hospital. At each institution, to different degrees of unpleasantness, doctors and nurses have demanded that I discuss my transsexuality whether I am in for pneumonia or stomach disease. When I was admitted to UNM Hospital, unable to breathe, an intake nurse, after trying to flatter me with "I had no idea you were transgender," talked to me about accepting his gay son and the challenges that came with that decision in rural New Mexico, while I gasped and shook my head empathetically. While at Duke University Hospital, a senior doctor brought 10 interns into my room to not just discuss my sex change but to eyeball my very sex. My patience curdling into frustration, I asked how this information mattered, and why it required an audience. Seemingly imperious, he said, "It does matter." Perhaps it does, but I could never get a good explanation as to exactly how nor why these sorts of encounters happened so often during my stays.

"My gesture was not simply a power play, Ph.D. versus M.D., but an insistence on being respected. Because without exception, every doctor who came into my room was fascinated to distraction to learn that I am transsexual."

My exasperation hardly ends with the medical establishment. When people know about my transition, there is an instant feeling of intimacy, as if I have surrendered my privacy to them and become a trusting friend. Acquaintances will confide their dreams to me or make unwarranted advances and otherwise feel over-familiar with me. And even folks I generally adore have a tendency to suppose something special or transgressive about my identity. As it happens, a dear friend and I have been engaged in an ongoing debate about "queerness." For her, to be queer is the highest of accomplishments, an exalted mode of existence. When I tell her that I am not so queer, that my identity is rather commonplace, she looks askance at me. But it is true: I don't have remarkable insight into the number of sex systems. I am not liberated from the conventions of gender, sex or sexuality. Nor do I represent the body's triumph over nature or godliness.

At one time in my life, not wanting to be ensnared in my past, I celebrated an unhindered present. I disowned who I had been for who I had become. I withdrew from family and old friendships and met new people without discussing my transition. Later it dawned on me that rather than dismissing my history, I was denying it, which felt isolating and self-effacing. Maybe we all have the feeling that we haven't quite lived our life until we have narrated it.

While I do not see sex change as extraordinary, I understand that my experience gives me a particular sensibility. And since I do not live in "stealth" — a word used by some to describe a life in which no one knows you are transgender — I have had to expect questions about my transition, even if I don't really want, nor know how, to answer.

Grateful as I am by nature, reluctant to tell it all, and surprisingly lucky in other respects, I find it difficult to dig through old miseries and doubts. I do my best, though, to be honest in discussions about transsexuality. I have written about sex change for academic and journalistic venues, but always my effort is to place transsexuality within an unsurprising sphere of experience. In this I share the sentiments of a young man who wrote to the Governor of Washington state, explaining how marriage equality matters to him: "No one should have to be extraordinary to be ordinary."

Several years ago I attended a show at the Exit Theatre in San Francisco. Veronica Klaus was performing her one-woman show *Family Jewels*. Veronica sums up frustrations and sentiments when she ponders, "People ask me if I feel like a woman. Do I feel like a woman? The truth is, I have no idea whether I feel like any other woman. I have no idea whether I ever felt like any other man. All I know is that I feel like me, Veronica, a person whose existence is partly innate, partly instinct, partly art, the art of creating."

As I tend to repeat, transsexuality is life loving itself, loving its capacity for invention, change and possibility. All that seems arcane about transsexuality — hormone replacement therapy, surgeries, name changes — can be understood as marks of healing and of the desire to live well. For me, and perhaps because it is my experience, there is something simple if indefinable about transsexuality, resisting blunt definitions and analyses. It just is. I accepted it as it happened and am sure I did the right thing.

Originally published in "The Independent Weekly," www.IndyWeek.com, 3/7/12, as Why a sex chnge is not extraordinary.

Angela

Do You Love Me?

Angela Palermo

Angela is a transgender activist, writer, performer, librarian and amateur film-maker. She would like to attend film school and dreams of making a documentary on the Hijras of India. Her work has been published in the *Main Street Free Press*, *Transgender Tapestry* and the Colorado GLBT anthology *Focus on the Fabulous*. She can be reached at liongirlden@hotmail.com

> Do you love me?
> Like I love you?
> —Nick Cave

I begin with a lyrical epigraph from Nick Cave not to establish my hipster credentials (Kate Bornstein aside, are trans women even allowed entrance into such august company?), but to ask an honest and sincere question. It's really quite simple, the sort of interrogative that all human beings ask at one time or another. But for transgender and genderqueer people, posing the question, "Do you love me like I love you?" can be especially thorny and problematic.

Of course, this state of affairs should not come as a surprise to anyone, whether amongst the cognoscenti or not. After all, (monotheistic) Western culture has long been hostile to any sort of gender and sexual diversity. Everything from biblical injunctions to sexist gender roles to Hollywood movies (Jonathan Demme, are you listening?) seems to condemn explorations of the multiverse of gender identities and expressions. Even today, in the early twenty-first century, stepping outside the rigid, "two box" gender system requires courage and endurance for the sometimes difficult road ahead. Donning the bulky, weighty armor of a "transgender warrior" is a risky business indeed. The battles can appear endless, while taking us far afield. And the return trip to Ithaca (if you'll pardon the reference), likely filled with churning seas and "monsters" of many sorts, may seem almost idyllic compared with what one finds in the place once called "home."

"As 'gender creative' folks, it's up to us to seek out supportive people and nurturing environments. In so doing, we will create spaces in which we can continue our explorations, seeking out our 'true selves,' however provisional these 'selves' may ultimately be."

Coming out as transgender or genderqueer makes us vulnerable to prejudice and discrimination of all sorts and emanating from seemingly every quarter of our lives. Parents and siblings may reject us, withholding their affections unless we conform to traditional gender norms. We may not be allowed to attend family functions/celebrations should we choose to present in the gender of our choice. The revelation of one's gender variant status may even result in complete ostracism, with parents turning their child onto the streets. Our spouses and lovers sometimes turn their backs, requiring us to squelch or abandon our deeply held identities and desires, however newly discovered. Employers may fire or demote us. Coworkers may carry out campaigns of harassment, creating a "hostile work environment." (Codified legal protections are only a first step in addressing rampant employment discrimination.) Trans people can (and do) lose housing and health care coverage. Even helping professionals sometimes get in on the transphobic game. A surprising number of therapists continue to pathologize us, claiming that being transgender is "unnatural" or "paraphilic" and can, even must, be "cured." And imagine being a young trans person (or not-so-young trans person) and hearing clergy condemn your very being week after week, as if God Himself can't wait to cast your weary, queer soul into the flames of everlasting Perdition. Bearing these considerations in mind, is it any wonder that suicide rates, substance abuse and depression run so much higher than average in the transgender/gender variant community?

This assessment may sound grim and forbidding, but all is not lost. Far from it. I know firsthand that there are many glimmers of light in what can, at times, seem like endless gloom. As "gender creative" folks, it's up to us to seek out supportive people and nurturing environments. In so doing, we will create spaces in which we can continue our explorations, seeking out our "true selves," however provisional those "selves" may ultimately be. Depending on where we live and work, we may well find a wealth of trans-focused or at least trans-friendly resources, including, but not limited to, transgender support groups, trans-friendly Human Resource professionals and trans-knowledge-able therapists. And, on the internet, there are even trans-focused "chat rooms" and trans-inclusive dating websites! (The Web has been such a boon to the transgender community, alleviating the isolation many of us feel. But that's an entirely different essay!)

In the early days of my own transition, I struggled to piece together a support network of organizations and individuals who truly had my best interests at heart, as a transsexual woman and just as a human being. I was eager to create my own "family of choice." My birth family was disappointing me in so many ways, but my friends, both trans and non-trans, were often loving and supportive. In what follows, I will lay out my own gender journey in a way that I hope is helpful and illuminating to both transgender/genderqueer folks and SOFFAs alike.

> I feel a force I've never felt before
> I can't hold it down I've just got to soar
> And laugh in the face that is vulture law
> I burst out — I'm transformed
> I burst right out — into a swan!
> —Siouxsie Sioux

I do not believe there is any such thing as a typical transgender journey. But my story may contain its share of unusual and quirky elements. For one, I have no memory of thinking, "I'm really a girl," as a young child. (I've heard many trans women say such things. Are some of these declarations "revisionist history?") I just knew I loved trying on my mother's shoes, skirts and dresses. And I wondered why my older brother didn't share sartorial enthusiasms. My father's clothes bored me, while the man himself generally inspired fear and dread. It would not be overstatement to say that he had "anger management" issues.

My mom had a cheerier, more inviting personality, but she had an icy streak of her own (her emotional frostiness has not decreased with advancing age). Both my parents were second generation Italian-Americans who came of age in a largely Italian-American neighborhood in New York City during the Fifties and Sixties. Neither attended college and, consequently, their "horizons" were not especially broad, a fact that was painfully reinforced during my coming-out process with my mother (my dad had already passed away by that time).

Sadly, my immediate family (namely, my mother and brother) have numbered among the least helpful people during my period of transition and in the years that have followed. I came out to my mother in July 2000, on the evening of my birthday, no less. I had spent nearly two weeks crafting what I believed was a very heartfelt and authentic letter about my transgender self. Even though I was very anxious, I felt I just had to tell my mother. My "true self," as a woman, was bursting out all over. Nothing and no one was going to stop this "new self," not even me.

On my birthday, at Common Grounds coffee house, and having my (now ex-) wife there for support, I read my mother my coming out letter. Trembling and with a quavering voice, I revealed a still very vulnerable part of myself to the woman I loved so dearly as a small child. She said little after I finished reading. She seemed in shock, as if my revelation caught her off guard and more than a little blindsided. She could only weakly muster that she "never knew," not seeing "any signs" of my transgender status.

"*Deep* down, I think my mother wants her 'son' back, but is realistic enough to know that 'he' is now a specter who cannot and will not return."

We put her on a plane back to Florida the next afternoon, with a copy of my letter in her bag. She kept her peace the next two days, but on the third day all hell really did break loose. She called me up that evening yelling, crying, berating and shrieking curses at my therapist (a trans woman herself; more about her soon) and me. Not surprisingly, I grew defensive under the barrage of verbally abusive attacks. I fired back in (what felt like) righteous anger. After all, hadn't I taken the time to compose and recite a sincere letter? I wondered how my own mother could brutalize me in such a willful and disrespectful manner. Had I not suffered enough in my three decades, as someone "out of phase" with her own body?

My mother and I continued arguing regularly over the phone. I felt a deep need to parry her blows, while she apparently felt empowered to continue her attacks against me (and my transgender friends and allies). After a month or so, I wearied of rhetorically battling my mother. I decided I would bring up my transness only in passing in future conversations. That way, I figured, the hostilities would cease, but not without gently reminding her that I was a transsexual woman who had no intention of ever "turning back."

In the months and years that followed, I sent her a steady stream of photos chronicling my evolving self. I wanted her to have visual confirmation of everything I had been saying. Eventually, my mother "made her peace" with who I am, but has never fully accepted me as a woman. Despite my pleas, she has never attended a PFLAG meeting nor read any material I sent along (not so far as I know, anyway). We talk on the phone on the six nodal points of the year (her birthday, my birthday, Mother's Day, Easter, Thanksgiving and Christmas), but she refuses to see me in person, even though, by her own admission, I "pass" quite well. (I would never make an issue of my "passibility," except in the context of my immediate family. My mother, no doubt, would be horrified if I looked like a "man in a dress.") She does not celebrate me as her newly found daughter nor does she easily refer to me as "Angela."

Deep down, I think my mother wants her "son" back, but is realistic enough to know that "he" is now a specter who cannot and will not return. And, honestly, I have largely given up on ever receiving her full acceptance. My mother's love, apparently, is not unconditional. So be it. I am strong enough in my own person that I no longer require her approval.

I wish I could say that my brother Joe stood behind me during my struggles with our mother. But that just was not to be. He initially stood on the sidelines and allowed the battles to rage unabated. He knew about my coming out as transgender the evening my mother arrived back in Florida in July 2000. She had handed him my letter, which he read and did not fully believe. When I called him that night, he spoke with a frightened tone in his voice. I knew that likely did not bode well. He would occasionally voice his incomprehension and dismay, but did not become openly hostile until June/July 2003. That summer, I found myself in a difficult economic situation. I was scheduled for genital surgery in late September in Thailand, but found myself at odds with my landlady. She refused to let me out of my lease so that I could move to Boulder, where I worked. I knew I needed to live close to my job if I was to dilate my surgically carved vagina four hours every day for the first three months post-operative. My brother initially promised to help me out financially, but then reneged. He became emotionally abusive, cursing a blue streak and swearing that he should fly to Colorado so he could "beat the piss" out of me. Thankfully, I was eventually able to work out an arrangement with my landlady and moved to Boulder in late July.

Shortly after the move, I swore to myself that I would never again pick up the phone to call my brother until he apologized, except in case of a family emergency or "act of God." Why should I ever again volunteer for such vicious and mean-spirited abuse? I held firm to my pledge. I engaged the "natural disaster" clause when Hurricane Charley slammed into my brother's hometown of Port Charlotte, Florida in August 2004, but I otherwise maintained "radio silence," birthday and Christmas cards excepted. Our relationship has defrosted somewhat in recent years. He called me in late July 2006, stating that he wanted the two of us to be "closer" again. It took his second divorce in 2009-2010 for that wish to become a full-fledged reality. For a time, we talked every few weeks. I wanted him to know that I "was there" for him, even if he had not done so in my time of great need.

> Love will tear us apart again.
> —Joy Division

My experiences with significant others have been a source of both great joy and heartbreaking conflict. Both the elation and sorrow, I believe, largely derived from my insecurities around intimate relationships and an inability to know what I really wanted in and from a partner. In my twenties and thirties, I was struggling so hard just to see clearly. My vision was clouded by all my (largely unacknowledged) baggage. Looking back, none of this is at all surprising. I had spent my youth stumbling around, especially when it came to gender roles and sexuality. I had a hard time understanding the budding sexual attractions of my peers and little comprehension of the behavior of my male classmates. All that teenage male strutting bordered on the incomprehensible. It was as if they were speaking a language that was largely foreign, a baffling emotional pantomime that was both impenetrable and ridiculous. Moreover, the "lack of fit" I experienced with my own body greatly complicated any sexual attractions that I did feel. I was attracted to girls but never felt secure enough in myself to ask any of them out on a date. Somehow I knew, even then, that being intimate with a woman would be a deeply problematic proposition.

I had only one girlfriend in my college years. She was from a semi-fundamentalist background and, thus, wanted to remain a virgin until marriage. Despite my grumblings against fundamentalist Christianity, I was secretly pleased that she did not expect me to have sexual intercourse with her. But I sure enjoyed kissing her breasts! I briefly dated another woman during a summer language program in Vermont. She had contracted herpes a short time prior and, I think, was too ashamed to ask me for sex. (At one point, she asked if

I thought her "damaged goods.") Again, I found myself reprieved from the looming demands of full sexual intimacy. Was I subconsciously broadcasting "signals" that attracted women who, for their own reasons, were only interested in a limited form of physical intimacy?

My blundering into a relationship with Margarita, the woman who would become my wife, forced me to face my fears around sexuality and gender, and then some. In many ways, we were a good fit. We shared similar interests and values. And we were both graduate students at the University of California, San Diego. I was pleased to have such a beautiful girlfriend, one who was actually attracted to me. (I still find that attraction puzzling. I did not make a very good "man!") She was not like my two previous girlfriends. She desired "all of me." Foreplay was fine by her, but she wanted more than the fondling of her breasts, expecting penis-in-vagina sex to be on the menu, and that I would dish it up upon request. I found myself caught in a dilemma with no simple solutions. On the one hand, my ego was incredibly gratified that she was physically attracted to me. I had never met any woman quite like her! On the other, I feared that this very same attraction would be my undoing. I thought it likely that I would not be able to satisfy her desires. And clearly, I was not the "man" for that particular job. Not by the proverbial long shot.

Intimacy with Margarita, whom I loved dearly (and still do, although in a different sort of way), was always fraught and difficult. Physical intimacy with her almost always made my "defenses" go on alert. I could never really relax with her in intimate situations. Fears, which even then I took to be "irrational," got a hold of me and would not let go. I could not seem to shake my fears and lack of comfort. And nothing seemed to help, certainly not with any consistency. On any given sexual encounter, I was generally somewhere between significant discomfort and full on "flipped out." I could only pleasure her unproblematically when, on the odd occasion, I was so thoroughly "horny" the bodily dysphoria subsided. Needless to say, my sexual performance was less than stellar.

Margarita thought I should consider seeing a therapist. I was too ashamed. I thought perhaps I was a gay, but I had never felt a significant attraction to men. It was all very confusing. (Almost no one in the Nineties held up being transgender as a "life option," or even discussed it at all.) Margarita sometimes interpreted my "sexual issues" as a lack of attraction for her; not at all true. She had long struggled with depression and anorexia/body issues. My discomfort in bed activated her fears and anxieties around her own body, sometimes tipping her into a depressive episode. She had a difficult time hearing me when I told her that I did indeed find her attractive. And so, round and round we went. This was not a marriage made in heaven. Sadly, Aphrodite granted us few of her favors.

Margarita and I, however, soldiered on as a couple, taking our troubled relationship from San Diego to the Bay Area to little Durango, Colorado. We loved and respected one another too much to call it quits too quickly. But that didn't stop Margarita from essentially commanding me to see a counselor just before the move to Durango. In the midst of a full-blown emotional breakdown, I readily agreed, shame be damned. I was desperate; pleased she had held out therapy as an option. From those seven sessions in June/July 1996, I learned that I had some smallish attraction to men, among other things. By this time, we were beginning to give one another the space to explore the multiplicity of queer identities. She had come out to me as bisexual, which literally made me think, "Thank God I'm not the only freak in this relationship."

It was in Durango, of all places, that I caught the first glimmers of my future trans identity. That October, we attended a fundraiser for the local college radio station called the "Transvestite Ball." I was very excited to attend "en femme" and spent weeks figuring out my costume. I had a great time, thrilled by all the compliments I received for my cowgirl outfit (I went as the country singer Patsy Cline!). Upon returning home, I simply could not take the female clothes off. It was the most amazing "high" of my life, and I had done my share of drugs in college! I pranced around for another two hours before finally disrobing and going to bed. This experience was crucial in my development.

I wondered why wearing women's clothes had such a profound and empowering effect on me. I began to consider the possibility I was a transgender person, of one sort or another. I read what I could find, both in print and on the then burgeoning internet. With some trepidation, Margarita gave me complete freedom to explore my gender identity. And, by that point, I was committed to discovering the full truth about myself, no matter the consequences. As I gradually moved toward a transsexual identity, our marriage, weakened as it was, began to collapse. This disintegration was not due to any transphobia on my wife's part. Quite the contrary. She had little problem with me starting female hormones or dressing as a woman in public. We had simply been through too many trials for our relationship to continue. Our time together was at an end, and we both recognized that fact. Although the first two or three years post-break up were, at times, tense, I am heartened that we have remained friends. Just in this last year, our former closeness as kindred spirits has returned.

I have been involved in two intimate relationships since that time. The first was with Sabrina, a troubled trans woman whom I am convinced has what is known as Borderline Personality Disorder. I dated her off-and-on for two years. She was controlling, sexually jealous and filled with a sometimes-frightening rage. One day I would be Queen of the Universe in her eyes, and the next a Horrible Bitch (a phenomenon known in the psychological literature as "splitting"). I tried to work things out with her, but ultimately to no avail. From the relationship with Sabrina, I learned never to put up with outrageously abusive behavior. But, on the positive side, I discovered I could have a comfortable and mostly satisfying sexual relationship, even though I still had a male body. That was a revelation, but I was not put off from surgically altering my body.

I had genital surgery between the close of my relationship with Sabrina and beginning another one year later with Sandra, a biological woman, self-identified lesbian and gifted painter. For a time, I was mesmerized by Sandra's artistic abilities. I never thought I would ever have such an artsy girlfriend. And I was delighted with her lesbian identity. For a woman-loving-woman to desire me felt very gratifying and validating. Sandra actually saw me as a woman and wanted to have sex with me! And I loved being pleasured as a woman. I was so excited (and a little amused) to be having "lesbian sex." I delighted in my female body, feeling liberated from the oppressive dysphoria of male identity and anatomy. Without caveat, sex was finally fun! And Sandra and I did have a good sex life for a few years. But by the time of our sixth anniversary, I felt restive with the relationship. We had been in couples' counseling for two separate stretches. I recognized that Sandra could be controlling and manipulative. I wanted out, so I broke things off with her in January 2011. Since then, I have learned, for the first time in my life, to be totally comfortable with being single. I've had a great time "dating myself." I feel confident that I will no longer fall into damaging or unsatisfying relationships. And that is a very liberating feeling indeed!

I get by with a little help from my friends.
—The Beatles

True friends and allies are so vitally important in the lives of transgender people. I say that from long personal experience. In fact, in my life, friends and allies have played a more significant and positive role than either my family or even significant others. They have helped me when others let me down or turned their backs and without expectation of quid pro quo "paybacks." And these folks have done so with great care, respect, grace and good humor. I don't think I can ever thank them enough for all their support and wise counsel.

I have had remarkable luck in my choice of "caring professionals." They have all been respectful and knowledgeable about trans people, or at least willing to learn. But two stand out for special mention. While still in Durango,

I found my first Denver area therapist, Rachael St. Claire, through a website dedicated to transgender issues. I was impressed with the blurb she provided in her listing and was later delighted to discover that she was a transsexual woman herself. I was nervous about meeting her for the first time in February 2000. I wasn't sure if I had what it took to be considered a "real" trans woman! She immediately put me at ease, and, at the end of the third session, promised to write a letter for me to obtain female hormones, commenting, "You're as much of a trans woman as anyone I've ever met." (She also connected me with a very trans-knowledgeable physician in Dr. Ingrid Justin, who remains my primary care doctor.) I was ecstatic that I had passed the "real tranny" test with such flying colors. I never doubted that Rachael cared a great deal about my welfare and me. She laughed with me in the good times and bucked me up in the bad (i.e. job loss, depression, suicidal ideations, etc.). She helped me to legally change my name, change the sex designation on my driver's license and wrote a letter so that I might have genital surgery. She did all this while never hesitating to "call me on my shit." I loved her dearly during the early years of my transition and still do. I would have continued seeing her if she had not been promoted to a mid-level management position at my HMO. I can't argue with a trans woman moving up the company ladder!

My present therapist, Rick Ginsberg, is likewise very dear to me. I have been seeing him since January 2010, upon the recommendation of a friend. At this point, I no longer require a therapist who is well schooled in transgender issues, as I have made it through my transitional period, certainly in the formal sense. While my transgender status is never too far from the surface, our sessions mostly concern general life issues, such as changing careers and dating (as a trans woman and just in general). Rick has helped me to see myself as a sexual being, and as someone who feels as if she is, in some real sense, going through a sexual awakening for the first time. It's truly liberating to have the professional counsel of someone who understands when I say, "I feel like I'm seventeen all over again." I come away from sessions with Rick feeling heard, respected and valued for every dimension of my identity. I value that sort of recognition in a very deep and profound way.

My longest standing friend and advocate has without a doubt been Jenny Scanlon. As I have told her many times, she is like the older sister I never had. I trust her opinion more than anyone else's and feel like I can tell her almost anything. I first met Jenny when I began working for the Colorado Coalition for the Homeless in late February 2000. She was employed as a Nurse Practitioner in CCH's Stout Street Clinic. She was the first person I came out to other than my wife and therapist Rachael. At that time, Jenny was advocating for a more trans inclusive policy at the Clinic, plus she set off my "gaydar," despite her mostly feminine presentation. Through careful discernment, I was nearly certain I could trust her with my secret revelation. When opening up to her in May 2000, I discovered my revelation wasn't so secret after all. She said she thought I might be a trans woman, because I told her about seeing a Kate Bornstein event in Boulder, and that I "rushed" to investigate reports of transgender "working girls" strolling the streets of south Denver (reports she had relayed to me). I was briefly stunned that she had puzzled me out (how could she possibly know when I had been so careful!), but was very quickly relieved that she was so understanding and supportive. Our friendship has grown and strengthened over the years. She even accompanied me when I flew to Thailand for genital surgery. I was so pleased to have a good friend and medical professional alongside me for an important surgical procedure. In the years since, we have talked and gotten together regularly, even during the three-year period when she split time between San Francisco and Tanzania doing HIV/AIDS work (thank goodness for Facebook!). I can never repay her enough for the love and kindness she has shown me over the last dozen years. What a wonderful friend and confidante!

I have a number of other friends and acquaintances, both trans and non-trans, who been supportive of me in my life's journey. I met a number of amazing people at the Colorado Anti-Violence Program (CAVP), where I was a crisis line volunteer for several years. Avi Skolnik, Kelly Costello and Crystal Middlestadt stand out as CAVP friends and queer fellow travelers. I also met my good friend CJ Carter through CAVP volunteering. CJ and I have become very close over the last two years. CJ was presenting as a femme lesbian when I first met her, but is now following a genderqueer path. Who knows, she may even transition to become a man. I think CJ sees me as something of a transgender mentor and guide. And I am only too happy to "give back" to other gender variant folks. Through CJ, I met Cindy, a kind and loving bisexual woman. My presence in Cindy's life seems to have given her "permission" to explore her own gender expression in a freer and more open fashion. I have maintained a long-distance friendship with Micki, a fellow transsexual woman, since 2001. We have shared our respective journeys, offering advice and giving comfort, when needed. Although briefly falling out of touch, we reconnected through Facebook three years ago. We met for the first time in March 2011.

My friend and coworker Beth and her boyfriend Leo are very supportive in all aspects of my life. Soon after learning of my transgender status, she took me out for lunch with the purpose of coming out as a bisexual. She saw me as a natural ally. I like the idea of being a trusted "old hand" at queerness! Lastly, I would like to note the transgender advocates who have made the University of Colorado campus (where I work) more trans friendly and inclusive. Bruce Smail and Steph Wilenchek both did great work as Director of the University's GLBT Resource Center. Steph, for one, was instrumental in establishing TRANSforming Gender, CU's transgender themed conference, as an annual campus event. I look forward to working more closely with Scarlet Bowen, the Resource Center's newly installed Director. Scarlet and I have become fairly close in the last few months, really hitting it off as friends. All my friends and allies acknowledge, respect and support me as a trans woman, but also recognize that I am much more than just one single identity.

> Spirit of the rising sun, lift me up
> Hold me there and never let me fall
> Love me 'til I die, my heart won't wait
> Soon I will be loved
> In this love song
> —U2

I began this essay asking the question, "Do you love me?" Over the dozen years since beginning my gender transition, I have received a variety of answers. My immediate family has sometimes answered with a harsh "No!" And that response is really too bad, for them more than me. I have grown so much since transitioning into my womanhood. The door, however, will remain open to them. I will not hold any grudges should they move into a place of full acceptance — the sort of acceptance all people deserve. I look forward to the day when I will find a long-term partner with whom I can share my joys and dreams. I feel like I am finally ready for a healthy intimate relationship. In the meantime, I will cherish all the wonderful friends and allies who have graced my life with their love, support and talents. I would like to make my life and all my relationships into the sort of "love song" that the U2 lyric suggests. Love is the most beautiful song we can sing, don't you think?

"Exit" by Jonas Jaeger © 2012

Appendix

"HIV" by Jonas Jaeger © 2012

Glossary

*Compiled by Cameron T. Whitley
and Eleanor A. Hubbard*

All words defined are **bolded**

Ally-an individual who is a member of a **dominant group** supporting members of a **subordinate group** and working to end oppression directed toward them, such as **homophobia, transphobia, heterosexism** or racism. Oppression may include prejudice, but refers, more importantly, to the institutionalization of discrimination; like sexism and **heterosexism**.

Androgyny-a gender presentation that includes both **masculine** and **feminine** characteristics, but the person is not **cross-dressing** or trying to **pass** as another gender; for instance, some male rock stars, like to be on stage wearing wigs and make-up.

Asexual (also known as nonsexuality)-a lack of sexual attraction to others or the lack of interest in **sexuality**.

Bigender-see **gender variant**.

Binary system-see **gender and sexual binary system**.

Birth sex-see **gender assignment**.

Bisexual-people who are primarily emotionally, physically, psychologically and/or spiritually attracted to members of both sexes; the sexual attraction may be concurrent or at different times in the person's life.

Bottom surgery-a surgical procedure to reconstruct the genitals to align with the desired sex. For **M2F** (male to female) individuals, this may involve the removal of the testicles (orchiectomy) in order to surgically construct a vagina. For **F2M** (female to male) individuals, the surgical reconstruction of genitals may involve a hysterectomy, the removal of internal sexual organs or vaginectomy (the removal of all of the parts of the vagina). Female to male individuals may also elect to have a penis constructed (phalloplasty or metoidioplasty) and testicular implants (scrotoplasty). **See also top surgery**.

Butch-an individual, usually a self-identified woman, who displays masculine qualities; this term may be used as an identity or as an adjective (I am butch, or she is acting butch). Masculine **gay** men may also use this term to describe themselves. Often contrasted with **femme**.

Cisgender-gender identity formed by a match between an individual's **gender identity** and the behavior or role considered appropriate for one's **sex** and/or **gender**. In this society, they would be members of the **dominant gender group**, and usually referred to as women and men (see **transgender**).

Closeted-usually this term refers to an individual who chooses to not disclose their **sexual orientation** and/or **gender identity**. A **GLBT** person may make this decision out of preference or out of fear in order to keep a job, housing, friends or in some other way to survive; many **GLBT individuals** are "out" in some situations and "**closeted**" in others.

Coming out-affirming and declaring one's sexual or **gender identity**. This is usually not a single event, but a life process because in each new situation, a **GLBT** person must decide whether or not to come out.

Conversion therapy-(also known as reparative or reorientation therapy)-an effort to change a person's **sexual orientation** from **homosexual** to **heterosexual** or to change a transgender person's **gender identity**. The American Psychological Association vigorously opposes these efforts, usually by conservative Christian groups. Many of those who have been through such therapy say that it does more harm than good.

Cross-dresser (also cross-dressing)-anyone who wears clothing of the other **sex** and/or **gender** for enjoyment or entertainment, and for some sexual pleasure. A drag cross-dresser sometimes performs for the purpose of parodying gender (see **cross-dressing, drag kings** and **drag queens**).

DSM-**D**iagnostic and **S**tatistical **M**anual of Mental Disorders, currently in its 4th edition, also referred to as DSM-IV, with another version due in 2013.

Dominant/Subordinate Group(s)-a social category which indicates social power and status. For instance, **heterosexuals** and **cisgender** individuals are members of the dominant group in our society, and **homosexuals** and **gender variants** are members of the subordinate group. Members of the dominant group receive privileges often denied to subordinate groups (like the legal right to marry), whereas subordinate groups may have prejudice and discrimination directed toward them.

Drag-see **drag show**.

Drag king-usually an individual who was born female and identifies as female, dressing in male clothing for the purpose of performance and entertainment. Individuals who identify and perform as drag kings may or may not be **transgender**, **gender variant**, **intersex**, **lesbian** or **gay**.

Drag queen-usually an individual, who was born male and identifies as male, dressing in female clothing for the purpose of performance and entertainment. Individuals who identify and perform as drag queens may or may not identify as **transgender**, **gender variant**, **intersex**, **gay** or **lesbian**.

Drag show (also known as **drag**)-a performance where **drag queens** and/or **drag kings** lip-sync to music and perform a parody of **gender**. Although sometimes **drag shows** are designed as fundraisers for nonprofit organizations or to raise awareness about a particular topic in the community, they are more often a commercial enterprise.

Dyke-a masculinized woman, who also has an emotional, sexual attraction to other women. This term can be used as a term of endearment among other women who identify the same way, however, it can also be used as a derogatory term (see **sissy boy**).

Erotic/erotica-arousing sexual desire or excitement; **erotica** is usually printed or visual material used to arouse sexual feelings.

Estrogen-hormone used by **M2F** individuals to produce female secondary sex characteristics, like stopping beard growth and growing breasts, in order to transition to the other sex.

F2M (also FTM)-designation used to identify an individual who was assigned female at birth, but who has transitioned or is in the process of transitioning, from female to male (see also **M2F**). If transgender persons consider themselves outside of the **gender system**, they may identify by a variety of terms (see **gender variant**).

Femme-an individual, usually a biological woman, who displays feminine qualities; often contrasted with **butch**.

Femininity-the social characteristics used to identify women; **gender identity**, psychological and emotional traits, as well as **gender roles** assigned to them by the society in which they live. For instance, women who are mothers are expected to dress conservatively, refrain from nursing in public and love their children unconditionally (see also **masculinity**).

GLBT (may also be GLBTQ or GLBTI)-refers to gay/lesbian/bisexual/transgender person(s); often used to signify the collective group of **sexual orientation** and **gender identity** minorities. The use of the term also refers to a political movement working to achieve equity for all individuals regardless of **sexual orientation** or **gender identity**. Sometimes the phrase includes a Q, which refers to **queer** or questioning, and other times the phrase may include an I, for **intersex**.

GQ-see **gender variant**.

Gay-men who are primarily emotionally, physically, psychologically and spiritually attracted to men (see **homosexual**). The term **gay** is sometimes used to describe a collective group of individuals (both male and female) who are attracted to a member or members of the same sex. Many **lesbians**, however, do not wish to be included in a word that predominately means men.

Gaydar-the purported ability of **gays** and **lesbians** (and some straight people) to recognize one another intuitively or by very subtle clues.

Gender-the social characteristics used to identify and differentiate women from men. Usually this term is associated with **masculine** and **feminine** qualities, activities and identities, as well as psychological and emotional characteristics, and roles assigned to them by the society in which they live. Many social scientists contrast this with sex, which are biological characteristics, but others argue that this is a false distinction and both **sex** and **gender** are biological and social at the same time.

Gender and **sexual binary system(s)**-socially constructed social systems in which men/women and gays/straights are thought to be dichotomous **polar** opposites. These systems are maintained by social norms, legal requirements and enforcement by social institutions, like schools. In other words, in this society, it is assumed that there are two, and only two, **genders**, so that if you are male, then you cannot be female. The same is true for **sexual orientation**: **gay** and straight are mutually exclusive. **Bisexual** and **transgender** persons illustrate that both **gender** and **sexual orientation** are more of a continuum, than dichotomies.

Gender assignment-assignment at birth of male or female, usually by a doctor, looking at an infant's genitalia. If the infant has ambiguous genitalia, the child is considered **intersex**.

Gender bending-playing with **gender** rules; for instance, a woman who enjoys a cigar after dinner.

Gender confirming surgery-see **bottom surgery**, **gender reassignment surgery**, **top surgery**.

Gender conforming-see **cisgender**.

Gender creative-a term suggested by Dr. Diane Ehrensaft as a positive alternative to **gender variant** or **gender non-conforming**.

Gender cues-female or male cues indicating to other persons how the individual wants to be perceived; for instance, hairstyles, clothing, jewelry, make-up, etc.

Gender dysphoria-see **Gender Identity Disorder**.

Genderfluid-see **gender variant**.

Gender identity-is the internal sense of **masculinity** and **femininity**; the self-identification of an individual with a **gender** category (usually male or female), as well as how their society views them. This identification may align with one's **gender assignment** or **birth sex** (see **cisgender**), or it may be misaligned (see **transgender**). Some individuals may not identify as male or female, or they may identify with both categories (see **gender variant**).

Gender Identity Disorder (**GID**, also known as Gender Dysphoria)- formal diagnosis used by psychologists to describe persons whose **gender identity** does not match the **gender** they were assigned at birth. The diagnosis from the **DSM** used to allow the **transgender** person to have **gender reassignment surgery** has evolved from **Transsexualism** (1980) to **Gender Identity Disorder** (1994). The term Gender Dysphoria will probably be used in **DSM-V**.

Genderless-see **gender variant**.

Gender norms-the usually unwritten rules of a society that determine how a male or female should act; such as, men often carve the turkey at Thanksgiving.

Gender-neutral pronouns-in English and most languages, pronouns are gendered. Some transgender people prefer to be referred to by a gender-neutral pronoun, see the chart below (from www.wikipedia.org).

	Nominative (subject)	Objective (object)	Possessive determiner	Possessive pronoun	Reflexive
Traditional Pronouns					
He	*He* laughed	I called *him*	*His* eyes gleam	That is *his*	He likes *himself*
She	*She* laughed	I called *her*	*Her* eyes gleam	That is *hers*	She likes *herself*
It	*It* laughed	I called *it*	*Its* eyes gleam	That is *its*	It likes *itself*
One	*One* laughed	I called *one*	*Ones* eyes gleam	That is *one's*	One likes *oneself*

Invented Pronouns

Ze (or zie or sie) and zir	*Ze* laughed	I called *zir/zem*	*Zir/Zes* eyes gleam	That is *zirs/zes*	*Ze* likes *zirself*
Ze (or zie or sie) and hir	*Ze* laughed	I called *hir*	*Hir* eyes gleam	That is *hirs*	*Ze* likes *hirself*
Ze and mer	*Ze* laughed	I called *mer*	*Zer* eyes gleam	That is *zers*	*Ze* likes *zemself*
Zhe, Zher, Zhim	*Ze* laughed	I called *zhim*	*Zher* eyes gleam	That is *zhers*	*Ze* likes *zhimself*

Gender non-conforming-any individual who does not obey the gender rules of a society; for instance, not dressing as the gender they were assigned at birth (see also **gender creative**, **gender variant** and **transgender**).

Gender presentation-how individuals present themselves so that they will be perceived as either male or female. This presentation includes **gender cues**, which enable transgender persons to present themselves as the **gender** they perceive themselves to be.

Gender(ed) pronouns-see **gender-neutral pronouns**.

Gender privilege-privileges accorded to **gender conforming** individuals, such as social recognition, jobs and religious affirmation (see also **heterosexual privilege**).

Genderqueer-see **gender variant**.

Gender Reassignment Surgery-(also known as SRS, sex affirmation surgery, sex realignment surgery, sex-change surgery) — surgical procedures to make one's sexual characteristics align with one's gender identity (see **bottom surgery**, **top surgery**).

Gender role-a social role is a group of behaviors, rights and obligations pertaining to a particular status position, such as doctor or teacher, which are socially prescribed (for instance, doctors wear a white coat). Many roles are gendered, such as mother and father (for instance, mothers nurture and fathers provide).

Gender spectrum-idea that **gender** is not dichotomous and oppositional, but is rather distributed across a wide range of behaviors, attitudes and values.

Gender variant-an umbrella term for any person who identifies outside of the **gender binary system** (one must be either male or female) and engages in behavior that does not align with their **gender assignment** (for instance, **transgender** persons). This includes those who do not consider themselves either male or female, those who transcend gender, those who fluctuate back and forth between masculine and feminine **gender presentation** and **gender identity** and those who do not identify with any **gender**. Other terms used by the **transgender** community are bigender, genderfluid, genderless, genderqueer, pangender, pansexual, F2X and M2X.

Harry Benjamin Standards of Care-outlines the usual, but non-binding, treatments for individuals who wish to undergo hormonal or surgical transitions to the other sex.

Hermaphrodite-see **intersex**.

Heteronormativity-the practices and institutions that legitimize and privilege **heterosexuality** and traditional **gender roles** as normal and natural.

Heterosexism-the structural enforcement of homophobia and the privilege of being **heterosexual** (for instance, the denial of gay marriage); the belief in the superiority of heterosexuality, and that everyone is or should be heterosexual. Thus, **GLBT** may be denied the rights and responsibilities, accorded to straights.

Heterosexual (also **straight**)-people who are primarily emotionally, physically, psychologically and spiritually attracted or committed to a person of the other sex. For instance, a woman who is attracted to men would be a **heterosexual**, as would a man who is attracted to women. Commonly thought of as the opposite of **homosexual**.

Heterosexual privilege-the benefits that a straight person receives automatically in this society because they are straight; these benefits are often invisible and "unmarked;" for instance, no one introduces their friend as my straight friend, although GLBT individuals are often introduced that way; for instance, "This is my new gay friend" (thus marked).

Homophobia-the irrational fear of **homosexuals**, homosexuality or any behavior, belief or attitude of self or others, which does not conform to rigid **gender role** stereotypes. It is the fear that enforces **sexism** as well as **heterosexism**. It is also used to mean prejudice against **GLBT** individuals (also see **transphobia**).

Homosexual (also **lesbian, bisexual** or **gay**)-people who are primarily emotionally, physically, psychologically and spiritually attracted or committed to a person of the same sex. For instance, a woman who is attracted to women would be **homosexual,** as would a man who is attracted to men. Research indicates this is not a choice, but rather a biological given (see **lesbian, gay**). Commonly thought of as the opposite of **heterosexual**.

Hormone Replacement Therapy (also known as HRT)-the use of hormones to produce secondary sex characteristics for **transgender** persons. For **M2F, estrogen** is primarily used. For **F2M, testosterone** (also called **T**) is primarily used.

Institutional heterosexism-the systematic arrangements of a society used to benefit straight and non-transgender individuals over **GLBT** persons; for instance, the use of language, the media, education, religion to enforce **heterosexual privilege** and gender conformity.

Internalized homophobia/heterosexism/transphobia-the process by which a **GLBT** individual comes to accept, internalize and live out the inaccurate myths and stereotypes applied to them by society, usually to their detriment.

Intersex (formerly known as hermaphrodites)-usually a child whose genitals are ambiguous at birth. Sometimes, the child has both male and female genitalia or neither. Intersexuality may also relate to atypical chromosomal, genital, morphologic or sex development characteristics. Most intersex adults had **gender reassignment surgery** at their birth and were raised as either a boy or a girl. Many intersex adults now believe that most of the surgeries performed on them were unnecessary and often unhealthy. Today, hermaphrodite is often considered a derogatory term. **In-**

tersex is sometimes included in GLBTI, for political and social purposes.

Lesbian-a woman who is primarily emotionally, physically, psychologically, and spiritually attracted to women (see **homosexual**).

LGBT-lesbian/gay/bisexual/transgender, emphasizing **lesbians** rather than **gay** men (see **GLBT**).

M2F (also MTF)-designation used to identify an individual who was assigned male at birth, but who has transitioned, or is in the process of transitioning, from male to female (see also **F2M**). If a **transgender** person considers themselves outside of the **gender system**, they may identify by a variety of terms (see **gender variant**).

Masculinity-the social characteristics used to identify men: **gender identity**, psychological and emotional traits, as well as **gender roles** assigned to them by the society in which they live. For instance, men who are fathers are expected to have jobs and be good providers (see **femininity**).

Out-a **GLBT** person who has told most or all of the people in their lives their **gender** and/or **sexual identity**. Many are **closeted** in some area of their lives; for instance, the person may be **out** at home but **closeted** at work.

Outed-someone other the **gay** or **trans** person themselves telling others. This is unacceptable in the **GLBT** community, although some would argue that if a politician who is making laws that harm the **GLBT** community, that person should be **outed**.

Pangender-see **gender variant**.

Pansexual-(also known as Omnisexual)-refers to an individual who is not necessarily attracted to a person based on their gender, but may be physically, emotionally and sexually attracted to persons of all genders and sexes.

Passing (also known as stealth)-the ability of an individual to be recognized in society as the gender they present themselves as (for instance, a **M2F**

living and accepted as female). Passing is a process of adhering to certain specific **gender cues** and behavioral and psychological tendencies associated with a particular gender.

Pre-op, Post-op, No-op-refers to the status of a **transgender** person who is **transistioning**, (see **transsexual**).

Questioning-refers to a person who is in the process of deciding whether or not they are **GLBT**.

Queer-a formerly derogatory word reclaimed by the **GLBT** community to describe people who do not fit gender or sexual norms. Some **GLBT** individuals still disapprove of the use of the term, whereas in other places, it becomes part of the phrase, GLBTQ.

Queer nation-a political movement that emerged out of **queer theory** for the purpose of political and social change.

Queer theory-a theoretical perspective, which emphasizes the fluidity of gender and sexual categories. Judith Butler (1999) is the prime theoretician of queer theory, and her most well-known resource is *Gender Trouble: Feminism and the Subversion of Identity*.

Restorative or Reorientation Therapy-see **Conversion therapy**.

Sensuality-the pleasures of the senses; visual, auditory, olfactory, taste and touch.

Sex-the physical sexual characteristics, usually genitals, which a doctor or mid-wife uses to assign the gender of a baby. This determination may not be as straightforward in some situations as is usually thought (see **gender assignment** and **intersex**). The term **sex** is often used by social scientists to mean the biological attributes of a person versus those that are socially constructed. In popular discussions, though this word usually means intercourse (for instance, "Would you have sex on your first date?").

Sexual and gender binary system(s)-see **gender and sexual binary system**.

Sexual behavior-how a person behaves out of their desire for and attraction to another person. In some cases, behavior does not determine sexual identity or orientation, meaning that a person may engage in same-sex sexual behaviors, but not consider themselves **gay** or **lesbian**.

Sexual identity-how and with whom a person identifies sexually; **sexual identity, sexual behavior** and **sexual orientation** may or may not match, meaning that a person may have sexual reltions with the other sex, but not perceive themselves as **straight** (see **homosexual, heterosexual, bisexual, gay, lesbian**).

Sexual orientation-who the person finds attractive; the pattern of attraction and desire to the same-sex (**homosexual** or **gay, lesbian**) other sex (**heterosexual** or **straight**) or both (**bisexual**), or open to attraction to any gender of person (**pansexual**). The desire for and attraction may be emotional, physical, psychological and/or spiritual. Some persons perceive themselves as **asexual**.

Sexuality-the capacity for sexual feelings (including **erotic** attitudes, values and beliefs), as well as how one acts on those sexual feelings. Attraction and desire may be emotional, physical, psychological and/or spiritual. Commonly, it is used as an umbrella term to identify one's sexual identity (for instance, "I'm straight!").

Sissy boy-an effeminate male, usually a derogatory term (see **dyke**).

SOFFA-an umbrella term that stands for Significant Others (SO), Family members (Fa), Friends (Fr) and Allies (A). This term is most prominently used within the **transgender** and/or **gender variant** community for their loved ones.

Standards of Care (SOC or **Harry Benjamin Standards of Care)**-outlines the usual, but non-binding, treatments for individuals who wish to undergo hormonal or surgical transitions to the other sex, issued in 2011 (version 7) by the World Professional Association for Transgender Health Standards of Care for the Health of Transsexual, Transgender, and Gender Nonconforming People. For more information, www.wpath.org

Stealth-see **passing**.

Stonewall riots-a series of spontaneous demonstrations against police raids of a gay and transgender bar, Stonewall Inn, in Greenwich Village, NYC, in 1969. It was police policy to raid such bars regularly, often beating up those who were at the bar. At Stonewall, the **drag queens** fought back and began what is not considered to be the defining event marking the start of the gay rights movement in the United States.

Straight-see **heterosexual**.

Subordinate group-see **dominant/subordinate groups**.

Testosterone (also known as T)-used by **F2M** individuals to produce male secondary sex characteristics, like beard growth, in order to transition to the other sex.

Top surgery (also known as chest reconstruction)- a surgical procedure for **F2M** where the breasts are removed. Usually the removal of the breasts is done to make a male-appearing chest and may involve what is often termed a mastectomy (also see **bottom surgery**).

Tranny-a slang term referring to **transgender**, may be used within the transgender community affectionately, but often considered derogatory.

Trans-Latin for crossing over; often used as slang for transgender, as in **trans** person or **trans-kin**.

Transgender (also known as **trans** or **transgendered**)-a term for people who perceive themselves as born into the wrong body. It may also be used as an umbrella term to include anyone who does not fit well into the gender they were assigned at birth (**gender assignment**), what gender they identify with (**gender identity**) and how they present themselves (**gender presentation**). Transgender is also used to refer to those who transcend or transgress **gender norms,** although those persons prefer **gender variant** or some other term. **Transsexual** is an older term, but still may be used for those **transgender** persons who use hormones and surgical procedures to **transition**. This term, however, does not indicate in any way the **sexual orientation** of the person (i.e., **transgender** persons are **gay, straight** and **bisexual**).

Transgender Day of Remembrance (also TDOR)-a day to honor and remember those who have been killed by tragic acts of violence against **transgender** individuals. The day was commissioned by Gwendolyn Ann Smith, a **transgender** activist, columnist and graphic designer, to memorialize Rita Hester, a **transgender** African American, who was murdered in Allston, Massachusetts, November 28, 1998. TDOR is held annually on November 20th.

Transgendered-The GLAAD Media Reference Guide notes that, "The word **transgender** never needs the extraneous "ed" at the end of the word. In fact, such a construction is grammatically incorrect. Only verbs can be transformed into participles by adding "-ed" to the end of the word, and **transgender** is an adjective, not a verb." However, some people within the **transgender** community still use **transgendered**, most unknowingly and some for self-reclamation.

Transgenderism-the condition of being transgender.

Trans-Kin-a word chosen by the editors' of this book to refer to **SOFFAs**. Kinship is usually referred to as blood relations or a sharing of common heritage or origins. This term is relevant in the **transgender** community, as many **transgender** people refer to their friends as family.

Transition-involves changing over time one's **gender presentation** and eventually living as the other sex.

Transphobia-the irrational fear of **transgender** persons, also any negative attitude or behavior directed toward **trans** people, such as stereotyping, name-calling and assault.

Transsensuals-typically used to describe a **cisgender** woman who is primarily attracted to **butch, transgender, transsexual** or **gender variant** masculine individuals. There is no comparable term for **cisgender** men.

Transsexual (also transsexualism)-an older term for people who believe that their genitals and other body parts do not reflect their true sex and are actively **transitioning** to the other sex through the use of surgery and/or **hormones**. It also includes individuals who do not intend to have surgery as well as those who do. In the **transitioning** phase, **transsexuals** may use **hormones**, live as their preferred **sex**, and may identify as **pre-op** (prior to **gender re-assignment surgery**), **post-op** (after the surgery) or **no-op** (choosing not to have any surgery) (see **gender reassignment surgery**). Most **transgender** persons now prefer **transgender** to **transsexual**.

Two Spirit-generally an individual of indigenous American descent who is said to house both a masculine and feminine spirit. This individual may dress and perform the work associated with one gender or with both.

"Untitled" by Troy Jones © 2012

Trans-Kin Reading List

Compiled by Cameron T. Whitley

This selection of books, is intended to provide additional information for trans-kin (SOF-FAs) and their transgender loved ones. This list is not intended to be comprehensive but rather a sampling of relevant literature. The categories are loose, as many books contain information that spans multiple categories.

Children of Transgender Parents

Allen, M. 1990. *Transformations: Cross-dressers and Those Who Love Them.* Hialeah, FL: Dutton.

Bornstein, K. 2006. *Hello Cruel World: 101 Alternatives to Suicide for Teens, Freaks and Other Outlaws.* New York, NY: Seven Stories Press.

Garner, A. 2004. *Families Like Mine: Children of Gay Parents Tell it Like it Is.* New York, NY: Harper Collins.

Girshick, L.B. 2009. *Transgender Voices: Beyond Women and Men.* Lebanon, NH: University Press of New England.

Howey, N. 2002. *Dress Codes: Of Three Girlhoods — My Mother's, My Father's, and Mine.* New York, NY: Picador Press.

Howey, N. and E. Samuels (eds). 2000. *Out of the Ordinary: Essays on Growing Up with Gay, Lesbian, and Transgender Parents.* New York, NY: St. Martin's Press.

Children's Books

Carr, J. 2010. *Be Who You Are.* Bloomington, IN: AuthorHouse.

Cheltenham Elementary School Kindergartners. 1991. *We Are All Alike… We Are All Different*. New York, NY: Scholastic Press.

Dyer, W. 2005. *Incredible You*. Carlsbad, CA: Hay House, Inc.

Ewert, M. 2008. *10,000 Dresses*. New York, NY: Seven Stories Press.

Kates, B. 1992. *We're Different, We're the Same*. New York, NY: Random House.

Kemp, A. 2010. *Dogs Don't Do Ballet*. New York, NY: Simon & Schuster Books.

Kilodavis, C. 2010. *My Princess Boy*. New York, NY: Simon & Schuster Books.

Kressley, C. 2005. *You're Different and That's Super*. New York, NY: Simon and Schuster Books.

Parr, T. 2009. *It's OK to be Different*. New York, NY: Little, Brown and Company.

Skeers, L. 2010. *Tutus Aren't My Style*. New York, NY: Dial Books for Young Readers.

Smith-Mansell, D. 2004. *Stop Bullying Bobby! Helping Children Cope with Teasing and Bullying*. Far Hills, NJ: New Horizon Press.

Wanzer, C.K. 2005. *Choose to Love*. Bloomington, IN: AuthorHouse.

Education, College and Classroom

Howard, K. and A. Stevens (eds). 2000. *Out & About Campus: Personal Accounts by Lesbian, Gay, Bisexual & Transgender College Students*. New York, NY: Alyson Publishers.

Sanlo, R. (ed). 1998. *Working with Gay, Lesbian, Bisexual and Transgender College Students*. Santa Barbara, CA: Greenwood Publishing Group.

✱ ✱ ✱ ✱ ✱

Parents of Transgender Children

Beam, C. 2008. *Transparent: Love, Family and Living the T with Transgender Teenagers.* Orlando FL: Harcourt Books.

Brill, S. and R. Pepper. 2008. *The Transgender Child: A Handbook for Families and Professionals.* San Francisco, CA: Cleis Press Inc.

Ehrensaft, D. 2011. *Gender Born Gender Made: Raising Healthy Gender-Nonconforming Children.* New York: The Experiment.

Just, Evelyn. 1998. *Mom, I Need To Be a Girl.* Second Edition. Longmont, CO: Just Evelyn.

Krieger, I. 2011. *Helping Your Transgender Teen: A Guide for Parents.* New Haven, CT: Genderwise Press.

Pepper, R (ed.) 2012. *Transitions of the heart: Stories of Love, Struggle and Acceptance by Mothers of Transgender and Gender Variant Children.* Berkeley, CA: Cleis Press.

Schor, E. 1999. *Caring for Your School-Age Child Ages 5 to 12.* Washington, D.C.: American Academy of Pediatrics.

Significant Others of Transgender Persons

Boyd, H. 2003. *My Husband Betty: Love, Sex, and the Life of a Crossdresser.* New York, NY: Thunder's Mouth Press.

Boyd, H. 2007. *She's Not the Man I Married: My Life with a Transgender Husband.* Berkeley, CA: Seal Press.

Cook-Daniels, L. 2000. "I Hope the Blood Never Washes Off Your Hands: Transgender Parenting Crossing the Lines" in *Home Front: Controversies in Nontraditional Parenting,* edited by Jess Wells. New York, NY: Alyson Books.

Erhardt, V. 2006. *Head Over Heels: Wives Who stay with Cross-dressers and Transsexuals*. Binghamton, NY: The Haworth Press.

Pratt, M.B. 1995. *S/He*. Ithaca, NY: Firebrand Books.

Rudd, P. 1999. *My Husband Wears My Clothes: Crossdressing from the Perspective of a Wife*. Katy, TX: P.M. Publishers.

Rudd, P. 2000. *Crossdressers: And Those Who Share Their Lives*. Katy, TX: P.M. Publishers.

Employers and Coworkers

Walworth, J. 1998. *Transsexual Workers: An Employer's Guide*. Bellingham, WA: Center for Gender Sanity.

Walworth, J. 1999. *Transsexual Workers: A Guide for Coworkers*. Bellingham, WA: Center for Gender Sanity.

Weiss, J. 2007. *Transgender Workplace Diversity: Policy Tools, Training Issues and Communication Strategies for HR and Legal Professionals*. North Charleston, South Carolina: BookSurge Publishing.

Family

Boenke, Mary. 2003. *Trans Forming Families: Real Stories About Transgendered Loved Ones*. Third Edition. Hardy, VA: Oak Knoll Press.

Brown, M. and C. Rounsley. 2003. *True Selves: Understanding Transsexualism — For Families, Friends, Coworkers, and Helping Professionals*. San Francisco, CA: Jossey-Bass Books.

Currah, R., R. Juang and S. Minter (eds). *2006. The Ties That (Don't) Bind: Transgender Family Law and the Unmaking of Families*, Minneapolis, MN: University of Minnesota Press.

Helping Professionals

Cohen-Kettenis, P.T. and F. Pfäfflin. 2003. *Transgenderism and Intersexuality in Childhood and Adolescence.* Thousand Oaks, CA: Sage Publications.

DeCrescenzo, T., and G.P. Mallon. 2002. *Serving Transgender Youth: The Role of the Child Welfare System: Proceedings of a Colloquium.* Washington, D.C.: Child Welfare League of America.

Ettner, R. 1999. *Gender Loving Care: A Guide To Counseling Gender-variant Clients.* New York, NY: W. W. Norton and Co.

Israel, Gianna and Donald Traver. 1997. *Transgender Care: Recommended Guidelines, Practical Information, and Personal Accounts.* Philadelphia, PA: Temple University Press.

Lev, A. I. 2004. *The Complete Lesbian and Gay Parenting Guide.* New York, NY: Berkley Publishing Group.

Lev, A.I. 2004. *Transgender Emergence: Therapeutic Guidelines for Working with Gender Variant People and Their Families.* Binghamton, NY: Haworth Clinical Practice Press.

Mallon, G.P. 1999. *Social Service with Transgendered Youth.* Binghamton NY: Harrington Park Press.

Stone Fish, L., and R.G. Harvey. 2005. *Nurturing Queer Youth: Family Therapy Transformed.* New York, NY: W. W. Norton & Company, Inc.

Vanderburgh, R. 2007. *Transition and Beyond: Observations on Gender Identity.* Portland, OR: Q Press.

Religion and Spirituality

Dzmura, N. 2010. *Balancing on the Mechitza: Transgender in Jewish Community.* Berkely, CA: North Atlantic Books.

Conner, R.P. 2004. *Queering Creole Spiritual Traditions: Lesbian, Gay, Bisexual and Transgender Participation in African Inspired Traditions in the Americas.* New

York, NY: Routledge.

Kaldera, R. 2009. *Hermaphrodeities: The Transgender Spirituality Workbook.* Hubbardson, MA: Asphodel Press.

Kreider, R. S. 2003. *From Wounded Hearts: Faith Stories of Lesbian, Gay, Bisexual and Transgender People and Those Who Love them,* Second Edition. New York, NY: Strategic Press.

Kron, K. and S.A. Gore. 2011. *Coming Out in Faith: Voices of LGBTQ Unitarian Universalists.* Boston, MA: Skinner House Books.

Kugle, S.A. 2010. *Homosexuality in Islam: Islamic Reflections on Gay, Lesbians, and Transgender Muslims.* New York, NY: Oneworld.

Ladin, J. 2012. *Through the Door of Life: A Jewish Between Genders.* Madison, WI: University of Wisconsin Press.

Mollenkott, V.R. 2001. *Omnigender.* Cleveland, OH: Pilgrim Press.

Mollenkott, V.R. and V. Sheridan. 2010. *Transgender Journeys.* San Jose, CA: Resource Publications.

Nyland, A. 2007. *Study New Testament for Lesbians, Gays, Bi, and Transgender: With Extensive Notes on Greek Word Meaning and Context.* Australia: Smith and Stirling Publishing.

Tanis, J. E. 2003. *Trans-Gendered: Theology, Ministry, and Communities of Faith.* Cleveland, OH: Pilgrm Press.

Tehuti, M. 2011. *Beautiful Prayers for Lesbians, Gays and Transgenders.* Australia: Smith and Stirling Publishing.

Tigert, L.M. and T.J. Brown. 2001. *Coming Out Young and Faithful.* Cleveland, OH: Pilgrim Press.

Trible, P. 1978. *God and the Rhetoric of Sexuality.* Minneapolis, MN: Fortress Press.

Sheridan, V. 2001. *Crossing Over: Liberating the Transgendered Christian.* Cleveland, OH: Pilgrim Press.

Waun, Maurine 1999. *More Than Welcome: Learning to Embrace Gay, Lesbian, Bisexual and Transgendered Persons in the Church.* Atlanta, GA: Chalice Press.

Wilhelm, A.D. 2010. *Tritiya-Prakriti: People of the Third Sex: Understanding Homosexuality, Transgender Identity, and Intersex Conditions Through Hinduism.* Bloomington, IN: Xlibris, Corp.

$$\star \quad \star \quad \star \quad \star \quad \star$$

Transgender Autobiographies and Biographies

Beatie, T. 2008. *Labor of Love: The Story of One Man's Extraordinary Pregnancy.* Berkeley, CA: Seal Press.

Boylan, J. F. 2003. *She's Not There: A Life in Two Genders.* New York, NY: Broadway Books.

Colpinto, J. 1999. *As Nature Made Him: The Boy Who Was Raised as a Girl.* New York, NY: Harper Collins.

Green, J. 2004. *Becoming a Visible Man.* Nashville, TN: Vanderbilt University Press.

Jorgensen, C. 2001. *Christine Jorgensen: A Personal Autobiography.* San Francisco, CA: Cleis Press.

Jones, Aphrodite. 2008. *All She Wanted (Brandon Teena Story).* New York, NY. Simon & Schuster.

Kailey, M. 2005. *Just Add Hormones: An Insider's Guide to the Transsexual Experience.* Boston, MA: Beacon Press.

Krieger, N. 2011. *Nina Here Nor There: My Journey Beyond Gender.* Boston, MA: Beacon Press.

McClosky, D. 2000. *Crossing: A Memoir.* Chicago, Il: University of Chicago Press.

Middlebrook, D.W. 1999. *Suits Me: The Double Life of Billy Tipton.* New York, NY: Mariner Books.

Rees. M. 1999. *Dear Sir or Madam: The Autobiography of a Female-to-Male Transsexual.* London: Cassel Academic Press.

Schofield, S.T. 2007. *Two Truths and a Life.* Ypsilanti, MI: Homofactus Press.

Scholinski, D. 1998. *The Last Time I Wore a Dress.* New York, NY: Riverhead Books.

Spray, J. 1997. *Orlando's Sleep: An Autobiography of Gender.* Chicago, IL: New Victoria Publishers.

Sullivan, L. 1990. *From Female to Male: The Life of Jack Bee Garland.* New York, NY: Alyson Publishers.

Thompson, R. and K. Sewell. 1995. *What Took You So Long: A Girl's Journey to Manhood.* New York, NY: Penguin Books.

Valerio, M.W. 2006. *The Testosterone Files: My Hormonal and Social Transformation From Female to Male.* Berkeley, CA: Seal Press.

Wilchins, R. 1997. *Read My Lips.* Ithaca, NY: Firebrand Books.

✶ ✶ ✶ ✶ ✶

Transgender Fiction (Teen and Adult)

Anders, C. 2005. *Choir Boy.* New York, NY: Soft Skull Press.

Beam, C. 2011. *I Am J.* New York, NY: Little, Brown and Company.

Bohjalian, C. 2000. *Trans-Sister Radio.* New York, NY: Vintage Press.

Edwards, H. and R. Kennedy. 2010. *F2M: The Boy Within.* Collingwood, VIC, Australia: Ford Street Publishing.

Eugenides, J. 2002. *Middlesex.* New York, NY: Picador Press.

Feinberg, L. *Stone Butch Blues.* 2004. Ithaca, NY: Firebrand Books.

Feinberg, L. 2006. *Drag King Dreams.* New York, NY: Carroll & Graf Publishers.

Peters, J.A. 2004. *Luna.* New York, NY: Megan Tingley Books.

St. James, J. 2008. *Freak Show.* New York, NY: Puffin.

Wittlinger, E. 2007. *Parrotfish.* New York, NY: Simon & Schuster Books.

Transgender Histry

Meyerowitz, J. 2002. *How Sex Changed: A History of Transsexuality in the United States.* Cambridge, MA: Harvard University Press.

Stryker, S. 2008. *Transgender History.* Berkeley, CA: Seal Press.

Transgender Recommendations

Bockting, W. and E. Coleman (eds.). 1992. *Gender Dysphoria: Interdisciplinary Approaches in Clinical Management.* Binghamton, NY: Haworth Press.

Bornstein, K. 1994. *Gender Outlaw: On Men, Women and the Rest of Us.* New York, NY: Routledge.

Bornstein, K. 1997. *My Gender Workbook: How to Become a Real Man, a Real Woman, the Real You or Something Else Entirely.* New York, NY: Routledge.

Bornstein, K. and S.B. Bergman. 2010. *Gender Outlaws: The Next Generation.* Berkeley, CA: Seal Press.

Bullough, V.L. and B. Bullough. 1993. *Cross-dressing, Sex, and Gender.* Philadelphia, PA: University of Pennsylvania Press.

Burke, P. 1996. *Gender Shock: Exploding the Myths of Male and Female.* New York, NY: Anchor Books/Doubleday.

Butler, J. 1990. *Gender Trouble: Feminism and the Subversion of Identity.* New York, NY: Routledge.

Califia, P. 1997. *Sex Changes: The Politics of Transgenderism*. San Francisco, CA: Cleis Press.

Carlisle, D.B. 1998. *Human Sex Change and Sex Reversal: Transvestism & Transsexualism*. Lewiston, NY: Edwin Mellen Press.

Cameron, L. 1996. *Body Alchemy: Transsexual Portraits*. San Francisco, CA: Cleis Press.

Currah, P., S. Minter and J. Green. 2000. *Transgender Equality: A Handbook for Activists and Policymakers*. Washington, D.C.: National Gay and Lesbian Task Force (NYAC).

Currah, P., R.M. Juang, and S.P. Minter, (eds). 2006. *Transgender Rights*. Minneapolis, MN:University of Minnesota Press.

Denny, D. 1990. *Deciding What To Do About Your Gender Dysphoria: Some Considerations for Those Who Are Thinking About Sex Reassignment*. Decatur, GA: AEGIS.

Denny, D. 1994. *Gender Dysphoria: A Guide to Research*. New York, NY: Garland Publishing.

Denny, D. 1994. *Identity Management in Transsexualism: A Practical Guide to Managing Identity on Paper*. King of Prussia, PA: Creative Design Services.

Denny, D. 1998. *Current Concepts in Transgender Identity*. New York, NY: Garland Publishing.

Devor, H. 1989. *Gender Blending: Confronting the Limits of Duality*. Bloomington, IN: Indiana University Press.

Devor, H. 1999. *FTM: Female-to-Male Transsexuals in Society*. Bloomington, IN: Indiana University Press.

Diamond, M. 2004. *From the Inside Out: Radical Gender Transformation, FTM and Beyond*. San Francisco, CA: Manic D Press.

Diamond, M. 2011. *Trans/Love: Radical Sex, Love & Relationships Beyond the Gender Binary*. San Francisco, CA: Manic D Press, Inc.

Ekins, R. 1997. *Male Femaling: A Grounded Theory Approach to Cross-dressing and Sex Changing*. New York, NY: Routledge.

Ekins, R. and D. King (eds). 1996. *Blending Genders: Social Aspects of Cross-dressing and Sex Changing*. New York, NY: Routledge.

Epstein, J. and K. Straub. 1991. *Body Guards: The Cultural Politics of Gender Ambiguity*. New York, NY: Routledge.

Fausto-Sterling, A. 1992. *Myths of Gender: Biological Theories About Women and Men*. New York, NY: Basic Books.

Fausto-Sterling, A. 2000. *Sexing the Body: Gender Politics and the Construction of Sexuality*. Basic Books.

Feinberg, L. 1996. *Transgender Warriors: Making History from Joan of Arc to RuPaul*. Boston, MA: Beacon Press.

Feinberg, L. 1998. *Trans Liberation: Beyond Pink or Blue*. Boston, MA: Beacon Press.

Garber, M. 1997. *Vested Interests: Cross-dressing and Cultural Anxiety*. New York, NY: Routledge.

Halbertstam, J. 1998. *Female Masculinity*. Durham, NC: Duke University Press.

Halbertstam, J. 2011. *The Queer Art of Failure*. Durham, NC: Duke University Press.

Herdt, G. (ed). 1996. *Third Sex, Third Gender: Beyond Sexual Dimorphism in Culture and History*. Cambridge, MA: Zone Books.

Irvine, J.M. 1990. *Disorders of Desire: Sex and Gender in Modern American Sexology*. Philadelphia, PA: Temple University Press.

Kessler, S.J. 1998. *Lessons from the Intersexed*. New Brunswick, NJ: Rutgers University Press, 1998.

Lesley, K. 2009. *How Stephen Became Stephanie and Other Transgender Tales*. Chesterfield, UK: Woodlord Publishing.

Nestle, J., R. Wilchins and C. Howell. (eds). 2002. *GenderQueer: Voices From Beyond the Sexual Binary.* New York, NY: Alyson.

Namaste, V.K. 2000. *Invisible Lives: The Erasure of Trassexual and Transgender People.* Chicago, IL: University of Chicago Press.

Nataf, Z. 1996. *Lesbians Talk Transgender.* London: Scarlet Press.

Prosser, J. 1998. *Second Skins (A Gender and Culture Reader).* New York, NY: Columbia University Press.

Queen, C. and L. Schimel (eds). 1997. *Pomosexuals: Challenging Assumptions About Gender and Sexuality.* San Francisco, CA: Cleis Press.

Ramet, S. (ed). 1997. *Gender Reversals and Gender Cultures: Anthropological and Historical Perspectives.* New York, NY: Routledge.

Rohrer, M. and Z. Keig. 2010. *Letters for My Brothers: Transitional Wisdom in Retrospect.* San Francisco, CA: Wilgefortis Press.

Rottnek, M. (ed). 1999. *Sissies and Tomboys: Gender Nonconformity and Homosexual Childhood.* New York, NY: New York University Press.

Roughgarden, J. 2004. *Evolution's Rainbow: Diversity, Gender, and Sexuality in Nature and People.* Berkeley, CA: University of California Press.

Schlesier, K.H. 1993. *Wolves of Heaven: Cheyenne Shamanism, Ceremonies, and Prehistoric Origins.* Norman, OK: University of Oklahoma Press.

Stuart, K.E. 1991. *The Uninvited Dilemma: A Question of Gender.* Portland, OR: Metamorphous Press.

Volcano, D.L. and J. Halberstam. 1999. *The Drag King Book.* London: Serpent's Tail.

Williams, W. 1992. *The Spirit and the Flesh: Sexual Diversity in American Indian Culture.* Boston, MA: Beacon Press.

Videos about Trans-Kin

Compiled by Eleanor A. Hubbard

This selection of videos is intended to provide additional information for Trans-Kin (SOF-FAs) and their transgender loved ones. This list is not intended to be comprehensive but rather a sampling of relevant videos

Adventures in the Gender Trade (1994)-Documentary

A good overview of what the transgender experience is like, with a wide range of stories from people who refuse to have their identity defined by either male or female. Kate Bornstein, writer and performer, is a M2F transgender person, and this documentary presents her frank account of her personal journey from unhappy boy child into liberated trans lesbian.

Adventures of Priscilla, Queen of the Desert (1994)-Fiction

Drag queens Mitzi (Hugo Weaving) and Felicia (Guy Pearce) and trans person Bernadette (Terence Stamp) hit the road in a broken-down lavender bus, Priscilla in order to perform at a casino in remote Alice Springs, Australia. Bernadette's former wife, and their son together, run the casino. Along with outrageous costumes and lip-synched disco tunes, this story is both incredibly funny and a poignant reminder that reconciliation is possible, now a musical on Broadway in New York.

The Adventures of Sebastian Cole (1998)-Fiction

Henrietta is the only parent that Sebastian really knows. His father is distant and his mother an alcoholic, so his stepfather, Henry provides him with love, acceptance and boundaries. At 17, when Sebastian is told that Henry is transitioning to Henrietta, his usual teen angst becomes turmoil. This unusual coming-of-age tale explores parent, stepparent and relationships with friends.

Beautiful Boxer (2005)-Docudrama

Kick boxer Parinaya Charoemphol (Asanee Suwan) harbors an unusual secret: He's transgender. Inspired by a famous Thai pugilist who lived two drastically different lives, this award-winning drama recounts Parinaya's painful attempts to exist in the paradoxical worlds of M2F fashion models and the ultimate masculine sport of kickboxing. His relationship with his mother is particularly well represented.

Becoming Chaz (2010)-Documentary

Chastity Bono, daughter of entertainers Sonny and Cher, grew up on her parents' TV show and was as a beautiful little girl well-loved by their fans. The story of how Chastity transitions to Chaz and how that affects his mother, his fiancé, and his fans is compelling. In addition, the documentary focuses on the emotional ramification of his decision as well as the hormone shots and his decision whether or not to have surgery.

Being Chaz (2011)-Documentary

This documentary shows Chaz embraceing his new life, while his fiancé Jen must deal with living with a man rather than a woman. In addition, his relationship with Jen is tested by his debut on "Dancing with the Stars," amidst controversy and threats to his life over his decision to participate in the show.

The Believers: The World First Transgender Gospel Choir (2006)-Documentary

Hallelujah — the world's first transgender gospel choir has taken the stage! The Believers revolutionizes popular conceptions about faith, gender identity and sexuality. Director Todd Holland is granted intimate access as choir members open up about the pain — and joy — that has brought them together. Buoyed by the transcendent force of music, we witness people who are brave enough to be their true selves, and we experience the healing power of acceptance in this moving film that quite literally sings.

A Boy Named Sue (2000)-Documentary

The F2M transgender experience is movingly portrayed as Sue transforms into Theo. During six years of taping the transformation, sex reassignment surgery is authentically portrayed, as well as how those in Theo's immediate circle are affected.

Bombay Eunuch (2001)-Documentary

Indian hijras were in the past revered as divine, but due to Western influence now are little more than relics in a rapidly modernizing world. Through the voice of Meena, a 37-year-old hijra and mother to her eunuch family, this documentary explores the challenges facing many in the Indian transgender community and the importance of remaining true to oneself. It also explores family that is created out of necessity rather than born into. We would identify hijras as M2F transgender persons, but that is not how they would identify themselves.

Boys Don't Cry (1999)-Docudrama

Based on actual events, Hilary Swank (in an Oscar-winning performance) inhabits Brandon Teena, a transgender young man searching for love and acceptance in a small Midwestern town. The social norms prohibit him from achieving his desire to become a man, even as he explores loving, and ultimately violent, relationships.

The Brandon Teena Story (1998)-Documentary

Brandon Teena, born as Teena Brandon, identified as a man. This documentary uses interviews, reenactments and news footage to tell his story. Although Brandon found happiness with a girlfriend and made a number of friends, he was brutally attached and murder, when his secret was discovered. His life served as the basis for the film, Boys Don't Cry, starring Hilary Swank.

Call Me Malcom (2005)-Documentary

Transgender student Malcolm Himschoot is about to begin his final year at seminary. Filled with anxiety about an uncertain future, Malcolm embarks on a cross-country road trip to connect with other transgender people and their loved ones. This poignant documentary examines Malcolm's inspiring journey toward self-acceptance, fortified by the support of his community at the Iliff Theological Seminary, Denver CO.

Gender Rebel (2006)-Documentary

This captivating documentary explores the lives of three biological females who reject the conventional concepts of gender and see themselves not as female or male, but something in between. We follow these individuals as they encounter challenges at every turn, including telling their families who they really are.

Girl Inside (2007)-Documentary

Madison is a M2F transgender person who through her crucial three-year transition, interacted with her 80-year-old grandmother, Vivien. Vivien insisted that not only was Madison's emotional, intellectual, physical and spiritual journey to self-discovery important, it was just as important to understand all things female. While Vivien's attempts to school Madison in old-fashioned codes of fashion and behavior are often hilarious, the juxtaposition of two vastly different experiences of womanhood, from very different generations, raises profound issues about the nature of gender, femininity and sexuality. Sometimes funny, sometimes painful, this heartwarming coming of age story is both an intimate portrait and a thoughtful exploration of what it means to be a woman.

Just Call Me Kade (2002)-Documentary

The inspiring true story of 14-year-old Kade Farlow Collins, F2M transgender teen, living with an incredibly understanding family in Tucson, Arizona.

Ma Vie en Rose: My Life in Pink (1997)-Fiction

Seven-year-old Ludovic regularly dons girls' clothing, putting a strain on his perplexed family and sending shockwaves among his bigoted neighbors. Ludovic innocently carries on; oblivious to the chaos he creates. This Belgian comedy was a smash at an international film festival and received a Best Foreign Film Golden Globe.

Middle Sexes: Redefining He and She (2006)-Documentary

Gore Vidal narrates this thought-provoking documentary highlighting interview with transgender, intersex and bisexual men and women. Scientific and academic experts shed light on the stigma of people whose gender does not fall in the gender binary system both in our society and around the world.

No Dumb Questions (2001)-Documentary

This funny and touching award-winning documentary profiles three sisters, six, nine and eleven, struggling to understand their beloved Uncle Bill, who they will now meet as Aunt Barbara for the first time. The conversations illustrate the girls' developmental stages and their personalities. If you need to talk to a child about being transgender, this is the movie to watch.

Normal (2003)-Fiction

Tom Wilkinson sensitively portrays Roy, a rural Normal, Illinois resident, who declares after his 25th wedding anniversary that he has always believed he was a woman trapped into a man's body. Jessica Lange, portrays all the emotions of his shell-shocked wife, Irma, coping with Roy's transition. His children and the friends in this small town react, in some cases with anger and in others with support. The film earned three Golden Globe nominations.

Prodigal Sons (2008)-Documentary

In high school, Kimberly Reed was male, a straight-A student and captain of the football team. But since leaving his rural Montana hometown, he's become a woman — and a filmmaker whose documentary could not be any more personal. Kimberly attends her high school reunion, and her community and family see her for the first time as a woman. The impact on her family is profound, all of who react differently, including her estranged mentally-ill, adopted brother.

Red Without Blue (2007)-Documentary

This provocative and insightful film documents three years in the lives of identical twins Mark and Alex Farley as they come to terms not only with their homosexuality, but also with Alex's decision to transition from male to female. As their parents divorced and they were increasingly stigmatized in school, they attempted a joint suicide in high school. Each of the brothers struggle to affirm their own identity, remain twins and learn what it means to be a family outside of traditional norms.

She's a Boy I Knew (2007)-Documentary

This auto-ethnography is not only an exploration into the filmmakers' process of transition from male to female, from Steven to Gwen, but also an emotionally charged account of the individual experiences, struggles and issues of her two sisters, mother, father, best friends and wife. Under Haworth's sensitive eye, each stepping stone in the process of transitioning becomes an opportunity to explore her family and friends and our own underlying assumptions about gender and sexuality.

Sir: Just a Normal Guy (2002)-Documentary

Jay Snider is a 30-year-old woman transitioning to a man. This film documents the process and includes interviews with him as well as his ex-husband Dave, his queer pal Sean Doig and Kari his lesbian girlfriend.

Southern Comfort (2001)-Documentary

This moving documentary chronicles the last year in the life of Robert Eads, a F2M transgender man dying of ovarian cancer. We're introduced to several prominent figures in Robert's life — most importantly, his life partner, Lola Cola. Lola is a transgender woman who's become Robert's life partner and caretaker. The two prepare to lead a panel at the annual Southern Comfort conference, a yearly event created for transgender individuals.

Still Black: A Portrait of Black Transmen (2008)-Documentary

African-American transgender males are often marginalized for being both black and trans. Six articulate black trans gender men — who are also artists, students, husbands, fathers, lawyers and teachers — speak candidly about race, gender, body image and status.

Trained in the Ways of Men (2007)-Documentary

Gwen Araujo was brutally murdered in 2002, after four men with whom she had been intimate, discovered she was a M2F transgender teen. Gwen's case became a rallying point for the transgender community, when the men claimed at their trial that her deception justified their actions. Gwen's mother portrays her daughter's pain and suffering in very moving terms.

Transamerica (2005)-Fiction

Bree (Felicity Huffman) gets the shock of her life a week before her final sex change surgery when she discovers a son she didn't know she had. After bailing him out of jail, the two set out on a cross-country journey riddled with road bumps. Huffman won numerous awards (and an Oscar nomination) for her role as a man longing to be a woman. This is a completely believable exploration of a mother and her son learning to live with change.

TransGeneration (2005)-Documentary

This absorbing Sundance Channel documentary series captures a year in the life of four college students who made a commitment to transition from their birth sex, despite the difficult consequences transgender individuals confront. Follow along as Lucas explains his decision to become a man, Raci seeks hormones on the black market, Gabbie celebrates her surgery with a pre-op dinner party and T.J. plans a trip to Greece to visit his parents. All of the college students explore their journey with family and friends.

Transparent (2005)-Documentary

Transparent focuses on 19 F2M transgender persons who gave birth to children while living full-time as men. The first-person stories explain how changing genders is dealt with and impacts family relationship. Even though these men may not be typical fathers, they deal with common and universal themes: single parenthood, teen pregnancy and their children's emotional and physical development. The film challenges the ways we relate to one another based on gender, particularly within our immediately families.

Two Spirits: Sexuality, Gender, and the Murder of Fred Martinez (2009)-Documentary

At age 16, transgender American Indian Fred Martinez became one of the youngest hate-crime victims in modern history, when a man who later bragged about the brutal crime savagely beat him to death. This documentary tells Martinez's story living in a small town in Western Colorado, particularly through the eyes of his family and community. In the process, it illuminates the Navajo Two Spirit tradition — which honors individuals who embody both the masculine and the feminine — and demonstrates how ancient values can inform (and improve) modern life.

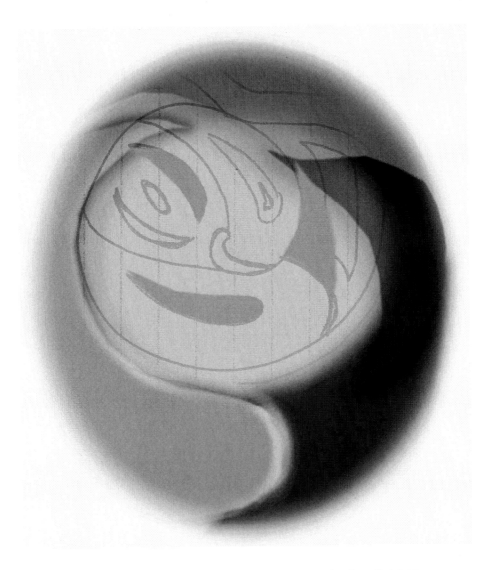

"The Creation of Art" by Cameron Whitley © 2012

Trans-Kin Organizations
Compiled by Eleanor A. Hubbard

This is a selection of diverse organizations which support trans and their kin in a variety of ways. It is not intended to be comprehensive but rather a sampling to encourage you to surf the internet for organizations that will fit your needs. Almost all of the blurbs are direct quotes of the organization's mission statement. Many of these organizations, particularly the educational ones, also have a bibliography of books and other sources to continue your study.

Ali Forney Center-dedicated to promoting awareness of the plight of homeless LGBT youth.

American Psychological Association-Answers to your Questions About Transgender People, Gender Identity, and Gender Expression (http://www.apa.org/topics/sexuality/transgender.aspx)

Camp Aranu'tiq-to provide transgender and gender variant youth with a safe, fun, and unique camp experience during which they are able to express gender however they are comfortable and connect with others in similar situations. Camps are in Southern New England and Southern California.

Campaign for Southern Equality-a national effort, based in the South, to assert the full humanity and equality of LGBT people in American life and to increase public support for LGBT rights.

COLAGE (People with a Lesbian Gay Bisexual Transgender or Queer parent)-a national movement of children, youth and adults with one or more LGBTQ parent, building community and working toward social justice through youth empowerment, leadership development, education and advocacy.

Dignity, USA-envisions and works for a time when GLBT Catholics are affirmed and experience dignity through the integration of their spirituality with their sexuality, and as beloved persons of God who participate fully in all aspects of life within the Church and society.

Forge-to support, educate and advocate for the rights and lives of transgender individuals and SOFFAs.

Friends of GLBT Youth-dedicated to eradicating homophobia and transphobia in order to allow all young GLBT people the opportunity to reach their full potential.

FTM International-The largest and longest running educational organization focusing on services for the FTMs and their SOFFAs.

Gay & Lesbian Leadership Institute-to increase the number of LGBT people in public office and to provide programming, service, and other support to help ensure their success.

Gender Spectrum-provides education, training and support to help create a gender-sensitive and inclusive environment for all children and teens.

Gender.org-a national organization focused on the needs, issues and concerns of gender variant people. It is an umbrella organization that includes the American Education Gender Information Service (AEGIS), Gender Education and Advocacy (GEA), the Remembering our Dead Project and Day of Remembrance.

GLAD (Gay & Lesbian Advocates & Defenders)-New England's leading legal rights organization dedicated to ending discrimination based on sexual orientation, HIV status and gender identity and expression.

GLAAD (Gay & Lesbian Alliance Against Defamation)-works with news, entertainment and social media to bring culture-changing stories of LGBT people into millions of homes and workplaces every day.

GLSEN (The Gay, Lesbian and Straight Education Network)-strives to assure that each member of every school community is valued and respected regardless of sexual orientation or gender identity/expression.

Human Rights Campaign-America's largest civil rights organization working to achieve lesbian, gay, bisexual and transgender equality...advocating for equal rights and benefits in the workplace, ensuring families are treated equally under the law and increasing public support among all Americans through innovative advocacy, education and outreach programs.

International Foundation for Gender Education (IFGE)-leading advocate in the promotion of free gender expression and identity, providing an excellent platform for national news.

Intersex Society of America (ISNA)-is devoted to systemic change to end shame, secrecy and unwanted genital surgeries for people born with an anatomy that someone decided is not standard for male or female.

It Gets Better Project-was created to show young LGBT people the levels of happiness, potential and positivity their lives will reach — if they just get through their teen years. It also reminds teenagers in the LBGT community that they are not alone — and it WILL get better.

Lambda Legal-is the oldest, founded in 1973, and largest national legal organization whose mission is to safeguard and advance the civil rights of lesbians, gay men, bisexuals, transgender people and those with HIV through impact litigation, education and policy work.

Metropolitan Community Churches-a global Christian church that has a specific outreach to GLBT members and friends.

National Black Justice Coalition-dedicated to empowering Black same-gender-loving, lesbian, gay, bisexual and transgender people. The Coalition works with communities and allies for social justice, equality and an end to racism, homophobia and transphobia.

National Center for Transgender Equality-a social justice organization dedicated to advancing the equality of transgender people through advocacy, collaboration and empowerment.

National Gay and Lesbian Task Force (NGLTF)-to build the grassroots power of the LGBT community.

National Transgender Advocacy Coalition (NTAC)-sponsors The Transgender Center (online), which provides information on the Bill of Gender rights, transgender basics, and action and how you can help.

National Youth Advocacy Coalition (NYAC)-a social justice organization that advocates for and with young people who are lesbian, gay, bisexual, transgender or questioning (LGBT) in an effort to end discrimination against these youth and to ensure their physical and emotional well-being.

Open and Affirming Churches-inclusive Protestant churches that welcome the full participation of LGBT people.

PFLAG (Parents, Families, & Friends of Lesbian and Gays)-promotes the health and well-being of lesbian, gay, bisexual and transgender persons, their families and friends through: support, to cope with an adverse society; education, to enlighten an ill-informed public; and advocacy, to end discrimination and to secure equal civil rights. Parents, Families and Friends of Lesbians and Gays provides opportunity for dialogue about sexual orientation and gender identity, and acts to create a society that is healthy and respectful of human diversity.

SAGA (Southern Arizona Gender Alliance-offers support, social and discussion groups that reflect various aspects of gender and society.

TNET (PFLAG's Transgender Network)-specifically focuses on support for transgender people and their parents, families and friends. It provides education on some issues unique to the transgender community, and focuses on issue advocacy to ensure equal rights for the transgender community at local and national levels.

TLDEF (Transgender Legal Defense & Education Fund)-committed to ending discrimination based upon gender identity and expression and to achieving equality for transgender people through public education, test-case litigation, direct legal services, community organizing and public policy efforts.

TYFA (TransYouth Family Allies)-empowers children and families by partnering with educators, service providers and communities, to develop supportive environments in which gender may be expressed and respected.

TransActive-to provide information that will help you better understand, accept, affirm and support a gender non-conforming or transgender child or youth on their unique journey through life.

Transgender at Work (TAW)-provides resources for innovative employers who want to set their company employment policies to help their transgender employees to be at their most productive, without spending energy hiding an important part of themselves and pretending to be something they are not.

Transgender Law and Policy Institute (TLPI)-dedicated to engaging in effective advocacy for transgender people in our society. The TLPI brings experts together to work on law and policy initiatives designed to advance transgender equality. Their website provides an amazing wealth of information and resources on legislation, case law, employer and college policies and other resources

TransKidsFamily (TKF)-an online forum for trans kids and their family to discuss issues in common.

Two Spirit National Cultural Exchange, Inc.-dedicated to the positive development of Two Spirit people and to seek to preserve a way of life that existed for hundreds and hundreds of years in order to rediscover and preserve the multi-tribal traditions of the Two Spirit community.

Unid@s (The National Latin@ LGBT Human Rights Organization)-dedicated to creating a multi-issue approach to advocacy, education and convening of and for Latin@ communities. Guided by economic justice, feminist, environmental and pro-peace values, Unid@s joins a global effort to transform systems and policies to support LGBT Latin@s and others.

"Untitled" by Liam Madden © 2011

Authors' List

Key: SO = Significant Other; Fa = Family; Fr = Friend; A = Ally;
*T = Transgender; * indicates Pseudonym*

Alyson, Jayne* (T)-*Growing Into Your SOFFAs.* p. 305

Baker, Katherine (Fr) *Educating My Family: Trans-Etiquette and Allyship.* p. 179

Beatie, Nancy (SO) *My Life with Thomas, the Pregnant Man.* p. 23

Beemyn, Genny (T)-*How to be an Ally to Transgender People.* p. 313

Bryant, Heather (Fa)-*The Trouble With Pronouns.* p. 89

Burke, The Most Rev. Bennett D.D. (A)-*Why Aren't You (Your Name Goes Here).* p. 225

Burton, Elijah Henry (T)-*From Oma to Daddy.* p. 317

Clark, Meg Whitlock (Fa)-*Pink China.* p. 97

Clark, Meg Whitlock (Fa)-*Janet's First Day of School as Ruthie.* p. 99

Cowan, Heather (SO)-*A Lesbian Who Hates Men Dating a Man Who Hates Lesbians.* p. 29

Dark, Kimberly (Fr)-*Revealing Ourselves.* p. 185

Daugherty, Rafi (T)-*I Love You and I Disagree With You, Pt. II.* p. 129

Diamond, Morty (T)-*Raised By Community.* p. 323

Feakins, Jonathan (Fa)-*Loveably Bizarre.* p. 85

Gates, Flora* (SO)-*Things That Matter.* p. 35

Cameron

Artists' List

Cover Art by Cameron T. Whitley

Outside of his academic pursuits, Cameron is a mixed-medium artist interested in the use of art (painting, drawing, photography and collective engagement) to convey complex problems and evoke emotions. Using acrylics on canvas, the cover art titled, "Trans-Kin" is a stylistic representation of how our relationships are interconnected. The purple piece at the center signifies those in the transgender community, where the other pieces represent significant others, family members, friends and allies. The color for the transgender piece was strategically chosen as purple and is often used as a symbol of pride and recognition in LGBTQ communities. The blue ribbon in the background symbolizes the movement embedded in our relational connections with others and in the transitional process of the transgender person. The five puzzle pieces fit neatly together enclosing the transgender person in what would ideally look like a supportive network. What is missing from this image, and what is been absent in past resources, is a recognition that significant others, family members, friends and allies need support as well as they come to terms with the transgender status of a loved one.

$$\star \quad \star \quad \star \quad \star \quad \star$$

Artists' List

Some of our artists provided photographs of themselves, biographies, and descriptions of their artwork; some did not. In this section, we are including the photographs and biographies of those artists who provided them and the art they contributed. On the page where the artwork resides, a description is provided if one was supplied to us.

Brenneman, Hilary (Ally)

p. 113-Ghost Leaf
p. 156-Bird of Paradise
p. 234-Fall
p. 249-Waves
p. 303-Hilary
p. 321-Heleconia

Francis, Jackie (Trans Woman)

Jackie Frances is an artist from Canton, Massachusetts. Jackie began her transition from male to female in May of 2010 and has been living full-time as her female self since November of 2010. Jackie's art comes from being raised on television, board games, 80's video games and horror movies. A few of my main influences are Sesame Street, The Muppets, Fraggle Rock, Candyland, Chutes and Ladders, Pac Man, Tetris, Stephen King and Clive Barker. You can see more of her work at http://jackiefrances.tumblr.com

p. 12-Behind Closed Eyes
p. 239-Church

Jaeger, Jonas (Trans Man)

Jonas Jaeger resides in Denver, Colorado where he is a massage therapist. He's an artist who is passionate about queerness, compassion, photography and enjoying each moment to the fullest. He loves traveling, photographing people and the everyday things they tend to overlook.

p. 73-Love Me
p. 178-Untitled
p. 294-Untitled
p. 347-Exit
p. 350-HIV

Jones, Troy (Trans Man)

Troy was born in Honduras and raised on one of its Bay Islands until he was 16. He then moved to Orlando, Florida for high school. Shortly after graduating, he joined the U.S. Army, serving in South Korea, Iraq and at Fort Lewis, Washington. He fell in love with Seattle, Washington and has been residing there ever since. He studied 3D art and animation for a little over a year and very quickly because bored with it. His art is now his full passion in life and has been since the summer of 2010.

p. 22-No. 12-November Challenge
p. 47-No. 24-November Challenge
p. 114-Untitled
p. 366-Untitled

Madden, Liam (Trans Man)

At the tender age of five, Liam moved to New York City from Panama with his family. He grew up in Queens and Brooklyn, but went to the School of Art and Design in Manhattan for high school. He has a degree in Studio Art from Hunter College. Liam's first love was analog or film photography; he uses both film and digital cameras. Visit Liam's website at www.photography-byliam.com

p. 34-Untitled
p. 392-Untitled

Perri, Dominic (Trans Man)

p. 139-Field

scholinski, dylan (Trans Man)

dylan currently resides in the Denver metro area and is a distinguished artist, author and public speaker on many issues, including suicide prevention, depression, art, etc. dylan has appeared on *20/20*, *Dateline* and *Today* to discuss his experiences and has been featured in a variety of newspapers and magazines. Recently his award-winning book (*The Last Time I Wore a Dress: A Memoir*) was listed in the Top 10 Must Reads in *Out Magazine's* first Transgender Issue. His work not only portrays the anguish of his earlier years but also his ultimate triumph.

dylan is the founder/witness for Sent(a)Mental Studios and frequently opens his studio to a variety of Denver metro youth to provide safe space to explore and discover ways of expressing and empowering themselves without bringing harm to themselves or others.

p. 15-12.31.11–from the daily shots of the "random morning series"
p. 85-Biography
p. 95-"no barbies" — from the daily shots of the "complex — learning to divide" series

Yamamoto, Autumn (Ally/Friend)

p. 41-The Archer's Violin
p. 57- Sleepy Joe
p. 165-Portrait #21
p. 283-Portrait #30
p. 285-Biography
p. 291-Portrait #4

Whitley, Cameron (Trans Man)

Cover-Trans-Kin
p. 5-8 Biography
p. 386-The Creation of Art
p. 396-Photograph of Cameron
p. 397-Description of Cover Art

Whitley, Melanie (Significant Other)

p. 74-75-Photograph and biography

p. 8-Fleur

p. 108-Mask of a Thousand Sorrows

p. 166-Coming Home